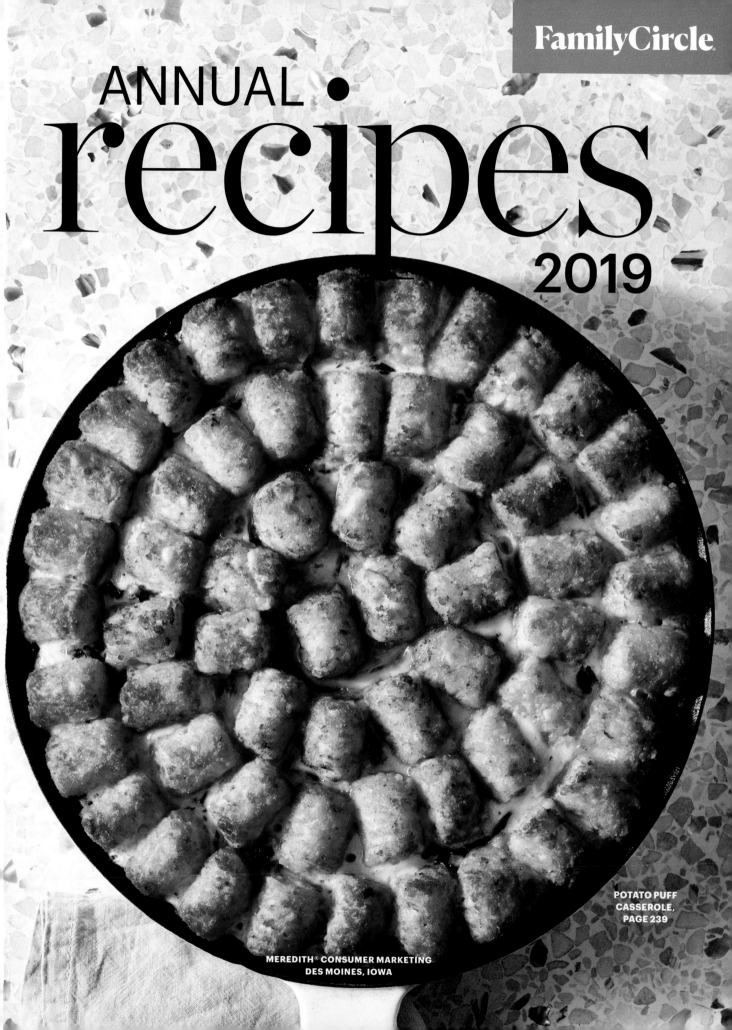

FamilyCircle.

ANNUAL recipes 2019

POTATO PUFF
CASSEROLE,
PAGE 239

MEREDITH® CONSUMER MARKETING
DES MOINES, IOWA

LEMON TART,
PAGE 132

At *Family Circle*® our goal is to make your life easier, starting with the meals you make.

A year ago January, determined to eat more veg and less carbs, I bought myself a spiralizer. Then it sat on my kitchen table, unopened, for *seven months*. The spiralizer isn't difficult to use—it had nothing to do with that. (And yes, you can buy veggie noodles at the supermarket, but I'm kind of known for making things challenging for myself.) It sat collecting dust because even the teeniest, tiniest change, like to your dinner routine or mind-set, is really, really hard.

When I did finally pull that spiralizer out of the box in July, it *did* get me to eat more veg, so it was a win regardless of how long it sat on my kitchen table. It was a lesson to myself that all of us here at *Family Circle* want to pass along to all of you: Be kind to yourself. Women (especially moms) feel so much pressure and guilt for what they're not getting done or not doing well enough. Let it go—you're one person, doing the best you can, which is usually already at superhuman levels. You will get to everything, just maybe not within the time frame you planned.

One of the biggest pressures of daily life is what to make for dinner. We know weeknights in particular present cooking challenges, so the foundation of the food section in every issue of *Family Circle* is a collection of recipes that helps you get delicious, nutritious food on the table fast. But we don't ignore the fact that sometimes you play host for the big game ("Two-Point Conversion," page 56), want to make a special seasonal dessert ("Make Me Blush," page 100) or do a little leisurely weekend grilling ("American Grill," page 148).

Go easy. Enjoy your life and those who share it with you. We're here to help.

Cheryl E. Brown

Cheryl E. Brown, Editor in Chief
Family Circle

Family Circle® Annual Recipes 2019

MEREDITH CONSUMER MARKETING

Director of Direct Marketing-Books: Daniel Fagan
Marketing Operations Manager: Max Daily
Assistant Marketing Manager: Kylie Dazzo

WATERBURY PUBLICATIONS, INC.

Editorial Director: Lisa Kingsley
Associate Editor: Tricia Bergman
Creative Director: Ken Carlson
Associate Design Director: Doug Samuelson
Graphic Designer: Mindy Samuelson
Contributing Copy Editors: Terri Fredrickson, Gretchen Kauffman
Contributing Indexer: Mary Williams

***FAMILY CIRCLE*® MAGAZINE**

Editor in Chief: Cheryl E. Brown
Executive Food Editor: Julie Miltenberger
Associate Food Editor: Sarah Wharton

MEREDITH NATIONAL MEDIA GROUP

President: Jon Werther

MEREDITH CORPORATION

President and Chief Executive Officer: Tom Harty

In Memoriam: E.T. Meredith III (1933–2003)

OPEN-FACED CRAB SANDWICH, PAGE 95

EAT FRESH! This collection of recipes from the 2019 issues of *Family Circle* makes it easier than ever to cook delicious food made with fresh, in-season ingredients. Whether it's a 30-minute weeknight meal, casual gathering, or a holiday celebration, we've got you covered. Recipes are organized by month to take advantage of what's in season and to make it easy to find the perfect recipe for any occasion. And you can count on our tested recipes and approachable cooking methods for dishes so reliable they'll quickly become family favorites.

**COCONUT RICE WITH
JERK CHICKEN AND
MANGO SALSA, PAGE 91**

Contents

JANUARY 8

FEBRUARY 36

MARCH 68

APRIL 86

MAY 108

JUNE 134

JULY 158

AUGUST 182

SEPTEMBER 198

OCTOBER 216

NOVEMBER 236

DECEMBER 268

INDEX 296

ROASTED CELERY
ROOT AND APPLE WITH
PORK, PAGE 30

January

11

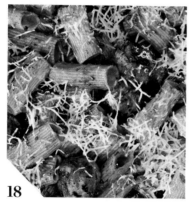

18

35

BALL OF ENERGY
PB Cup, 11
Cocoa-Coconut Almond, 11
Very Berry, 11

FAMILY DINNERS
Moo Shu Pork Noodles, 13
Curried Lentil Soup, 14
Chicken Piccata, 17
Baked Rigatoni and Meatballs, 18
Stuffed Flank Steak, 21

ROASTED
Roasted Broccoli and White Bean
  Pasta, 24
Roasted Brussels Sprouts with
  Poached Egg and Parmesan, 24
Roasted-Vegetable Chicken
  Soup, 27
Roasted Potatoes and Parsnips
  with Steak, 27
Roasted Celery Root and Apple
  with Pork, 30

START THE YEAR HEALTHY
Spice-Roasted Chicken Thighs, 31

BUILD A BETTER SMOOTHIE
Berry-Beet-Banana-Basil, 33
Coffee-Chocolate-PB, 33

WHILE YOU WERE SLEEPING
Overnight Oatmeal, 35

PB CUP

VERY
BERRY

COCOA-
COCONUT
ALMOND

BALL OF ENERGY

Need an afternoon pick-me-up? Don't reach for coffee—roll with one of these instead. The best part is you can make 'em ahead. They'll keep up to two weeks in the fridge or up to three months in the freezer.

PB Cup

Serves 20 **Prep** 15 min **Chill** 30 min

5   pitted dates
¾   cup old-fashioned oats
½   cup peanut butter
½   cup mini chocolate chips
⅓   cup peanut butter powder, plus more for rolling
¼   tsp salt

1 Soak dates in hot water 5 min. Add to a mini chopper along with 2 tbsp of the soaking liquid and puree.

2 Transfer to a bowl and add oats, peanut butter, chocolate chips, ⅓ cup peanut butter powder and the salt. Stir to combine, adding more oats if mixture is very sticky. Wrap and refrigerate 30 min.

3 Form into 20 balls (1 tbsp each), then roll balls in more peanut butter powder to coat.

PER SERVING 82 **Cal** | 5 g **Fat** (1 g **Sat**) | 3 g **Pro** | 8 g **Carb** | 4 g **Sugars** | 1 g **Fiber** | 76 mg **Sodium**

Cocoa-Coconut Almond

Serves 20 **Prep** 15 min **Chill** 30 min

⅔   cup chunky almond butter
½   cup dark chocolate chips
½   cup old-fashioned oats
¼   cup cocoa powder
2   tbsp agave syrup
½   tsp almond or coconut extract
¼   tsp salt
½   cup finely shredded coconut, plus more for rolling

1 In a large bowl, stir first seven ingredients with ½ cup finely shredded coconut. Continue mixing ingredients until dough comes together. Wrap and refrigerate 30 min.

2 Form into 20 balls (1 tbsp each), then roll balls in more finely shredded coconut to coat.

PER SERVING 118 **Cal** | 9 g **Fat** (4 g **Sat**) | 3 g **Pro** | 9 g **Carb** | 5 g **Sugars** | 2 g **Fiber** | 55 mg **Sodium**

Very Berry

Serves 20 **Prep** 15 min **Chill** 30 min

½   cup freeze-dried raspberries
⅔   cup crunchy sunflower seed butter (well stirred)
⅔   cup old-fashioned oats
½   cup white chocolate chips
½   cup sweetened dried cranberries
2   tbsp honey
¼   tsp salt

1 In a small ziptop bag, crush freeze-dried raspberries. Transfer half to a large bowl and add remaining ingredients. Stir until combined and dough comes together. Wrap and refrigerate 30 min.

2 Form dough into 20 balls (1 tbsp each), then roll balls in remaining crushed raspberries to coat.

PER SERVING 105 **Cal** | 5 g **Fat** (1 g **Sat**) | 3 g **Pro** | 12 g **Carb** | 8 g **Sugars** | 2 g **Fiber** | 61 mg **Sodium**

To form the Cocoa-Coconut Almond balls, thin vinyl or latex gloves will help the dough stick to itself, not to your hands. You may need to compress all doughs so balls hold their shape.

MOO SHU PORK
NOODLES

FAMILY DINNERS

Because you've gotta get food on the table. Fast weeknight meals!

Moo Shu Pork Noodles

Serves 6 **Prep** 10 min **Cook** 20 min

- **8   oz dry thin spaghetti**
- **3   tbsp vegetable oil**
- **1½ lb ground pork**
- **½   tsp salt**
- **1   bag (14 oz) tricolor coleslaw mix**
- **6   oz snow peas, thinly sliced**
- **½   cup moo shu hoisin sauce, plus more for drizzling**
- **2   tbsp sambal oelek (Indonesian hot chile sauce)**

1 Bring a large pot of lightly salted water to a boil. Add spaghetti and cook 9 minutes. Drain. Meanwhile, heat oil in a large skillet over high.

Add ground pork, season with ¼ tsp salt and cook, breaking apart with a spoon, 5 minutes. Remove to a bowl and reduce heat to medium-high.

2 Add coleslaw mix and snow peas to skillet. Sauté 3 minutes, sprinkling with ¼ tsp salt. Whisk hoisin sauce with 2 tbsp water and the sambal oelek; add to skillet with pork. Cook 1 minute and toss with spaghetti. Serve with additional hoisin.

PER SERVING 439 **Cal** | 12 g **Fat** (2 g **Sat**) | 31 g **Pro** | 51 g **Carb** | 15 g **Sugars** | 2 g **Fiber** | 862 mg **Sodium**

3 MOO SHU TWISTS

Substitute Broccoli slaw for the cabbage.

Make it gluten-free Opt for oyster sauce instead of hoisin and toss pork and veggie mixture with rice noodles.

Add some crunch Stir in drained and chopped water chestnuts when you add the sauce.

Moo shu pork is traditionally served with scrambled eggs in thin pancakes. This quick-to-the-table version is tossed in thin spaghetti.

Creamy and hearty, this pressure cooker soup delivers richness and depth of flavor in under 30 minutes.

Curried Lentil Soup

Serves 6   **Prep** 10 min   **Cook** 7 min   **Pressure cook** 10 min   **Release** 5 min

- **2   tbsp vegetable oil**
- **1   medium onion, chopped**
- **1   tbsp curry powder**
- **2   tsp sugar**
- **¾   tsp salt**
- **½   tsp black pepper**
- **6   cups vegetable broth**
- **1½ cups dried red lentils**
- **2   medium russet potatoes, peeled and cut into 1-inch pieces**
- **1   cup packed baby kale, chopped**
- **Plain yogurt**
- **Naan**

1 In an electric pressure cooker, heat oil on Sauté setting. Add onion and cook 4 minutes. Sprinkle with curry powder, sugar, salt and pepper. Cook 1 minute. Stir in broth, lentils and potatoes.

2 Seal lid and cook on Manual 10 minutes. Use natural release 5 minutes, then quick-release the steam. Uncover, stir in kale and season to taste. Simmer 2 minutes on Sauté until kale is wilted. Serve with yogurt and naan on the side.

PER SERVING 292 **Cal** | 7 g **Fat** (1 g **Sat**) | 14 g **Pro** | 47 g **Carb** | 5 g **Sugars** | 7 g **Fiber** | 960 mg **Sodium**

CURRIED
LENTIL
SOUP

Chicken Piccata

Serves 4 **Prep** 20 min **Cook** 15 min

½	**cup all-purpose flour**
½	**tsp salt**
½	**tsp black pepper**
4	**small skinless, boneless chicken breasts, cut in half crosswise (1½ lb total)**
2	**tbsp butter**
2	**tbsp vegetable oil**
½	**cup white wine**
2	**tbsp lemon juice**
2	**tbsp capers**
1	**tbsp butter**
1	**cup instant polenta**
	Steamed green beans

1 In a shallow dish, combine flour with salt and pepper. Dredge chicken in seasoned flour. Heat butter and oil in a large stainless skillet over medium-high. Add 3 to 4 pieces of chicken and cook 2 to 3 minutes per side. Transfer to a sheet pan and keep warm in a 200° oven. Continue with remaining chicken.

2 Reduce heat under skillet to medium. Add wine, lemon juice, capers and butter, scraping up browned bits; simmer 2 minutes. Prepare polenta per package directions and spoon onto a platter. Place chicken on top of polenta and pour sauce over chicken. Serve with steamed green beans.

PER SERVING 534 **Cal** | 17 g **Fat** (6 g **Sat**) | 45 g **Pro** | 44 g **Carb** | 1 g **Sugars** | 4 g **Fiber** | 927 mg **Sodium**

This comfort food casserole can be adjusted to your family's liking: Swap marinara for the vodka sauce and/or shredded Parmesan for the Asiago.

SHAPESHIFTERS

Rigatoni not your family's jam? Try one of these awesome swaps. We switched up the proteins and sauces too!

Medium shells + pesto + heavy cream + medium peeled shrimp

Orecchiette + sliced cooked sausage + roasted red peppers + marinara sauce

Bow ties + shredded chicken + roasted garlic + Alfredo sauce

Baked Rigatoni and Meatballs

Serves 6   **Prep** 10 min   **Cook** 14 min
Bake 30 min

1	**lb rigatoni**
1	**pkg (12 oz) chicken meatballs, thawed if frozen**
1	**jar (24 oz) vodka sauce**
½	**tsp salt**
¼	**cup fresh parsley, chopped**
1	**cup ricotta**
¾	**cup shredded Asiago cheese**

1 Heat oven to 350°. Bring a large pot of lightly salted water to a boil. Add rigatoni and cook 14 minutes. Drain.

2 Meanwhile, cut meatballs in fourths. Return rigatoni to pot; add meatballs, vodka sauce, salt and parsley. Pour half into a 3-qt baking dish. Top with spoonfuls of ricotta. Add remaining rigatoni mixture and sprinkle with Asiago cheese. Bake 30 minutes or until golden and bubbly.

PER SERVING 610 **Cal** | 24 g **Fat** (9 g **Sat**) | 30 g **Pro** | 68 g **Carb** | 11 g **Sugars** | 0 g **Fiber** | 1,216 mg **Sodium**

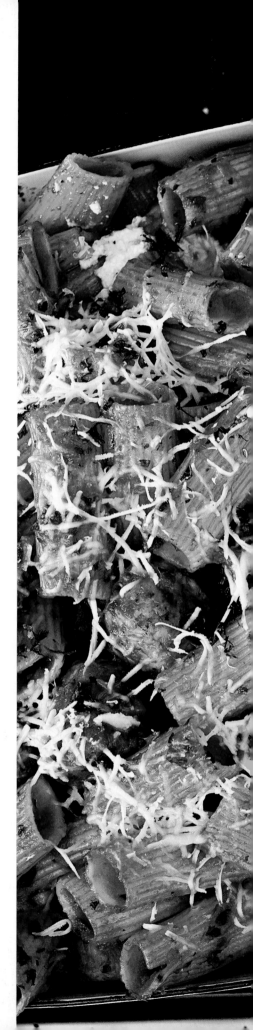

BAKED
RIGATONI AND
MEATBALLS

STUFFED
FLANK
STEAK

Stuffed Flank Steak

Serves 6 **Prep** 20 min **Cook** 10 min **Bake** 35 min **Rest** 10 min

6	**oz pkg herb stuffing mix**
1½	**cups water**
3	**tbsp butter**
4	**oz pkg sliced mixed mushrooms, coarsely chopped**
1¾ to 2 lb flank steak	
½	**tsp salt**
¼	**cup fresh parsley leaves, chopped**
3	**tbsp olive oil**
1	**tsp garlic salt**
2½	**lb sweet potato wedges**
½	**tsp black pepper**

1 Heat oven to 425°. Prepare herb stuffing mix per pkg directions, using 1½ cups water and 2 tbsp butter. Cool slightly.

2 Meanwhile, heat 1 tbsp butter in a medium skillet over medium-high. Add mushrooms and cook 5 minutes. Stir into stuffing.

3 Holding a sharp knife parallel to work surface and starting at a long side, slice steak in half horizontally without cutting all the way through. Open up steak like a book and season with salt. Press stuffing onto steak, leaving a 1-inch border on all sides. Sprinkle with parsley. Starting at a short side, roll up to enclose filling. Tie with kitchen twine, spacing 2 inches apart. Place on a rimmed baking sheet, rub with 1 tbsp oil and sprinkle with ½ tsp garlic salt.

4 On a large baking sheet, toss sweet potato wedges with 2 tbsp olive oil and ½ tsp garlic salt and the pepper. Roast steak and potatoes 35 minutes, turning once. Let steak rest 10 minutes. Remove twine before slicing.

PER SERVING 578 **Cal** | 21 g **Fat** (7 g **Sat**) | 37 g **Pro** | 60 g **Carb** | 10 g **Sugars** | 6 g **Fiber** | 1,115 mg **Sodium**

MAKE IT WORK!

If you don't have cotton twine for tying up the steak, use 2 skewers to hold the roll shut.

Skip the sweet potato wedges and sub in a bag of frozen sweet potato fries. Keep in mind: They'll cook faster than the steak.

If you won't have enough time after work to prep the stuffing and roll up the steak, you can make it a day ahead and refrigerate it (well wrapped) overnight. Add 15 to 20 min to roasting time.

Instead of rolling up the flank steak, buy a large sirloin steak and cut a pocket in the meat. Fill with as much stuffing as you can and secure opening with toothpicks or skewers. Season with salt and pepper and roast as per recipe.

ROASTED

It's January. Summer's colorful farmers' markets are a distant memory. But winter vegetables are just as delicious as their warm-weather counterparts with very little effort. It's amazing what a little oil, seasoning and a high-heat oven can do.

ROASTED BROCCOLI AND WHITE BEAN PASTA, PAGE 24

RULES OF THE ROAST

Roasting is very simple. But these best practices will help ensure that you don't wind up with a pan of both burnt and undercooked vegetables.

One size fits all. Cut your vegetables the same size so that pieces cook evenly. Bite-size, about 1½ inches, is good, but smaller or larger is fine.

Season before cooking. Sprinkle raw vegetables liberally with salt and pepper, then taste and season again after roasting. A squeeze of lemon or a dash of vinegar really brightens the flavor of caramelized veggies (or, for super-deep flavor, toss with a bit of balsamic vinegar before roasting).

Preheat the pan. For the best caramelization, place the pan in the oven while it heats, then add oil to the pan before carefully adding oil-coated veggies.

Side matters. Take the time to arrange veggies cut sides down. You'll expose the most surface area to the hot pan and get great browning and flavor.

Choose high-heat oils. Use an oil that won't scorch at high heat. Vegetable and canola are good bets. Olive oil works too, but save the nice extra virgin stuff for dressing and finishing.

Be hands-off. There's no need to stir if you're fine with one side of the veggies being very caramelized. For less-deep color but more even browning, stir or shake midway through cooking, then spread into one layer again.

Roasted Broccoli and White Bean Pasta

Serves 6 **Prep** 20 min **Roast** 25 min **Cook** 8 min

- 2 lemons
- 4½ tbsp extra virgin olive oil
- ¾ tsp salt
- 2 lb broccoli, cut into florets, stems peeled and cubed
- 4 to 5 shallots, peeled, halved lengthwise and sliced thickly crosswise
- ½ lb whole wheat spaghetti
- ¼ cup unsalted butter, cubed
- ¼ cup finely grated pecorino, plus more for serving
- 1 can (15 oz) butter beans, drained and rinsed

  Black pepper

1 Heat oven to 400°. Slice 1 lemon into ¼-inch-thick slices. Brush all over with ½ tbsp oil and sprinkle with ¼ tsp salt. Arrange lemon slices in a single layer on a rimmed baking sheet.

2 Toss broccoli and shallots with 2 tbsp oil and ½ tsp salt. Arrange in a single layer next to lemon slices and on a second rimmed baking sheet. With pan including lemon on bottom oven rack, roast 25 minutes. Remove lemon slices and quarter.

3 Meanwhile, bring a large pot of salted water to a boil. Add spaghetti and cook until almost al dente, about 8 minutes Reserve 1 cup pasta cooking water, drain pasta and return to pot. Juice remaining lemon.

4 Over low, melt butter into spaghetti. Stir in lemon juice, pasta water and pecorino. Mix in broccoli, shallots and half the roasted lemon. Stir in butter beans and 2 tbsp oil.

5 Sprinkle with pecorino and pepper to taste. Serve topped with remaining roasted lemon.

PER SERVING 439 **Cal** | 21 g **Fat** (7 g **Sat**) | 15 g **Pro** | 54 g **Carb** | 7 g **Sugars** | 12 g **Fiber** | 416 mg **Sodium**

Roasted Brussels Sprouts with Poached Egg and Parmesan

Serves 4 **Prep** 10 min **Roast** 35 min **Cook** 4 min

- 1½ lb large Brussels sprouts, trimmed and halved
- 2 tbsp extra virgin olive oil
- ½ tsp salt, plus more for serving
- ¼ tsp black pepper, plus more for serving
- 8 large eggs
- ¼ cup shaved Parmesan cheese

  Toasted bread

1 Heat oven to 400°. On a rimmed baking sheet, toss Brussels sprouts with oil, salt and pepper. Roast 30 to 35 minutes.

2 Meanwhile, fill a large, deep skillet three-fourths full with water. Bring water to barely simmering over medium-low. Crack each egg into a small bowl, then slip carefully into water. Cook 3 to 4 minutes; transfer with a slotted spoon to a paper-towel-lined plate. Season with salt and pepper.

3 Divide sprouts among 4 plates and sprinkle with Parmesan; top with eggs. Serve with toast.

PER SERVING 492 **Cal** | 20 g **Fat** (6 g **Sat**) | 28 g **Pro** | 53 g **Carb** | 6 g **Sugars** | 7 g **Fiber** | 1,003 mg **Sodium**

ROASTED BRUSSELS
SPROUTS WITH
POACHED EGG AND
PARMESAN

**ROASTED-VEGETABLE
CHICKEN SOUP**

Roasted-Vegetable Chicken Soup

Serves 10 **Prep** 20 min **Roast** 35 min **Cook** 9 min

- **1** lb rainbow carrots, peeled and halved lengthwise
- **1** lb turnips, peeled and cut into 1½-inch cubes
- **¼** cup vegetable oil
- **2¼** tsp salt
- **½** tsp black pepper
- **2** small yellow onions, quartered
- **4** cloves garlic, sliced
- **3** qt (12 cups) unsalted chicken broth
- **2** bay leaves
- **2** cups shredded rotisserie chicken
- **½** cup parsley, roughly chopped
- **5** cups cooked pasta (or rice or barley)

1 Heat oven to 425°. On a rimmed baking sheet, toss carrots and turnips with 2 tbsp oil, 1 tsp salt and the pepper. On a foil-lined rimmed baking sheet, toss onions with 1 tbsp oil and ¼ tsp salt. Roast carrots and turnips 15 minutes, then add pan with onions to oven and roast 20 minutes more.

2 Meanwhile, heat 1 tbsp oil in a large Dutch oven over medium. Add garlic and ¼ tsp salt; cook 4 minutes. Add broth, bay leaves and ¾ tsp salt; bring to a simmer.

3 Chop carrots and onions. Stir into soup with chicken and parsley. Simmer until heated through, about 5 minutes. Adjust seasoning if needed. Stir in cooked pasta.

PER SERVING 197 **Cal** | 7 g **Fat** (1 g **Sat**) | 15 g **Pro** | 19 g **Carb** | 7 g **Sugars** | 3 g **Fiber** | 763 mg **Sodium**

Roasted Potatoes and Parsnips with Steak

Serves 4 **Prep** 20 min **Roast** 30 min **Cook** 8 min

- **1** lb tricolor baby potatoes, scrubbed and halved (quartered if large)
- **1** lb slender parsnips, halved lengthwise
- **¼** cup vegetable oil
- **1¾** tsp salt
- **1** tbsp chili powder
- **1** lb skirt steak
- **1** avocado, peeled, pitted and cubed
- **2** tbsp fresh lime juice
- **2** tbsp roughly chopped cilantro leaves
- **2** tbsp Pickled Red Onion (recipe below)

1 Heat oven to 450°. On a rimmed baking sheet, toss potatoes and parsnips with 2 tbsp oil, 1 tsp salt and the chili powder. Roast 30 minutes.

2 Meanwhile, pat steak dry. Sprinkle all over with ½ tsp salt.

3 Heat 2 tbsp oil in a stainless skillet over medium-high. Add steak and cook 7 to 8 minutes, turning once, until temp reaches 130°. Transfer to a plate to rest 5 minutes; slice thinly on the bias.

4 While meat rests, stir avocado with lime juice, cilantro, ¼ tsp salt and Pickled Red Onion. Serve veggies with steak and avocado relish.

Pickled Red Onion In a small resealable container, combine ½ small red onion, halved lengthwise and thinly sliced; ¾ cup apple cider vinegar; 1½ tbsp sugar; and ½ tsp salt. Let stand at room temp at least 1 hour or up to overnight. Store in fridge up to 1 month.

PER SERVING 551 **Cal** | 33 g **Fat** (8 g **Sat**) | 29 g **Pro** | 41 g **Carb** | 7 g **Sugars** | 12 g **Fiber** | 1,118 mg **Sodium**

ROASTING TEMPS & TIMES
(FOR 1½-INCH PIECES)

If you roast at high heat—400° and above—you'll get deep, flavorful browning and a mix of textures in about 30 minutes or less. But what if you've also got something else cooking in the oven? You can roast at 350° or lower for a longer amount of time. Assume you'll need to add about 5 minutes of roasting time for each 25° difference in temperature.

400°

Broccoli 25 min

Brussels Sprouts 25 min

Cauliflower 30 min

Garlic 45 min

Lemons 25 min

Shallots 25 min

Sweet Potatoes 35 min

425°

Apples 10 min

Carrots 30 min

Celery Root 25 min

Onions 25 min

Turnips 30 min

450°

Butternut Squash 25 min

Parsnips 30 min

Potatoes 30 min

**ROASTED POTATOES AND
PARSNIPS WITH STEAK,
PAGE 27**

Roasted Celery Root and Apple with Pork

Serves 4 **Prep** 15 min **Roast** 25 min **Cook** 16 min

1¼ lb celery root, peeled and cut into 2-inch sticks

3 tbsp vegetable oil

1⅛ tsp salt

2 firm sweet apples (such as Braeburn or Honeycrisp), cored and cut into 8 wedges

4 bone-in pork chops (about 2 lb)

¼ tsp black pepper

2 tbsp all-purpose flour

1 cup unsalted chicken broth

½ tsp chopped fresh thyme

1 Heat oven to 425°. On one side of a rimmed baking sheet, toss celery root with ½ tbsp oil and ½ tsp salt. On a sheet of foil, toss apple wedges with ½ tbsp oil and ¼ tsp salt. Roast celery root 15 minutes. Remove from oven, add foil with apples to baking sheet and roast 10 minutes more.

2 Meanwhile, pat pork dry. Sprinkle all over with ¼ tsp each salt and pepper.

3 Working in 2 batches, heat 1 tbsp oil per batch in a large stainless skillet over high. Add pork and cook, turning once, 7 to 8 minutes, until golden brown and temp reaches 140°. Transfer to a plate to rest 5 minutes.

4 Return skillet to stovetop over low heat. Carefully whisk in flour, then broth, stirring to scrape up browned bits. Stir in thyme and ⅛ tsp salt. Taste and adjust seasoning if needed. Serve pork with celery root, apples and gravy.

PER SERVING 496 **Cal** | 28 g **Fat** (5 g **Sat**) | 34 g **Pro** | 28 g **Carb** | 13 g **Sugars** | 5 g **Fiber** | 892 mg **Sodium**

START THE YEAR HEALTHY

Try spiralizing—the trick to getting everyone to eat more vegetables.

Spice-Roasted Chicken Thighs

Serves 4   **Prep** 20 min
Roast 25 min   **Broil** 3 min

8	**small chicken thighs (2 lb)**
5	**tbsp vegetable oil**
1	**tbsp shawarma seasoning**
1	**tsp salt**
	Black pepper
	Lemon and/or orange slices
1½	**lb spiralized sweet potatoes**
3	**tbsp vegetable oil**
	Spinach

1 Heat oven to 450°. On a large rimmed baking sheet, rub chicken thighs with 2 tbsp oil, shawarma seasoning and ½ tsp salt. Sprinkle with pepper. Add a few lemon and/or orange slices to one side of pan. Spread sweet potatoes on a second large rimmed baking sheet and toss with 3 tbsp oil, ½ tsp salt and pepper.

2 Roast chicken and sweet potatoes 25 minutes. Remove citrus slices from pan and cut in half. Check chicken temp (should be 165°) and potatoes. If either needs more time, return to oven 5 minutes. Remove sweet potatoes to a platter.

3 Heat broiler. Broil chicken 3 minutes or until browned. Serve chicken over spinach with sweet potatoes and roasted citrus.

PER SERVING 537 **Cal** | 27 g **Fat** (4 g **Sat**) | 31 g **Pro** | 44 g **Carb** | 11 g **Sugars** | 8 g **Fiber** | 814 mg **Sodium**

BUILD A BETTER SMOOTHIE

Blend up the best version of your breakfast or lunch with these tips and tricks from nutritionist and author Megan Gilmore.

Step One: Pick a Low-Sugar, High-Nutrition Base Liquid

Adding the right amount of liquid will help create a perfect consistency for your smoothie. And that consistency is a major reason why smoothies are such great meal choices. One study found that the same ingredients served separately were less filling than when served blended together. Use 1 cup liquid per 2 cups frozen fruit, 1 to 2 big handfuls leafy greens, 1 to 2 tbsp fat/protein. Try…

Soy or regular milk Either can double as your protein source. Trendier milks have less protein but still deliver benefits: Almond milk has vitamins A, D and E, and oat milk is rich in soluble fiber.

Coffee Its flavor works especially well with banana-based smoothies. Maybe don't give this one to your teen, though!

Juice No-sugar-added OJ, pomegranate and pineapple work well, particularly if you're using a stronger-flavor green like kale or arugula.

Water Save yourself some calories and sugar, especially if your other ingredients create a thick texture and are packed with flavor.

Step Two: Add Fruits and Veggies

Fruit should be your primary source of sweetness since it contains lots of vitamins and minerals, as well as added fiber to keep you full. "If I wind up with a smoothie that tastes off one morning—when produce isn't ripe, it can taste chalky—I'll add a splash of maple syrup," says Gilmore, who is also the author of *The Fresh and Healthy Instant Pot Cookbook*. Honey works too.

Step Three: Add Protein (So You're Not Hungry 20 Minutes Later)

Protein will definitely make your smoothie substantial, and studies have also found that it can help your muscles and bones stay stronger longer. Both Gilmore and Keri Gans, RDN, author of *The Small Change Diet,* recommend hemp hearts and hemp seeds. Nut butters can also be good protein sources, and your healthy fat will be built right in. Powdered proteins, such as pea protein, can be good alternatives if you're vegan, lactose-intolerant or sensitive to ingredients like soy and nuts.

Berry-Beet-Banana-Basil

Serves 2   Prep 10 min

- **1** cup frozen sliced strawberries
- **4** oz cooked beets, chopped
- **1** large ripe banana, chopped and frozen
- **½** cup frozen cauliflower florets
- **6** to 8 large leaves basil, or to taste
- **1** tbsp hemp hearts (hulled hemp seeds) or flax or chia seeds
- **1¼** cups pomegranate juice

1 Combine all ingredients in blender and blend until smooth.

PER SERVING 225 **Cal** | 2 g **Fat** (0 g **Sat**) | 4 g **Pro** | 49 g **Carb** | 37 g **Sugars** | 5 g **Fiber** | 69 mg **Sodium**

Coffee-Chocolate-PB

Serves 2   Prep 20 min

- **¼** cup old-fashioned oats
- **½** cup cold brew coffee (or 1 shot espresso, cooled, plus water to equal ½ cup)
- **1** container (5.3 oz) vanilla or coffee yogurt
- **½** cup peanut butter (not natural)
- **2** tbsp raw cacao powder
- **1** tbsp honey
- **1½** cups ice

1 Soak oats in coffee 15 minutes. Add to blender with remaining ingredients and blend until smooth.

PER SERVING 337 **Cal** | 17 g **Fat** (3 g **Sat**) | 12 g **Pro** | 39 g **Carb** | 15 g **Sugars** | 4 g **Fiber** | 189 mg **Sodium**

BERRY-BEET-BANANA-BASIL

WHILE YOU WERE SLEEPING

Overnight oatmeal that's ready when you get up.

Overnight Oatmeal

Serves 6 **Prep** 5 min **Slow cook** 9½ hr on LOW

- **3   cups 1% milk**
- **3   cups water**
- **1½ cups steel-cut oats**
- **½   cup packed brown sugar**
- **¾   tsp salt**
- **Toppings, right**

1 Combine milk, water, oats, ¼ cup brown sugar and salt in a 5- to 6-qt slow cooker. Cover and cook overnight on LOW 9½ to 10 hours. Uncover and stir in ¼ cup brown sugar until smooth. (For looser oatmeal, stir in up to 1 cup additional milk.) Spoon about 1 cup oatmeal into each bowl and add toppings.

PER SERVING 275 **Cal** | 4 g **Fat** (1 g **Sat**) | 11 g **Pro** | 50 g **Carb** | 22 g **Sugars** | 4 g **Fiber** | 356 mg **Sodium**

Dairy Swaps Sub in an equal amount of almond or oat milk in place of the 1% milk.

Tip Cut down on cleanup by using a slow cooker liner.

OATMEAL TOPPING INSPIRATION

Take your breakfast to the next level with interesting flavor combos—sweet, savory or somewhere in between. For fully savory slow cooker oatmeal, omit the brown sugar called for in the recipe.

sliced strawberries + thinly sliced crystallized ginger

mini chocolate chips + chopped toasted hazelnuts

toasted coconut + finely diced fresh pineapple + cinnamon

dried tart cherries + chopped pistachios + honey

crumbled bacon + maple syrup

shredded cheddar + finely diced Gala apple

sliced bananas + blueberries + maple syrup

sautéed spinach + chopped breakfast sausage

sliced scallions + shredded pepper Jack + sour cream

Table for two? If you have a small family, make individual batches in your fridge instead. Combine equal parts milk and old-fashioned oats (steel-cut oats need cooking) in a jar with a pinch of salt and sugar to taste. Stir and seal. Refrigerate overnight.

MARBLED VANILLA
SUGAR COOKIES,
PAGE 51

February

39

55

58

BREAKFAST
Sheet Pan Egg Sandwiches, 39

FAMILY DINNERS
Slow Cooker Pulled Pork, 41
Stuffed Mac and Cheese, 42
Chicken and Barley Stew, 45
Chicken Enchiladas, 46
Instant Pot Quick Shrimp
    Risotto, 49

MODERN LOVE
Marbled Vanilla Sugar Cookies, 51
Pistachio and Raspberry White
    Chocolate Bark, 52
Chocolate Ganache Cupcakes, 55

TWO-POINT CONVERSION
Pork Meatballs with Hoisin
    Sauce, 57
Saté Dip, 57
Chicken Meatballs with Buffalo
    Sauce, 58
Blue Cheese Dip, 58
Beef Meatballs with Marinara, 61
Parmesan-Artichoke Dip, 61

**KITCHEN GEAR YOU'LL
ACTUALLY USE**
Instant Pot Slow-Cooked
    Honey-Ginger Pork, 65
Mustard-Olive Roast Chicken and
    Potatoes, 65
Instant Pot "Roast" Beef, 65
Green Goddess Dressing, 67
Chimichurri, 67
Tzatziki, 67
Romesco, 67

SHEET PAN EGG SANDWICHES

BREAKFAST

One and done—bake all the components on a single pan,
and your family can grab and go.

Sheet Pan Egg Sandwiches

Serves 5 **Prep** 5 min **Bake** 15 min

Nonstick cooking spray

Butter

5 **eggs**

5 **English muffins, split**

5 **slices cheddar cheese**

1 Coat five 3½-inch egg rings with cooking spray and a large rimmed baking sheet with butter. Place rings on pan.

2 Put pan in oven and heat oven to 350° (the hot rings and pan help the eggs set).

3 Remove pan from oven, crack 1 egg into each ring and sprinkle with salt and black pepper.

4 Add 5 split English muffins to pan; bake 10 minutes, adding 1 slice cheddar to 5 of the muffin halves for last 3 minutes of baking time.

PER SERVING 287 **Cal** | 14 g **Fat** (6 g **Sat**) | 16 g **Pro** | 26 g **Carb** | 1 g **Sugars** | 0 g **Fiber** | 522 mg **Sodium**

DIY A.M.

This method works for scrambled eggs as well. You can even stir in ingredients like onion or spinach to customize sandwiches.

Set up a breakfast bar. While the eggs bake, microwave sandwich fixin's like fully cooked bacon or sausage.

Nonstick egg rings are the secret to perfectly shaped eggs and pancakes. If you don't have them, use a well-greased muffin tin.

SLOW COOKER
PULLED PORK

FAMILY DINNERS

Because you've gotta get food on the table. Fast weeknight meals!

Slow Cooker Pulled Pork

Serve 8 **Prep** 15 min **Slow cook** 6 hr on HIGH or 9 hr on LOW

3¾ to 4 lb **boneless pork shoulder roast**

2 tbsp **spicy brown mustard**

¼ cup **packed dark brown sugar**

1 can (8 oz) **tomato sauce**

½ cup **apple cider vinegar**

2 tsp **liquid smoke**

1 tsp **garlic powder**

½ tsp **salt**

Pinch of cayenne

¾ cup **bottled barbecue sauce, optional**

Salad greens, black beans and/or sliced red onions, optional

1 Brush roast with mustard, then rub with brown sugar. In a slow cooker, whisk tomato sauce with vinegar, liquid smoke, garlic powder, salt and cayenne. Add roast.

2 Cook on HIGH 6 hours or LOW 9 hours. Remove pork to a cutting board. If roast is tied, remove and discard twine. Shred meat with 2 forks, discarding fat. Skim fat from cooking liquid. Drizzle pork with 1 cup cooking liquid. If desired, stir in barbecue sauce and serve over salad greens with black beans and red onion slices.

PER SERVING 462 **Cal** | 30 g **Fat** (11 g **Sat**) | 35 g **Pro** | 10 g **Carb** | 8 g **Sugars** | 2 g **Fiber** | 816 mg **Sodium**

3 OTHER WAYS TO SERVE PULLED PORK

Burrito Bowl Spoon Pulled Pork over rice and offer customize-your-own toppings: avocado, cheese, scallions, hot sauce.

BBQ Pork Pizza Spread bottled barbecue sauce on a pizza crust. Scatter Pulled Pork over sauce and add pickled jalapeño slices and shredded cheddar. Bake at 400° 15 minutes.

Pork Sammies Spoon Pulled Pork onto slider rolls and top with coleslaw and/or sweet pickle slices.

Boneless pork shoulder roast is sometimes called pork butt or Boston butt. Choose a roast with some marbling for flavor, but trim excess fat.

Cheese and pasta are an irresistible pair—
add a layer of filling and it takes mac and
cheese to another level.

SUPER STUFFERS

Amp up your mac and cheese with one of these awesome fillings.

Meat Sauce Sauté 1 lb lean ground beef, breaking apart, 5 minutes. Drain off fat and stir in 1 cup jarred marinara plus a pinch of salt and black pepper.

Mushroom Melt 2 tbsp butter in a large skillet over medium. Add two 8 oz pkg sliced mushrooms and 1 tbsp minced dried onion; cook 4 minutes. Season with ½ tsp salt and ¼ tsp black pepper.

Broccoli Heat 2 tbsp olive oil in a large nonstick skillet. Add one 12 oz bag frozen chopped broccoli, thawed, and 2 cloves garlic, chopped. Cook 3 to 4 minutes. Season with salt, black pepper and a pinch of red pepper flakes.

Stuffed Mac and Cheese

Serves 8 Prep 10 min Cook 10 min
Broil 4 min

1	pkg (16 oz) dry cavatappi
3	tbsp butter
3	tbsp all-purpose flour
3	cups milk
1	tsp onion powder
1	tsp salt
½	tsp black pepper
3	cups packed shredded white cheddar cheese

1 Bring a large pot of salted water to a boil. Add the cavatappi and cook 7 minutes. Drain. Meanwhile, melt butter in a large pot over medium. Sprinkle in flour and cook 1 minute, stirring constantly. Whisk in milk, onion powder, salt and pepper. Bring to a simmer; cook 2 minutes, whisking occasionally. Remove from heat and whisk in 2 cups cheese.

2 Stir cooked pasta into cheese sauce. Spoon half the mac and cheese into a greased 3-qt baking dish. Top with one of the fillings (see "Super Stuffers," at left) and remaining mac and cheese. Sprinkle 1 cup cheddar on top. Heat broiler. Broil until cheese is melted and lightly browned, about 4 minutes.

PER SERVING 525 **Cal** | 25 g **Fat** (12 g **Sat**) | 22 g **Pro** | 52 g **Carb** | 7 g **Sugars** | 1 g **Fiber** | 669 mg **Sodium**

STUFFED MAC
AND CHEESE

Chicken and Barley Stew

Serves 8   **Prep** 20 min   **Cook** 1 hr

1   cup pearled barley

1½ tsp salt

½   cup all-purpose flour

¾   tsp black pepper

1¾ lb skinless, boneless chicken thighs, cut into 1-inch pieces

¼   cup vegetable oil

8   oz baby bella mushrooms, quartered

3   large carrots, peeled and cut into ½-inch pieces

2   ribs celery, cut into ½-inch pieces

1   medium onion, diced

2   qt low-sodium chicken broth

2   tbsp fresh sage, chopped

1 In a saucepan, combine barley with ½ tsp salt and 3½ cups water. Bring to a boil, then simmer 25 minutes.

2 Combine flour with ½ tsp each salt and pepper. Toss chicken in flour mixture, shaking off and discarding excess. Heat 3 tbsp oil in a large heavy pot over medium-high. Add chicken; brown 5 minutes. Remove with a slotted spoon. Reduce heat to medium. Add 1 tbsp oil, the mushrooms, carrots, celery and onion; cook 8 minutes. Return chicken to pot. Add broth, barley with any liquid and sage. Bring to a boil over medium-high; reduce heat and simmer 20 minutes. Stir in 1 tsp salt and ¼ tsp pepper.

Tip Browning chicken in the large pot and then removing it to cook the mushrooms and veggies in the same pot helps build flavor. The more flavor you build in the pan, the more flavor your stew will have.

PER SERVING 314 **Cal** | 11 g **Fat** (1 g **Sat**) | 24 g **Pro** | 30 g **Carb** | 5 g **Sugars** | 5 g **Fiber** | 1,037 mg **Sodium**

When a recipe calls for a large amount of cilantro, don't just pick off the leaves—use the tender stems too. They have just as much flavor, and you'll save prep time.

Chicken Enchiladas

Serves 6 **Prep** 15 min **Bake** 25 min **Broil** 3 min

2	**cups salsa verde**
⅔	**cup fresh cilantro, plus leaves, for serving**
8	**oz sour cream**
2	**tbsp lime juice**
2½	**cups shredded rotisserie chicken**
1	**pkg (8 oz) shredded Mexican cheese blend**
12	**corn tortillas**

1 Heat oven to 350°. Add salsa verde, cilantro, sour cream and lime juice to blender; cover and blend until smooth. In a medium bowl stir 1 cup sauce with chicken and ¾ cup cheese.

2 Wrap tortillas in damp paper towels; microwave 1 minute. Spread ½ cup sauce in bottom of a 13 x 9 x 2-inch dish. For each tortilla, spoon 2 tbsp chicken filling into center of a tortilla. Roll up to enclose filling; place in baking dish. Pour on remaining sauce; top with remaining cheese.

3 Bake 25 minutes. Heat broiler. Broil enchiladas 3 minutes or until cheese is browned. Top with cilantro leaves.

PER SERVING 389 **Cal** | 19 g **Fat** (11 g **Sat**) | 20 g **Pro** | 31 g **Carb** | 6 g **Sugars** | 0 g **Fiber** | 959 mg **Sodium**

CHICKEN
ENCHILADAS

INSTANT POT
QUICK SHRIMP
RISOTTO

Instant Pot Quick Shrimp Risotto

Serves 6 **Prep** 10 min **Cook** 10 min **Pressure cook** 9 min

- ¼ **cup butter**
- 2 **large shallots, chopped**
- 1½ **cups Arborio rice**
- 2 **cloves garlic, minced**
- ½ **cup dry white wine**
- 1 **qt seafood stock**
- 1 **lb peeled, deveined medium shrimp (thawed if frozen)**
- ¼ **tsp salt**
- ¼ **tsp black pepper**
- 1 **cup frozen peas, thawed**
- ¼ **cup grated Parmesan**
- 2 **tbsp minced chives**

1 In multicooker, heat 2 tbsp butter on Sauté. Add shallots and cook, stirring, 5 minutes. Add rice and garlic. Stir to coat with butter and stir in wine. Cook 1 minute. Add stock. Seal and cook on Manual 9 minutes.

2 Meanwhile, heat remaining 2 tbsp butter in a large nonstick skillet over medium-high. Add shrimp. Season with salt and pepper. Cook 3 minutes. Stir in peas. Cook 1 minute.

3 Quick-release pressure and uncover. Stir in shrimp and peas, Parmesan and chives. Season with additional salt and pepper.

Tip To reheat leftover risotto, place in a small saucepan over medium, adding a little water, broth or wine to loosen it up but not so much that it gets mushy. Take off heat as soon as it's just warm.

PER SERVING 365 **Cal** | 10 g **Fat** (5 g **Sat**) | 22 g **Pro** | 45 g **Carb** | 3 g **Sugars** | 3 g **Fiber** | 827 mg **Sodium**

RISOTTO AND THE INSTANT POT

Risotto has a reputation of requiring too much hands-on time to make the cut for a weeknight dinner. Enter Instant Pot risotto, which requires less broth (because no steam is escaping) and almost no stirring while still producing perfectly cooked results.

What is Arborio rice? This rice has shorter, fatter kernels than long rice, with a high starch content that makes this dish creamy. Whether making traditional risotto on the stovetop or using a multicooker, Arborio is the preferred rice.

MARBLED VANILLA
SUGAR COOKIES

MODERN LOVE

Valentine's Day sweets that look like works of art but are unbelievably easy to make (and they'll impress even the toughest critics: teens).

Marbled Vanilla Sugar Cookies

Makes 24 **Prep** 15 min **Refrigerate** 1 hr, 30 min **Stand** 10 min
Freeze 15 min **Bake** 15 min

2	**cups all-purpose flour**
½	**tsp baking powder**
¼	**tsp coarse salt**
1	**stick unsalted butter, softened**
1	**cup sugar**
1	**large egg**
½	**tsp vanilla extract**
	Black, gray and burgundy gel food coloring
	Prepared white fondant
	Prepared vanilla frosting
	Sheets of edible gold leaf

1 Sift flour, baking powder and salt into a bowl. In a separate bowl, beat butter and sugar with an electric mixer on medium speed until pale and fluffy, about 3 minutes. Beat in egg and vanilla. Reduce speed to low. Gradually mix in flour mixture. Turn out dough and divide in half. Flatten each half into a rectangular disk and wrap in plastic. Refrigerate until firm, at least 1 hour.

2 Heat oven to 325°. Remove dough from fridge and let stand at room temp until just soft enough to roll, about 10 minutes Roll out 1 disk on a lightly floured surface to about ¼ inch thick, adding flour as needed to keep from sticking. Refrigerate until firm, about 30 minutes. Cut with heart cookie cutters. Transfer to parchment-lined baking sheets as you work.

Reroll scraps and continue cutting. Repeat with remaining disk of dough. Chill cookies in freezer until very firm, about 15 minutes.

3 Bake cookies, rotating halfway through, until just start to turn golden, 12 to 15 minutes. Let cool completely.

4 Meanwhile, with food coloring, tint ½ cup fondant black, ½ cup gray and ½ cup burgundy. Knead each until color is fully blended. Fold each ball of tinted fondant into a larger ball of white fondant 2 or 3 times. With a rolling pin, roll out fondant into ¼-inch-thick pieces (colors will bleed into each other, creating a marbled effect). Cut with heart cookie cutter. Let dry out as you repeat.

5 Spread a thin layer of frosting on top of each cookie to act as glue. Place a fondant heart over each frosted cookie and gently press down. Brush water lightly on fondant where you want to place gold leaf. Cut small pieces of gold leaf from sheets and apply to cookies with tweezers or a small paintbrush.

PER SERVING 253 **Cal** | 3 g **Fat** (1 g **Sat**) | 1 g **Pro** | 55 g **Carb** | 45 g **Sugars** | 0 g **Fiber** | 62 mg **Sodium**

TIPS FOR WORKING WITH FONDANT

If at all possible, pick up pretinted fondant so you can skip the step of tinting it yourself. If you do have to work the food coloring in, put on a pair of thin plastic gloves to avoid staining your hands.

Always keep fondant covered— either in a sealed bag or under a damp towel. When rolling or patting out fondant, use confectioners' sugar or cornstarch to keep it from sticking to the work surface, rolling pin or your hands.

TIPS FOR USING GOLD LEAF

Gold leaf can be difficult, but the payoff worth it! Two helpful tools are a set of fine-detail food-grade paintbrushes and some tweezers. Check amazon.com and crafts stores for both.

Once your cookie surface is dry, paint a little water on the fondant where you'd like to add the gold leaf. Pick up a small piece of gold and place it on the wet area. Tap down the gold leaf for a smooth finish or leave it bumpy for some 3-D glam.

Read labels carefully when buying real white chocolate for melting: It must contain at least 20% cocoa butter. Impostors will result in a clumpy mess.

TIPS FOR WHITE CHOCOLATE BARK

When breaking bark into pieces, hold it over a rimmed pan in case any toppings fall off.

Two other flavor combos to sprinkle over the white chocolate (in place of raspberries, pistachios and cocoa nibs—keep the flaky salt, because… salt!): freeze-dried strawberries and toasted chopped almonds; freeze-dried mango and toasted coconut flakes.

Pistachio and Raspberry White Chocolate Bark

Serves 12   **Prep** 10 min
Cook 5 min   **Stand** 30 min

16	**oz white chocolate, roughly chopped**
⅓	**cup shelled pistachios, roughly chopped**
¼	**cup freeze-dried raspberries, lightly crushed**
1	**tsp cocoa nibs**
½	**tsp flaky salt**

1 Line a baking sheet with parchment paper.

2 Over a double boiler or working in intervals in a microwave, melt chocolate until smooth, about 5 minutes. Pour chocolate onto prepared baking sheet and, with a small offset spatula, quickly spread into an even layer about ¼ inch thick. Sprinkle remaining ingredients over entire surface. Let bark stand completely until firm, about 30 minutes. Remove from tray and break apart.

PER SERVING 228 **Cal** | 13 g **Fat** (8 g **Sat**) | 4 g **Pro** | 29 g **Carb** | 27 g **Sugars** | 2 g **Fiber** | 112 mg **Sodium**

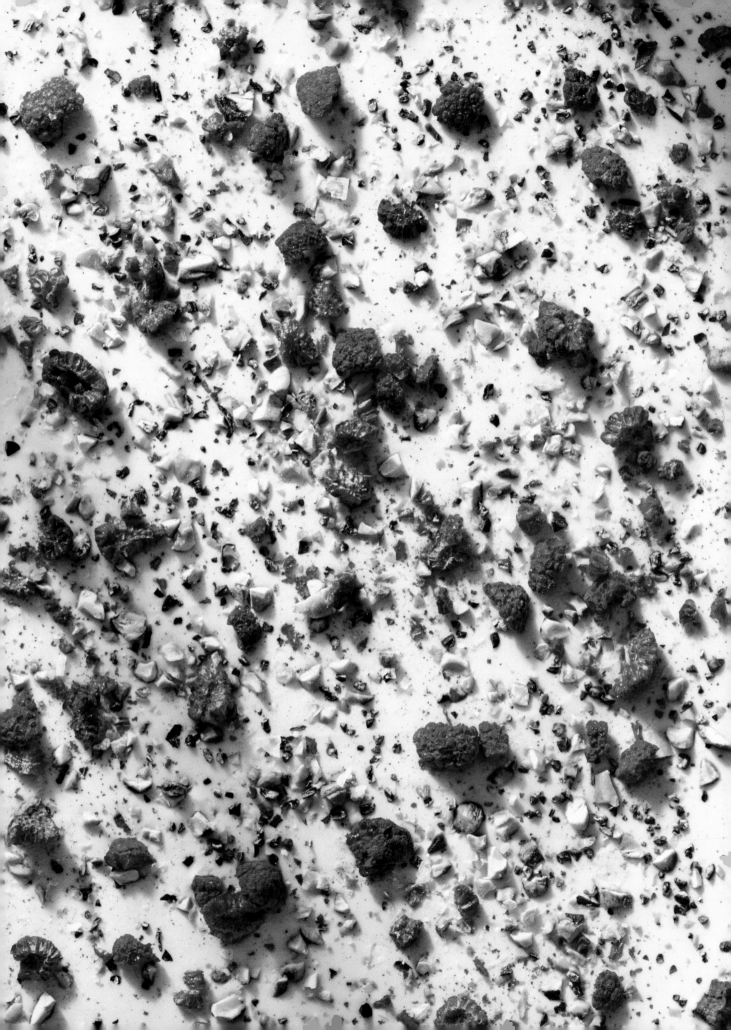

CHOCOLATE GANACHE
CUPCAKES

Chocolate Ganache Cupcakes

Serves 24 **Prep** 25 min **Bake** 20 min **Stand** 12 min

1½ **cups all-purpose flour**

1½ **cups granulated sugar**

¾ **cup unsweetened cocoa powder**

1½ **tsp baking soda**

¾ **tsp baking powder**

¾ **tsp salt**

2 **large eggs**

¾ **cup buttermilk**

3 **tbsp safflower or vegetable oil**

1 **tsp vanilla extract**

GLAZE

⅔ **cup heavy cream**

4 **oz bittersweet chocolate, chopped**

1 **tbsp corn syrup**

ICING

2 **tbsp unsalted butter**

¾ **cup confectioners' sugar**

2 **tbsp milk**

1 Heat oven to 350°. Line twenty-four 2½-inch muffin cups with paper liners. Sift first 6 ingredients into a large bowl. Add eggs, ¾ cup warm water, buttermilk, oil and vanilla. Beat with an electric mixer on medium speed until smooth.

2 Divide batter among muffin cups, filling each two-thirds full. Bake 20 minutes or until toothpick inserted in centers comes out clean. Transfer cupcakes to a rack and let cool.

3 Meanwhile, make glaze: Heat cream in a small saucepan over medium. Place chocolate and corn syrup in a small bowl. Pour cream over chocolate mixture and let stand 2 minutes. Whisk until smooth.

4 Dip tops of cupcakes into glaze, shaking off any excess. Let stand 10 minutes.

5 Make icing: Whip butter in a medium bowl with an electric mixer on medium-high speed until light and fluffy. Gradually add confectioners' sugar until incorporated. Add milk and whip until fluffy. (If too stiff, add a little more milk.) Place in a pastry bag with a small round tip. Write messages on cupcakes.

PER SERVING 182 **Cal** | 8 g **Fat** (4 g **Sat**) | 3 g **Pro** | 27 g **Carb** | 19 g **Sugars** | 1 g **Fiber** | 169 mg **Sodium**

PORK MEATBALLS
WITH HOISIN SAUCE

TWO-POINT CONVERSION

You are the ultimate multitasker—and now your Super Bowl buffet is too. We've got meatballs and dips that do double duty: They work on their own as appetizers, or they can go together on a bun if anyone in the cheering section is hungry for a meal. Talk about win-win.

Pork Meatballs with Hoisin Sauce

Serves 10 **Prep** 30 min
Slow cook 2½ hr on HIGH or 4½ hr on LOW

- **1 cup hoisin sauce**
- **¼ cup duck sauce**
- **¼ cup rice vinegar**
- **¼ cup sriracha**
- **¼ cup toasted sesame oil**
- **2½ tbsp soy sauce**
- **6 cloves garlic, grated**
- **4 scallions, finely chopped**
- **2 tbsp grated ginger (from a 4-inch piece)**
- **2 lb ground pork**
- **1 large egg**
- **1 cup panko breadcrumbs**
- **½ tsp salt**
- **Hoagie buns, Asian slaw, pickled ginger and/or sriracha, optional**

1 In a slow cooker, whisk together first 5 ingredients. Whisk in 1½ tbsp soy sauce and half the garlic, scallions and ginger.

2 In a large bowl, add pork and remaining garlic, scallions and ginger. Add egg, panko, 1 tbsp soy sauce and salt. Mix well.

3 Form into 1½-inch balls and add to slow cooker. Cover and cook 2½ hours on HIGH or 4½ hours on LOW. If desired, serve on buns with Asian slaw, pickled ginger and/or sriracha.

PER SERVING 362 **Cal** | 20 g **Fat** (6 g **Sat**) | 20 g **Pro** | 25 g **Carb** | 11 g **Sugars** | 0 g **Fiber** | 1,084 mg **Sodium**

Saté Dip

Serves 10 **Prep** 10 min

- **1 cup creamy peanut butter**
- **¾ cup unsweetened coconut milk**
- **2 tbsp soy sauce**
- **2 tsp light brown sugar**
- **3 cloves garlic**
- **1 2-inch piece peeled ginger, roughly chopped**
- **½ serrano chile or 1 whole jalapeño**
- **Juice of 1 lime**
- **1 to 2 tbsp water**
- **Sliced daikon radish, steamed asparagus, carrot sticks, rice crackers and/or sesame sticks, optional**

1 Combine all ingredients and 1 tbsp water in blender. Cover and blend until smooth. Add 1 tbsp water if needed for desired consistency.

2 If desired, serve dip with sliced daikon radish, steamed asparagus, carrot sticks, rice crackers and/or sesame sticks.

PER SERVING 191 **Cal** | 16 g **Fat** (6 g **Sat**) | 6 g **Pro** | 8 g **Carb** | 3 g **Sugars** | 2 g **Fiber** | 300 mg **Sodium**

PARTY MATH

Pro tips on hosting from George Duran, chef and TV host.

Appetizers Always offer a minimum of 2 kinds of appetizers. Prepare 6 pieces per person if you're also serving a "main course" like chili or pizza, 12 pieces per person if the whole party is apps.

Meat ½ lb per person. We're talking about the total of all the meat you're offering, whether that's charcuterie, deli meat or ground meat in cooked dishes.

Pizza 2 to 3 slices per person

Cheese 4 oz per person

Chips 1 family-size bag per 3 people

Salsa & Dips 4 oz per person. It's good to have spicy and mild options.

Alcohol Per person: 4 beers or ½ bottle of wine or ¼ bottle of liquor

Ice 2 lb per person

Sweets 2 to 4 pieces per person. If you're serving more than 1 kind of dessert, cut each into bite-size pieces so people can sample.

PAPER AND PLASTIC

Napkins For thin napkins, 3 per person. For the thicker kind, 2 should suffice. Add several extra as a buffer.

Paper Towels 1 roll per 6 people. Don't waste napkins on big spills.

Toilet Paper 1 roll per 4 people. Leave backup rolls in view (and within grabbing distance!) in your bathroom so guests don't have to search.

Paper Plates 2 regular-size paper plates per person, 2 smaller paper plates per person for desserts.

Plastic Utensils 2 of each utensil per person ensures there's a supply of backups in case anyone loses a fork.

Stain Remover Pens 2—some shirts and laps will thank you!

Chicken Meatballs with Buffalo Sauce

Serves 10 **Prep** 30 min
Slow cook 2 hr on HIGH or 4 hr on LOW

2¼ cups buffalo sauce (such as Frank's RedHot Wings Buffalo)

1 stick unsalted butter, melted

2 lb ground chicken

4 scallions, finely chopped

3 cloves garlic, grated

2 ribs celery, finely chopped

1 large egg yolk

1 cup plain breadcrumbs

1 tsp salt

Hoagie buns, leaf lettuce or celery leaves, optional

1 In a slow cooker, whisk 2 cups buffalo sauce with butter.

2 In a large bowl, mix ground chicken with ¼ cup buffalo sauce and all remaining ingredients until well combined.

3 Form into 1½-inch balls and add to slow cooker. Cover and cook 2 hours on HIGH or 4 hours on LOW.

4 If desired, serve on hoagie buns with leaf lettuce or celery leaves.

PER SERVING 280 **Cal** | 18 g **Fat** (8 g **Sat**) | 18 g **Pro** | 11 g **Carb** | 2 g **Sugars** | 0 g **Fiber** | 1,625 mg **Sodium**

Blue Cheese Dip

Serves 10 **Prep** 10 min

1 clove garlic

1 small shallot, quartered

8 oz cream cheese, cubed

4 oz Roquefort or blue cheese, crumbled

3 tbsp milk

¼ tsp cayenne pepper

Celery sticks, sliced cucumber, cherry tomatoes and/or potato chips, optional

1 Combine all ingredients in a food processor and process until creamy, scraping down sides as needed. If desired, serve dip with celery sticks, sliced cucumber, cherry tomatoes and/or potato chips.

PER SERVING 127 **Cal** | 11 g **Fat** (7 g **Sat**) | 4 g **Pro** | 2 g **Carb** | 1 g **Sugars** | 0 g **Fiber** | 279 mg **Sodium**

CHICKEN MEATBALLS
WITH BUFFALO SAUCE
AND BLUE CHEESE DIP

PARMESAN-
ARTICHOKE DIP

BEEF MEATBALLS
WITH MARINARA

Beef Meatballs with Marinara

Serves 10 **Prep** 30 min
Slow cook 2 hr on HIGH or 4 hr on LOW

1	**can (28 oz) crushed tomatoes**
1	**tsp sugar**
½	**tsp crushed red pepper**
1¾	**tsp Italian herb blend**
¾	**tsp salt**
½	**small onion, grated**
6	**cloves garlic, grated**
2	**lb ground beef**
2	**large eggs**
1	**cup plain breadcrumbs**
2	**tbsp chopped parsley**
2	**tbsp finely grated Parmesan**
	Giardiniera (pickled vegetables) and/or pretzels, optional

1 In a slow cooker, whisk tomatoes, sugar and red pepper with ¾ tsp Italian herb blend, ¼ tsp salt and half the onion and garlic.

2 In a large bowl, combine beef with remaining onion and garlic, 1 tsp Italian herb blend and ½ tsp salt. Add eggs, breadcrumbs, parsley and Parmesan. Mix until well combined.

3 Form into 1½-inch balls and add to slow cooker. Cover and cook 2 hours on HIGH or 4 hours on LOW. If desired, serve with giardiniera and/or pretzels.

PER SERVING 288 **Cal** | 12 g **Fat** (4 g **Sat**) | 23 g **Pro** | 22 g **Carb** | 6 g **Sugars** | 2 g **Fiber** | 486 mg **Sodium**

Parmesan-Artichoke Dip

Serves 10 **Prep** 15 min **Bake** 30 min **Broil** 3 min

6	**cloves garlic**
1	**cup shredded Swiss cheese**
6	**oz cream cheese, cubed**
⅓	**cup mayonnaise**
2	**tsp lemon juice**
¾	**tsp salt**
¼	**tsp cayenne pepper**
6	**tbsp finely grated Parmesan cheese**
2	**boxes (9 oz each) frozen artichoke hearts, thawed and patted dry**
2	**tbsp finely chopped parsley**
	Italian bread toasts, endive and/or fennel

1 Heat oven to 375°. Coat an 8 x 8-inch broiler-safe baking dish with cooking spray.

2 In a food processor, combine garlic, Swiss cheese, cream cheese, mayonnaise, lemon juice, salt and cayenne with ¼ cup Parmesan. Process until mostly smooth, about 20 seconds. Add artichoke hearts and 1 tbsp parsley; pulse until mixture is chunky but spreadable, stopping to scrape down sides of bowl as needed.

3 Transfer to prepared baking dish. Smooth top and sprinkle with remaining 2 tbsp Parmesan.

4 Bake until lightly browned around the edges, about 30 minutes.

5 Broil dip until top is browned in spots, about 3 minutes. Sprinkle with remaining parsley and serve with Italian bread toasts, endive and/or fennel.

PER SERVING 206 **Cal** | 17 g **Fat** (7 g **Sat**) | 7 g **Pro** | 7 g **Carb** | 1 g **Sugars** | 3 g **Fiber** | 410 mg **Sodium**

Easiest-yet-smartest party trick ever: Make a platter of all different shapes of pretzels—rods, twists, nuggets, you name it—and serve with as many different kinds of mustard as you can manage.

SATÉ DIP,
PAGE 57

CHICKEN
MEATBALLS
WITH BUFFALO
SAUCE, PAGE 58

BEEF MEATBALLS
WITH MARINARA,
PAGE 61

PORK MEATBALLS
WITH HOISIN SAUCE,
PAGE 57

**BLUE CHEESE
DIP, PAGE 58**

KITCHEN GEAR YOU'LL ACTUALLY USE

Overwhelmed with myriad devices that are supposed to make kitchen work easy and are truly worth their space in your drawers and on your counters? These items earn their keep.

Better for batches

FOOD PROCESSOR WITH MINI-CHOPPER BOWL

The food processor deserves all the real estate it takes up. Leave it on the counter and follow these tips to ensure you use it: (1) Keep the chopping blade and the shredding disk handy. When they're nearby, you're more likely to remember to shove veggies and cheese down the chute. Save your arm strength for more important things! (2) Invest in a mini-chopper bowl (if your machine didn't come with one) that lets you chop a tiny portion of food. If you process small amounts in the regular bowl, food will just get flung against the walls, away from the blade.

Less knife work

HANDHELD MANDOLINE

Don't be afraid of this razor-sharp tool! It makes slicing so easy. Some models have changeable blades, but a fixed blade is great for everyday slicing. A mandoline is faster than a knife and keeps slices a consistent thickness, so they all cook evenly. Plus, you can slice right over a bowl or pot or serving dish; no cutting board needed. Choose a mandoline that lets you choose among three thicknesses for more versatility.

Easier garlic prep

ZESTER and GRATER

Forget mincing sticky cloves: Grate your garlic. A good zester and grater is a winner for that option alone, but it's handy for ginger, chiles, hard spices (like nutmeg and cinnamon), cheeses and chocolate as well. You can also perfectly zest your citrus while leaving bitter pith behind. It's fast to use and easy to clean.

Faster, cooler vegetables

SPIRALIZER

Not just an infomercial gadget, the spiralizer makes it easier—and less boring—to eat vegetables. Think beyond subbing for pasta: Raw veggie noodles make a great salad base. And the thinness means hearty veg (like sweet potatoes and beets) cook faster when roasting or sautéing.

SPIRALIZER

FOOD PROCESSOR WITH MINI-CHOPPER BOWL

ZESTER AND GRATER

HANDHELD MANDOLINE

Mandoline and Microplane

Instant Pot Slow-Cooked Honey-Ginger Pork

Serves 6 **Prep** 25 min
Slow cook 3½ hr on HIGH or 6 hr on
LOW **Cook** 4 min

2 lb boneless pork shoulder for stew, cut into medium chunks

1 tsp salt

¼ tsp black pepper

3 carrots, peeled and thinly sliced on the bias with mandoline

1 small onion, halved and sliced on mandoline

1 red bell pepper, seeded and sliced

½ cup honey

6 tbsp unsalted chicken broth

2 tbsp finely grated ginger

1 tsp crushed red pepper

2 tbsp cornstarch

Hot cooked brown rice

1 In multicooker, toss pork with ½ tsp salt and the pepper. Add carrots, onion and bell pepper. Stir honey with ¼ cup broth, ginger, crushed red pepper and ½ tsp salt. Stir into pork mixture.

2 Seal and slow cook on HIGH (or MORE setting) 3½ hours or LOW 6 hours.

3 Remove lid and switch to Sauté. Bring mixture to a boil.

4 Stir cornstarch with 2 tbsp chicken broth. Add to multicooker and cook, stirring, until sauce is thickened, 4 minutes. Serve with hot cooked rice.

PER SERVING 418 **Cal** | 19 g **Fat** (6 g **Sat**) |
29 g **Pro** | 32 g **Carb** | 27 g **Sugars** | 1 g **Fiber** |
545 mg **Sodium**

Toaster Oven and
Digital Thermometer

Mustard-Olive Roast Chicken and Potatoes

Serves 4 **Prep** 30 min
Roast 1 hr, 20 min **Rest** 10 min

⅔ cup jarred large pitted Spanish olives (not stuffed), plus 2 tbsp olive brine

1½ lb tricolor baby potatoes, halved

3 tbsp Dijon mustard

½ tsp dried thyme

1 whole chicken (4 lb)

1 tbsp olive oil

½ tsp salt

¼ tsp black pepper

1 Halve ½ cup olives. Combine in a medium bowl with potatoes. Toss with 2 tbsp mustard and the olive brine. Spread evenly on foil-lined toaster oven tray.

2 Very finely chop remaining olives. Stir with 1 tbsp mustard and the thyme. Rub mixture under skin of chicken breasts. Pat chicken dry and rub with oil. Sprinkle all over with salt and pepper. Truss legs.

3 Place chicken breast side down on top of potato mixture. Roast in toaster oven at 450° (or on Rotisserie setting) 40 minutes, then turn breast side up. Roast 30 to 40 minutes more, until potatoes are tender and chicken temp reaches 165°. Rest chicken 10 minutes, then carve.

PER SERVING 439 **Cal** | 12 g **Fat** (2 g **Sat**) |
49 g **Pro** | 29 g **Carb** | 2 g **Sugars** | 5 g **Fiber** |
1,158 mg **Sodium**

Electric Multicooker

Instant Pot "Roast" Beef

Serves 8 **Prep** 10 min **Sauté** 8 min
Pressure cook 5 min
Natural release 8 min **Rest** 20 min

1 eye round beef roast (2 lb), fat trimmed

1 tsp salt, plus more for serving

¼ tsp black pepper

1 tbsp vegetable oil

1 cup beef broth

1 small onion, halved and sliced

3 cloves garlic, smashed

Chimichurri (recipe on page 67)

1 Sprinkle beef all over with salt and pepper. With multicooker on Sauté, heat oil and cook beef until lightly browned in spots, 2 minutes per side. Set aside.

2 In multicooker, combine broth, onion and garlic. Place rack over mixture.

3 Place meat on rack. Seal and cook 5 minutes on Manual. Let pressure release naturally, 7 to 8 minutes. Remove meat and tent with foil. Rest until temp reaches 120° for rare, about 20 minutes.

4 Slice very thinly and sprinkle with salt. Serve with Chimichurri or jus.

PER SERVING 163 **Cal** | 6 g **Fat** (2 g **Sat**) |
27 g **Pro** | 1 g **Carb** | 0 g **Sugars** | 0 g **Fiber** |
405 mg **Sodium**

Cooking doesn't have to be daunting:
The right tool can make time in the
kitchen a breeze.

STANDING BLENDER

A blender is worth your time and money because it helps you get the finished meal on the table. You can easily produce soups, smoothies and shakes (as well as the occasional margarita). And it's great for making super-fast, versatile sauces that will elevate even simple dinners.

IMMERSION BLENDER

If you're going to have only one blender, go for a standing model. But if you're willing to indulge in two, get an immersion blender. The biggest selling point? Less mess and fewer things to wash because there's no transferring—you just stick the blender right into a pot or bowl.

ELECTRIC MULTICOOKER

Multicookers have won hearts and minds—including ours!—primarily by serving as electric pressure cooker, slow cooker and rice cooker all rolled into one. But they can also sauté (try that, average slow cooker!), steam and sterilize. Not only do they save time on traditionally long-cooking braises, but they're also great for fast recipes like soups since cooking is mostly hands-off.

TOASTER OVEN

This appliance is awesome because you can completely skip preheating, saving time. It won't make your kitchen feel like an oven, either, even at high temperatures. Yes, you may know and love it for its wonderful way with toast, frozen pizza and appetizers. But think bigger: In a larger model, you can bake a cake or even roast a whole chicken (see recipe on page 65). It's also a handy backup oven during the holidays.

INSTANT-READ DIGITAL THERMOMETER

You use an app to check the weather rather than guessing. So why guess at the temperature of your food? Get an instant-read digital thermometer and a guide to doneness and always have your meat (and eggs and bread!) exactly how you want it.

IMMERSION BLENDER

ELECTRIC MULTICOOKER

STANDING BLENDER

TOASTER OVEN

INSTANT-READ DIGITAL THERMOMETER

Sauces that go with almost everything

Standing Blender

Green Goddess Dressing

Makes 1⅓ cups **Prep** 10 min

½	cup reduced-fat mayonnaise
½	cup reduced-fat sour cream
	Zest of 1 lemon plus 1 tbsp lemon juice
2	scallions, white and green parts, roughly chopped
2	tbsp fresh parsley stems and leaves
2	tbsp chopped chives or fresh dill
¼	tsp salt
¼	tsp black pepper

1 Add mayonnaise, sour cream; lemon zest and juice, scallions, parsley, chives, salt and pepper to blender. Cover and blend until smooth, stopping to scrape sides as needed.

Standing Blender

Chimichurri

Makes ⅔ cup **Prep** 10 min

2	large cloves garlic
1	cup packed roughly chopped parsley stems and leaves
¼	cup packed fresh cilantro stems and leaves
3	tbsp red wine vinegar
¼	tsp salt
¼	tsp black pepper
½	cup extra virgin olive oil

1 Add garlic, parsley, cilantro, vinegar, salt and pepper to blender. Cover and blend until well combined. With blender running, slowly add oil and blend until smooth.

Standing Blender

Tzatziki

Makes 3 cups **Prep** 10 min

1	seedless cucumber, peeled
2	cloves garlic
2	tbsp fresh dill
2	tbsp white wine vinegar
1	container (16 oz) plain Greek yogurt
½	tsp salt
⅛	tsp black pepper

1 Dice half of the cucumber; set aside. Add other half to blender along with garlic, dill and vinegar. Cover and blend until smooth. Transfer to a bowl and whisk in yogurt, salt and pepper. Fold in diced cucumber.

Standing Blender

Romesco

Makes 2 cups **Prep** 10 min **Cook** 10 min

4	cloves garlic, sliced
1	cup sliced almonds
1	jar (16oz) roasted red peppers, drained and liquid reserved
1	slice white bread, toasted and cubed
2	tbsp tomato paste
1	tbsp sherry or red wine vinegar
1	tsp smoked paprika
¾	tsp salt
¼	tsp cayenne pepper
2	tbsp extra virgin olive oil

1 In a dry skillet over medium-high, toast garlic and almonds until golden in spots, stirring frequently, about 10 minutes. Add to blender with roasted red peppers, bread, tomato paste, vinegar, smoked paprika, salt and cayenne pepper. Cover and blend well. With blender running, slowly add oil and reserved pepper liquid as needed until almost smooth.

ROMESCO

CHIMICHURRI

TZATZIKI

GREEN GODDESS DRESSING

SHRIMP AND
SAUSAGE SKILLET,
PAGE 74

March

74

82

85

FAMILY DINNERS
Soy-Glazed Chicken Thighs, 71
Spinach-Ricotta Lasagna, 74
Beef and Bean Chili, 74
Shrimp and Sausage Skillet, 74
Chicken Marsala, 76

STAY FULL WHILE FASTING
Mediterranean Bowl, 79
Beef and Sweet Potato Stew, 80
Veggie-Feta Egg Cups, 82

SNACKING
Nut Clusters, 83

DESSERT
Seriously Sneaky Chocolate
    Cake, 85

**SOY-GLAZED
CHICKEN THIGHS**

FAMILY DINNERS

Because you've gotta get food on the table. Fast weeknight meals!

Soy-Glazed Chicken Thighs

Serves 4 **Prep** 15 min **Cook** 8 min **Roast** 35 min

- 8 **small bone-in chicken thighs, skin removed**
- ¼ **tsp salt**
- ⅛ **tsp black pepper**
- 4 **tbsp low-sodium soy sauce**
- 2 **tbsp honey**
- 1 **pkg (12 oz) spaghetti**
- ¼ **cup rice vinegar**
- 3 **tbsp vegetable oil**
- 3 **tbsp peanut butter**
- 2 **tsp sesame oil**
- 3 **sliced scallions**
   Baby bok choy or other green vegetable

1 Heat oven to 400°. Place chicken on a large rimmed foil-lined baking sheet. Season with salt and pepper. Roast 20 minutes.

2 In a small bowl, whisk together 1 tbsp soy sauce and 1 tbsp honey; brush on chicken. Roast 15 minutes.

3 Meanwhile, bring a large pot of salted water to a boil. Add spaghetti and cook per pkg directions. Drain and rinse in cool water. Place spaghetti in a large bowl.

4 In another small bowl, whisk together vinegar with remaining 3 tbsp soy sauce, vegetable oil, peanut butter, remaining 1 tbsp honey, sesame oil and scallions. Pour over spaghetti and toss to coat. Brush chicken with pan drippings and serve with spaghetti and bok choy or your favorite green vegetable.

PER SERVING 706 **Cal** | 26 g **Fat** (4 g **Sat**) | 42 g **Pro** | 76 g **Carb** | 11 g **Sugars** | 4 g **Fiber** | 914 mg **Sodium**

PREP AHEAD

Weekend prep work makes fast weeknight dinners even speedier. A few shortcuts for your Sunday afternoon:

Spinach Lasagna Thaw spinach and combine marinara and diced tomatoes.

Beef and Bean Chili Clean cilantro and wrap in a paper towel; drain and rinse kidney beans; chop onion and garlic.

Soy-Glazed Chicken Thighs Slice scallions; cook noodles; make dressing and store separately.

For perfectly cooked pasta, use at least 4 quarts water for every 16 ounces pasta and stir after it begins to cook so it doesn't stick together. Taste pasta before draining to make sure the texture is al dente—a little chewy.

**SPINACH-RICOTTA
LASAGNA, PAGE 74**

BEEF AND BEAN CHILI, PAGE 74

Spinach-Ricotta Lasagna

Serves 8 **Prep** 20 min **Bake** 50 min
Stand 10 min

1 container (32 oz) part-skim ricotta

1 pkg (10 oz) frozen chopped spinach, thawed and squeezed dry

1 large egg

¾ cup grated Parmesan cheese

2 cups Italian cheese blend

½ tsp salt

   Freshly ground black pepper

1 jar (24 oz) chunky marinara or arrabbiata sauce

1 can (15 oz) fire-roasted diced tomatoes with garlic

12 no-boil lasagna noodles

1 Heat oven to 375°. Coat a 13 x 9 x 2-inch baking dish with nonstick spray. In a large bowl, combine ricotta with spinach, egg, ½ cup Parmesan cheese, ½ cup Italian cheese blend, salt and a few grinds of pepper.

2 In a second bowl, combine marinara sauce with diced tomatoes. Spoon ½ cup marinara mixture over bottom of prepared dish. Top with 3 lasagna noodles, one-fourth of the ricotta mixture and ¾ cup marinara mixture. Repeat 3 more times, topping with any remaining marinara mixture. Sprinkle with remaining 1½ cups Italian cheese blend and ¼ cup Parmesan cheese.

3 Cover dish with foil. Bake 25 minutes. Uncover and bake 25 minutes more. Let stand 10 minutes before cutting.

PER SERVING 484 **Cal** | 22 g **Fat** (12 g **Sat**) | 31 g **Pro** | 41 g **Carb** | 11 g **Sugars** | 1 g **Fiber** | 1,078 mg **Sodium**

Beef and Bean Chili

Serves 6 **Prep** 15 min **Cook** 35 min

2 lb ground round

1 sweet onion, chopped

3 cloves garlic, chopped

¼ cup chili powder

¾ tsp salt

½ tsp black pepper

1 can (15 oz) petite cut diced tomatoes

1 can (15 oz) tomato sauce

1 can (29 oz) or two cans (15 oz each) dark red kidney beans, drained and rinsed

   Diced avocado, sour cream, fresh cilantro and/or hot sauce, optional

1 Cook ground round and onion in a large heavy pot over medium-high until browned, 10 minutes. Add garlic; cook 3 minutes. Add chili powder, salt and pepper. Cook 1 minute. Stir in tomatoes, tomato sauce and ½ cup water.

2 Bring to a simmer, partially cover and cook 20 minutes. Stir in kidney beans and heat through. If desired, serve topped with avocado, sour cream, cilantro and/or hot sauce.

PER SERVING 418 **Cal** | 16 g **Fat** (6 g **Sat**) | 37 g **Pro** | 30 g **Carb** | 7 g **Sugars** | 8 g **Fiber** | 1,056 mg **Sodium**

Shrimp and Sausage Skillet

Serves 4 **Prep** 15 min **Cook** 11 min

2 tbsp extra virgin olive oil

1 red bell pepper, cored and sliced

2 ribs celery, chopped

1 small onion, halved and sliced

2 large cloves garlic, sliced

1 pkg (13 oz) turkey kielbasa, sliced

1 lb medium raw shrimp, peeled and deveined

½ tsp smoked paprika

⅛ tsp salt

2 cups hot cooked brown rice

1 Heat oil in a large skillet over medium-high. Add bell pepper, celery, onion and garlic. Cook, stirring, 4 minutes. Add kielbasa and cook 3 minutes. Stir in shrimp, smoked paprika and salt. Cover and cook 3 minutes, then stir in brown rice and cook 1 minute more.

PER SERVING 512 **Cal** | 17 g **Fat** (4 g **Sat**) | 41 g **Pro** | 49 g **Carb** | 4 g **Sugars** | 4 g **Fiber** | 915 mg **Sodium**

CLEANING MUSHROOMS

So…you need to wash mushrooms, right? Or wrong? If they're packaged presliced button mushrooms or premixed exotics, no—but everything else needs a quick cleaning. Here's the proper approach for each type.

Exotic mushrooms (oyster, shiitake and enoki): Wipe the tops with a damp paper towel.

White button and brown cremini (aka baby bella) mushrooms: Trim stems and rinse in a colander under cool water. Pat dry.

Large stuffing mushrooms and portobellos: Wipe the top of each cap with a damp paper towel or soft brush. Remove stems if you plan on grilling or stuffing. If not, just cut off any parts with visible soil.

Chicken Marsala

Serves 4　**Prep** 15 min　**Cook** 20 min
Roast 30 min

1½	lb small potatoes, halved if large
2	tbsp extra virgin olive oil
¾	tsp salt
¾	tsp black pepper
1	lb broccoli rabe
⅓	cup all-purpose flour
1½	lb thinly sliced chicken cutlets
2	tbsp butter
2	pkg (4 oz each) sliced mixed mushrooms
½	cup Marsala wine
½	cup beef broth

1 Heat oven to 425°. Toss potatoes with 1 tbsp oil and ¼ tsp each salt and pepper on a large rimmed sheet pan. Roast 10 minutes. Toss broccoli rabe with 1 tbsp oil and ¼ tsp each salt and pepper. Push potatoes to one side of pan and add broccoli rabe. Roast 20 minutes.

2 Meanwhile, on a plate, stir flour with remaining ¼ tsp each salt and pepper. Coat chicken in flour mixture (reserve leftover mixture). Heat 1 tbsp butter in a large lidded skillet over medium-high. Brown half the chicken, 3 minutes per side. Remove to a plate; repeat with 1 tbsp butter and remaining chicken. Reduce heat to medium, add mushrooms and sprinkle with 2 tsp flour mixture. Cook 3 minutes. Remove from heat and add wine. Return to heat; cook 1 minute and add broth. Return chicken to pan. Cover and cook 2 minutes. Serve with potatoes and broccoli rabe.

PER SERVING 549 **Cal** | 18 g **Fat** (6 g **Sat**) | 48 g **Pro** | 44 g **Carb** | 3 g **Sugars** | 7 g **Fiber** | 688 mg **Sodium**

CHICKEN
MARSALA

MEDITERRANEAN BOWL

STAY FULL WHILE FASTING

Intermittent fasting (IF) is one of the most-buzzed diets these days, and it's far more sustainable if you make smart choices when you do eat. Avoid hunger pangs with our breakfast, lunch or dinner.

Mediterranean Bowl

Serves 4 **Prep** 20 min **Cook** 12 min **Stand** 15 min

- **1 cup quinoa**
- **1 tsp salt**
- **1 cup packed parsley, finely chopped**
- **½ cup pistachios, roughly chopped**
- **1 cup grape tomatoes, halved**
- **1 cup drained and rinsed chickpeas**
- **⅓ cup pitted Kalamata olives, halved**
- **¼ English cucumber, diced**
- **8 oz shredded cooked chicken**
- **1 lemon, cut into wedges**

1 In a medium saucepan, bring 2 cups water to a boil. Add quinoa and salt and stir. Cover and reduce heat to low; simmer 12 minutes, until water is absorbed. Remove from heat. Fluff quinoa and let stand, covered, 15 minutes. Remove lid and cool to room temp.

2 Stir parsley and pistachios into cooled quinoa.

3 Divide quinoa evenly among 4 bowls. Top with tomatoes, chickpeas, olives, cucumber and chicken. Serve with lemon wedges.

PER SERVING 452 **Cal** | 17 g **Fat** (2 g **Sat**) | 31 g **Pro** | 47 g **Carb** | 5 g **Sugars** | 7 g **Fiber** | 1,030 mg **Sodium**

IF OPTIONS

Whole-Day Fasting Fast for 24 hours once or twice a week.

5:2 Eat normally five days a week, then drop down to 500 to 600 calories the other two nonconsecutive days.

Time-Restricted Feeding You eat only during an 8-hour window each day.

The basic premise of IF is that if you stop eating long enough, your body begins burning fat instead of carbs. It's not for everyone though—check with your doctor first.

Beef and Sweet Potato Stew

Serves 8 **Prep** 25 min **Cook** 41 min **Bake** 2½ hr **Stand** 10 min

¾ cup all-purpose flour

2 tsp salt

½ tsp black pepper

¼ cup vegetable oil

2 lb beef stew meat

1 medium onion, diced

3 ribs celery, sliced

4 cloves garlic, sliced

1 tbsp tomato paste

½ cup dry red wine

1 can (14.5 oz) low-sodium beef broth

6 sprigs parsley

6 sprigs thyme

2 dried bay leaves

1 lb sweet potatoes, peeled and cut into 1-inch cubes

10 oz mushrooms, quartered

1 can (14.5 oz) diced tomatoes

1 Heat oven to 325°. Whisk flour with 1½ tsp salt and the pepper. Heat 1½ tbsp oil in a large heavy ovensafe pot over high. Toss half the beef with flour mixture and add to pot. Cook, turning, until browned all over, 3 to 4 minutes per side. Transfer to a bowl. Add 1½ tbsp oil to pot and repeat with remaining beef, transferring to bowl when browned.

2 Reduce heat to medium-high. Add 1 tbsp oil to pot and stir in onion and celery. Cook 4 to 5 minutes. Add garlic and cook 1 minute. Stir in tomato paste and cook, stirring, 1 minute, until browned. Add wine and simmer until reduced, about 2 minutes, scraping up any browned bits.

3 Return beef to pot. Stir in broth and top with parsley, thyme and bay leaves.

4 Cover pot and transfer to oven. Bake 1½ hours.

5 Remove from oven; stir in sweet potatoes, mushrooms, tomatoes and remaining ½ tsp salt. Return to oven and bake, covered, 30 minutes. Remove lid and bake, uncovered, 30 minutes more. Let stand 10 minutes. Remove herbs and serve.

PER SERVING 328 **Cal** | 12 g **Fat** (3 g **Sat**) | 29 g **Pro** | 23 g **Carb** | 5 g **Sugars** | 3 g **Fiber** | 865 mg **Sodium**

BEEF AND SWEET POTATO STEW

Veggie-Feta Egg Cups

Serves 6 **Prep** 15 min **Bake** 20 min

12 eggs, lightly beaten

1 box (10 oz) frozen spinach, thawed, squeezed dry and chopped

½ cup chopped roasted red pepper

¾ cup crumbled feta cheese

1 tsp salt

½ tsp black pepper

Toast, optional

1 Heat oven to 375°. Coat twelve 2½-inch muffin cups with cooking spray.

2 In a large bowl, combine eggs, spinach, red pepper, feta, salt and black pepper. Divide evenly among muffin cups. Bake 18 to 20 minutes or until eggs are puffed and set. Serve with toast if desired.

PER SERVING 211 **Cal** | 14 g **Fat** (6 g **Sat**) | 17 g **Pro** | 4 g **Carb** | 2 g **Sugars** | 1 g **Fiber** | 834 mg **Sodium**

SNACKING

Nuts are so tasty, they don't need much gussying up. And these clusters are addictive and versatile—good as a snack, crumbled over yogurt or sprinkled on your salad.

Nut Clusters

Makes 40 **Prep** 15 min **Bake** 25 min
Stand 5 min

1	**cup toasted whole almonds**
1	**cup toasted pecan halves**
1	**cup toasted walnut halves**
¾	**cup Grape-Nuts**
¾	**cup Rice Krispies**
3	**egg whites**
6	**tbsp maple syrup**
½	**to ¾ tsp salt**

1 Heat oven to 325°. In a food processor, combine nuts; pulse to roughly chop. Add to a large bowl with Grape-Nuts and Rice Krispies.

2 In a small bowl, whisk egg whites, maple syrup and salt; pour over nut mixture and mix well.

3 Spoon loose tablespoonfuls onto 2 parchment-lined cookie sheets.

4 Bake 23 to 25 minutes, rotating pans halfway through. Cool on pans 5 minutes, then remove to cool completely on rack. Store in an airtight container up to 1 week. Makes about 40 clusters.

PER SERVING 77 **Cal** | 6 g **Fat** (1 g **Sat**) | 2 g **Pro** | 6 g **Carb** | 2 g **Sugars** | 1 g **Fiber** | 62 mg **Sodium**

Swap It Sub in 3 cups of any nuts. And try honey instead of maple syrup.

DESSERT

What they don't know won't kill them.
And they would never in a million years guess
this crazily delicious cake gets its moistness
from black beans…and that there's a sweet
potato in the frosting.

Seriously Sneaky Chocolate Cake

Serves 9   Prep 30 min   Bake 1 hr, 35 min   Cool 10 min

- ⅓ **cup all-purpose flour**
- ⅓ **cup unsweetened cocoa powder**
- 1 **tsp baking powder**
- ½ **tsp baking soda**
- 1 **can (15 oz) low-sodium black beans, drained and rinsed**
- 1 **cup sugar**
- 1 **tbsp vanilla**
- ½ **tsp salt**
- 4 **large eggs, room temperature**
- ⅓ **cup warm water**
- ¼ **cup vegetable oil**

GANACHE

- 1 **8 oz sweet potato**
- 1 **cup milk, semisweet or bittersweet chocolate chips**

1 Heat oven to 350°. Coat a 9-inch square baking pan with cooking spray. Line bottom with parchment; coat with more spray.

2 Whisk flour, cocoa powder, baking powder and baking soda in a bowl. In food processor, combine black beans, sugar, vanilla and salt. Process until smooth.

3 Add eggs, water and oil. Process until smooth. Add flour mixture and process until blended. Pour into pan.

4 Bake 35 minutes or until cake springs back when pressed. Cool 10 minutes, then run a thin knife between pan and cake. Flip cake onto a rack; remove parchment and cool completely. Frost cake with Ganache.

Ganache Heat oven to 375°. Bake sweet potato until tender, 45 minutes to 1 hour. Cool 10 minutes, then slice in half. Scoop out flesh (you'll need 1 cup) and place in food processor. Process until smooth. Add chocolate chips and process until smooth, scraping sides occasionally (the warm sweet potato puree will melt the chocolate). Cool 10 minutes, then spread on cake. Makes 1½ cups.

PER SERVING 357 **Cal** | 15 g **Fat** (4 g **Sat**) | 8 g **Pro** | 53 g **Carb** | 36 g **Sugars** | 7 g **Fiber** | 360 mg **Sodium**

RASPBERRY
CREPE CAKE,
PAGE 107

April

91

99

101

BREAKFAST
Bell Pepper, Cheddar and
  Sausage Quiche, 88

FAMILY DINNERS
Coconut Rice with Jerk Chicken
  and Mango Salsa, 91
Orzo Salad with Grilled
  Shrimp, 92
Open-Faced Crab Sandwich, 95
Spinach Salad with Warm
  Sausage Dressing, 96
Ground Turkey Quesadilla, 99

MAKE ME BLUSH
Rhubarb Tart, 101
Strawberry, Grapefruit and
  Coconut Pavlova, 102
Milk Chocolate Marshmallow
  Cake, 106
Raspberry Crepe Cake, 107

BREAKFAST

This recipe lends itself to endless riffing. Just remember the basics: the egg-milk mixture, 1 cup shredded or crumbled cheese and 2½ cups of the other stuff (cooked first).

Bell Pepper, Cheddar and Sausage Quiche

Serves 6 **Prep** 15 min **Bake** 40 min **Cool** 10 min

1	refrigerated pie crust
½	cup thin red bell pepper strips
2	cups crumbled cooked sausage
2	scallions, sliced
1	cup shredded sharp cheddar
6	large eggs
1	cup milk
½	tsp salt
¼	tsp black pepper

1 Heat oven to 375°. Fit pie crust into a greased 10-inch quiche pan or 9-inch deep-dish pie plate, fluting the edge. Line pie crust with foil and bake 15 minutes. Remove foil.

2 Meanwhile, in a bowl, microwave bell pepper strips with 2 tbsp water 1 minute, until softened. Drain. Scatter sausage, bell pepper strips, scallions and cheese into pie crust.

3 In a large bowl, whisk eggs, milk, salt and black pepper and pour into crust. Bake 15 minutes, then reduce temp to 350°. Bake 25 minutes or until center is set. Cool 10 minutes before slicing.

Tip To prevent rips, let crust come to room temp before unrolling.

PER SERVING 437 **Cal** | 32 g **Fat** (13 g **Sat**) | 18 g **Pro** | 21 g **Carb** | 3 g **Sugars** | 0 g **Fiber** | 1,017 mg **Sodium**

OTHER COMBINATIONS

poblano peppers + corn + pepper Jack

broccoli + bacon + cheddar

hash browns + chives + crumbled feta

MAKE IT VEGETARIAN

Go for chopped veggie sausage instead of pork.

MAKE IT GF

Skip the crust Just pour mixture into a greased pie plate. (Use GF sausage too!)

**BELL PEPPER, CHEDDAR
AND SAUSAGE QUICHE**

**COCONUT RICE WITH
JERK CHICKEN AND
MANGO SALSA**

FAMILY DINNERS

Because you've gotta get food on the table. Fast weeknight meals!

Coconut Rice with Jerk Chicken and Mango Salsa

Serves 6 **Prep** 20 min **Cook** 30 min **Stand** 5 min

- **2   cans (13.5 oz each) coconut milk**
- **3¼ tsp salt**
- **2   cups jasmine rice**
- **1   medium lime**
- **½   cup chopped cilantro**
- **6   small boneless, skinless chicken breasts**
- **2   tbsp jerk seasoning**
- **2   tbsp vegetable oil**
- **2   mangoes, halved, pitted, peeled and diced**
- **¼   cup diced red onion**
- **¼   tsp cayenne pepper**

1 In a medium saucepan, bring coconut milk, ⅔ cup water and 2 tsp salt to a boil. Reduce heat to low, stir in jasmine rice, cover and cook 15 minutes (or per pkg directions), stirring occasionally.

Let stand 5 minutes; fluff with a fork. Zest and juice the lime. Stir zest and ⅓ cup chopped cilantro into rice.

2 Meanwhile, sprinkle chicken with the jerk seasoning and 1 tsp salt. Heat oil in a skillet over medium-high. Add chicken and cook, covered, turning halfway through, until browned and temp reaches 165°, 12 to 15 minutes, depending on thickness.

3 Stir mangoes with lime juice, red onion, remaining ¼ cup chopped cilantro, the cayenne and ¼ tsp salt. Top rice with chicken and mango salsa.

PER SERVING 715 **Cal** | 35 g **Fat** (26 g **Sat**) | 33 g **Pro** | 69 g **Carb** | 16 g **Sugars** | 2 g **Fiber** | 1,330 mg **Sodium**

MANGO KNOW-HOW

Mangoes have a large flat pit the length of the fruit. To cut a mango, set it on a narrow side and hold with one hand. Position a large sharp knife off center, then slice through the flesh. Repeat on the opposite side.

Use a paring knife to score the flesh in a dice pattern up to, but not through, the skin. Press the flesh inside out and cut off the diced fruit.

For an easy bowl option, use ground chicken instead of breasts and cook with the jerk seasoning. Then stir chicken into cooked rice with the zest and cilantro.

This salad easily adapts to your family's taste. Not a fan of shrimp? Use scallops or shredded chicken. Swap broccoli florets for asparagus and rice for orzo.

Orzo Salad with Grilled Shrimp

Serves 4 **Prep** 10 min **Cook** 9 min **Grill** 13 min

- **1**   large lemon
- **1**   lb shrimp, peeled and deveined
- **2½** tbsp extra virgin olive oil
- **½**   tsp plus ⅛ tsp salt
- **¼**   tsp plus ⅛ tsp black pepper
- **¾**   lb asparagus, trimmed
- **1½** cups orzo
- **4**   oz feta, crumbled
- **⅓**   cup packed dill, minced

1 Heat grill to medium-high. Bring a large pot of salted water to a boil.

2 Zest and juice the lemon. In a large bowl, toss shrimp with 1 tbsp oil, ¼ tsp salt, ⅛ tsp pepper and half the lemon zest. Thread onto 4 metal skewers. Toss asparagus with ½ tbsp oil, ⅛ tsp salt, ⅛ tsp pepper and remaining zest.

3 Add orzo to boiling water and cook 9 minutes; drain. Meanwhile, grill asparagus 7 to 9 minutes, turning halfway through. Add shrimp and grill 2 minutes per side.

4 Chop asparagus and stir into orzo. Add dill, lemon juice, remaining 2 tbsp oil, remaining ¼ tsp salt and ⅛ tsp pepper and stir. Sprinkle with feta and top with shrimp.

PER SERVING 552 **Cal** | 20 g **Fat** (6 g **Sat**) | 30 g **Pro** | 40 g **Carb** | 5 g **Sugars** | 4 g **Fiber** | 1,267 mg **Sodium**

ORZO SALAD
WITH GRILLED
SHRIMP

**OPEN-FACED CRAB
SANDWICH**

Open-Faced Crab Sandwich

Serves 4   Prep 20 min

- **1**   lb lump crab meat
- **2**   scallions, sliced
- **1**   rib celery, finely diced
- **½**   red bell pepper, seeded and finely diced
- **2**   tsp lemon zest plus 2 tbsp lemon juice
- **6**   tbsp scallion cream cheese
- **¼**   tsp salt
- **⅛**   tsp cayenne pepper, plus more for topping
- **4**   slices toasted sourdough bread

  Shaved radishes

  Mixed greens, optional

1 Pick through crab meat for shells, then squeeze dry. Combine crab with scallions, celery, bell pepper, lemon zest and juice, 2 tbsp cream cheese, salt and cayenne pepper.

2 Spread about 1 tbsp cream cheese on each slice of sourdough. Divide crab mixture evenly among toasts. Top with shaved radishes and sprinkle with additional cayenne. Serve with mixed green salad.

PER SERVING 318 **Cal** | 4 g **Fat** (2 g **Sat**) | 29 g **Pro** | 40 g **Carb** | 4 g **Sugars** | 3 g **Fiber** | 1,240 mg **Sodium**

The warm sausage dressing (a little sweet, a little tangy, a lot delicious) wilts the spinach and will convert even the pickiest eater into a salad lover.

Spinach Salad with Warm Sausage Dressing

Serves 4   **Prep** 10 min   **Cook** 10 min

1	**container (10 oz) baby spinach**
10	**oz cremini mushrooms, sliced**
2	**shallots, halved and thinly sliced**
1	**tbsp extra virgin olive oil**
12	**oz smoked beef sausage, sliced into coins**
3	**tbsp honey**
2	**tbsp red wine vinegar**
1	**tbsp Dijon mustard**
	Crusty bread, optional

1 In a large bowl, toss spinach, mushrooms and shallots.

2 Heat oil in a large stainless skillet over medium-high. Add sausage and cook until browned, 10 minutes. Remove skillet from heat. Transfer sausage with a slotted spoon to a paper-towel-lined plate, reserving drippings. In the same skillet, whisk honey, vinegar and mustard. Pour warm dressing over salad and toss well.

3 Divide evenly among 4 bowls. Serve with crusty bread if desired.

PER SERVING 472 **Cal** | 35 g **Fat** (13 g **Sat**) | 17 g **Pro** | 21 g **Carb** | 16 g **Sugars** | 3 g **Fiber** | 850 mg **Sodium**

SPINACH SALAD WITH
WARM SAUSAGE
DRESSING

GROUND TURKEY QUESADILLA

Ground Turkey Quesadilla

Serves 4   **Prep** 10 min   **Cook** 6 min   **Bake** 15 min

2   **burrito-size (10-inch) flour tortillas**

1   **bag (8 oz) shredded Mexican cheese blend**

1   **tbsp vegetable oil**

1   **lb ground turkey**

1   **tsp ground cumin**

1   **tsp garlic salt**

¾   **cup salsa**

Shredded leaf lettuce

Sliced plum tomato, avocado and red onion

1 Heat oven to 350°. Place 1 tortilla on a parchment-lined baking sheet. Sprinkle tortilla with half the cheese.

2 Heat oil in a large nonstick skillet over medium-high. Add turkey, cumin and garlic salt. Cook, stirring to break up turkey, until cooked through, 5 to 6 minutes. Stir in salsa and cook until warm, 30 seconds. Spoon turkey mixture over cheese on tortilla and sprinkle with remaining cheese.

3 Top with a second tortilla. Bake until cheese is melted and tortilla is warm, 15 minutes. Top quesadilla with lettuce, tomato, avocado and onion.

PER SERVING 549 **Cal** | 33 g **Fat** (13 g **Sat**) | 40 g **Pro** | 24 g **Carb** | 4 g **Sugars** | 3 g **Fiber** | 1,388 mg **Sodium**

3 QUESADILLA TWISTS

Make it Italian with mozzarella, cooked sausage and marinara. Top with spinach, roasted red peppers and grated Parmesan.

Keep it vegetarian Use black beans or veggie crumbles instead of turkey.

Go spicy with pepper Jack, shredded chicken and hot sauce. Top with lettuce, pickled onion and diced pickled jalapeño.

RHUBARB TART

MAKE ME BLUSH

Spring desserts that are pretty (and delicious) in pink.

Rhubarb Tart

Serves 8 to 10 **Prep** 20 min **Stand** 30 min **Roast** 22 min **Bake** 40 min **Cool** 10 min

1   **lb fresh rhubarb, cut into 2-inch lengths (about 4 stalks)**

⅔   **cup plus 1¼ cups sugar**

2   **sticks unsalted butter**

3   **large eggs plus 2 yolks**

1   **tsp vanilla extract**

½   **tsp salt**

    Grated zest of ½ lemon

1½ **cups cake flour (not self-rising) or all-purpose flour**

¼   **cup fine yellow cornmeal (not stone-ground)**

    Whipped cream or crème fraîche, for serving

1 Grease and flour a 9-inch deep-dish fluted tart pan with removable bottom or round cake pan. In a 13 x 9 x 2-inch baking pan, toss rhubarb with ⅔ cup sugar. Let sit at least 30 minutes or up to 3 hours.

2 Heat oven to 400°. Cover rhubarb pan with foil and roast 10 minutes. Uncover and baste with accumulated juices. Roast 10 to 12 minutes, until rhubarb is tender but not falling apart and juices have become a glaze. Remove from oven and reduce heat to 350°.

3 Meanwhile, beat butter and 1¼ cups sugar with an electric mixer on medium-high speed, until light and fluffy. Beat in eggs and yolks one at a time, beating well after each addition. Beat in vanilla, salt and lemon zest. Stir together flour and cornmeal and beat in gradually at medium speed, scraping down sides of bowl halfway through.

4 Pour into prepared pan and bake until top springs back when touched lightly, about 40 minutes.

5 Remove from oven and cool 10 minutes. Turn pan upside down onto a serving dish and remove sides and bottom. While tart is still warm, arrange roasted rhubarb in a faux lattice pattern on top. Brush top and sides with remaining glaze. Serve warm or at room temperature with whipped cream or crème fraîche.

PER SERVING 507 **Cal** | 28 g **Fat** (16 g **Sat**) | 5 g **Pro** | 61 g **Carb** | 40 g **Sugars** | 1 g **Fiber** | 149 mg **Sodium**

Strawberry, Grapefruit and Coconut Pavlova

Serves 8 **Prep** 20 min **Bake** 3 hr **Cool** 5 hr

You'll need to start this the day before you plan to serve it.

- **2 cans (15 oz each) coconut milk, chilled overnight**
- **1 tbsp cornstarch**
- **1 cup superfine sugar**
- **4 large egg whites, room temperature**
- **1 tsp white vinegar**
- **¾ cup shredded unsweetened coconut, toasted**
- **2 large ruby red grapefruit**
- **2 tbsp confectioners' sugar**
- **1 tsp vanilla extract**
- **Handful of strawberries, topped and halved**
- **Mint, for garnish, optional**

1 Heat oven to 300°. Line a baking sheet with parchment. Using a 9-inch plate as a guide, trace a circle on parchment (turn parchment over so meringue doesn't come in contact with pencil).

2 In a small bowl, stir cornstarch with 3 tbsp superfine sugar.

3 With an electric mixer, beat egg whites on high speed until soft peaks start to form. Add remaining superfine sugar 1 tbsp at a time while beating until stiff and glossy. Beat in cornstarch mixture, then fold in vinegar and ½ cup toasted coconut.

4 Pour out onto baking sheet within circle and, using a spoon, spread meringue out to edges. Build up outer edge an inch higher than the middle, creating a shallow center for fruit and cream.

5 Place in oven and immediately lower temp to 225°. Bake meringue 3 hours. Turn off oven and let meringue cool in oven with door ajar 1 hour. Close door and leave meringue in oven at least 4 hours or up to overnight.

6 To serve, peel grapefruit, removing white membrane, then cut out segments, leaving connecting membrane intact. Separate coconut cream from coconut milk by pouring into a fine-mesh strainer lined with a paper towel or paper coffee filter (reserve milk for another use).

7 Place coconut cream in a bowl and add confectioners' sugar and vanilla. Beat with an electric mixer on high speed until stiff, about 5 minutes. Transfer meringue to a serving platter. Pile whipped coconut cream into center and scatter strawberries and grapefruit segments around it. Sprinkle with remaining toasted coconut and, if using, garnish with mint. Serve immediately.

PER SERVING 299 **Cal** | 3 g **Fat** (1 g **Sat**) | 1 g **Pro** | 55 g **Carb** | 45 g **Sugars** | 0 g **Fiber** | 62 mg **Sodium**

Simple swap: To replicate cake flour, combine ¾ cup plus 2 tablespoons all-purpose flour and 2 tablespoons cornstarch.

**STRAWBERRY,
GRAPEFRUIT AND
COCONUT PAVLOVA**

MILK CHOCOLATE
MARSHMALLOW CAKE,
PAGE 106

If you don't have superfine sugar, you can pulse 1 cup granulated sugar in a food processor until the crystals are broken up and almost powdery.

Milk Chocolate Marshmallow Cake

Serves 14 **Prep** 1 hr **Bake** 30 min **Refrigerate** 1 hr or overnight

You'll need a 9-inch-diameter 2½-qt mixing bowl to make this domed cake.

CAKE

- **2 sticks unsalted butter**
- **1 cup brewed coffee**
- **4 tbsp unsweetened cocoa**
- **1 cup granulated sugar**
- **½ cup packed brown sugar**
- **½ tsp salt**
- **1 tsp vanilla extract**
- **1 tbsp white vinegar**
- **Scant ½ cup milk**
- **2 large eggs**
- **2 cups all-purpose flour**
- **Filling and Frosting**

1 Heat oven to 350°. Line bottom of two 9-inch round cake pans with parchment and grease bottom and sides.

2 In a medium saucepan, melt butter. Remove from heat and whisk in coffee and cocoa until smooth. Whisk in both sugars, salt and vanilla. Place vinegar in a 2-cup liquid measure and add enough milk to equal ½ cup liquid; stir in eggs. Add flour to butter mixture, alternating with milk-egg mixture, whisking just until combined.

3 Pour 1½ cups batter in one prepared pan and 1 cup in the other pan.

4 Bake smaller cake 20 minutes and larger cake 25 to 30 minutes. Remove from oven and cool 15 minutes. Turn larger cake out onto a rack.

5 On a work surface, place two 20-inch lengths of plastic wrap side by side, overlapping by 1 inch. Turn smaller cake out onto middle of plastic. Immediately ease cake, plastic side down, into a 9-inch diameter 2½-qt mixing bowl. Cool completely while you make filling and frosting

Filling and Frosting

- **2 jars (7 oz each) marshmallow creme**
- **4 sticks unsalted butter, softened**
- **1 cup confectioners' sugar**
- **1 bar (3.5 oz) dark chocolate, melted**
- **½ cup pink sanding sugar**

1 In a standing mixer fitted with a whip attachment, whip marshmallow creme, butter and confectioners' sugar until fluffy and smooth. Remove half to a bowl; cover and refrigerate. Beat melted chocolate into remaining half. Reserve ½ cup chocolate filling and pour remaining into cavity of cake in bowl. Top with larger cake and pull excess plastic wrap up and over to cover. Refrigerate at least 1 hour or up to overnight.

2 Peel back plastic wrap and turn cake out onto a serving platter. Remove plastic and use reserved chocolate filling to fill in gap where cake layers meet.

3 Spread reserved white frosting over cake and sprinkle with a thick layer of pink sugar, using a spatula or clean hands to cover sides.

PER SERVING 704 **Cal** | 43 g **Fat** (26 g **Sat**) | 4 g **Pro** | 78 g **Carb** | 55 g **Sugars** | 2 g **Fiber** | 129 mg **Sodium**

Raspberry Crepe Cake

Serves 16 **Prep** 25 min **Refrigerate** at least 1 hr

- **1** **pkg (1.2 oz) freeze-dried raspberries**
- **½** **cup confectioners' sugar**
- **4** **cups heavy cream**
- **2** **pkg 9-inch ready-to-serve crepes (such as Melissa's Produce; 10 per pkg)**
- **½** **tsp vanilla extract**

1 In a blender or food processor, pulverize raspberries with ¼ cup confectioners' sugar. Reserve 1 tbsp in an airtight container.

2 Make dark pink layers: In a large bowl, combine half the remaining raspberry sugar with 1 cup cream and beat with a mixer on medium-high speed until stiff, about 1 minute. Place 1 crepe, dark side down, on a serving plate. Top with ⅓ cup of the raspberry cream, spreading it all the way to the edges. Continue with 4 more crepes and remaining raspberry cream. (Cream layers will be almost as thin as crepes.)

3 Make light pink layers: Using the same bowl and beaters, combine 2 cups cream with remaining raspberry sugar and beat with a mixer on medium-high until stiff. Continue layering 10 more crepes with ⅓ cup cream per layer.

4 Make white layers: In a large bowl, combine remaining 1 cup cream and ¼ cup confectioners' sugar with vanilla and beat with a mixer on medium-high until stiff. Continue layering 5 crepes with ⅓ cup cream per layer, ending with cream. Cover and chill at least 1 hour and up to 6 hours.

5 When ready to serve, sift or sprinkle reserved raspberry sugar over top. This is best served the same day but will keep, covered and chilled, for 1 more day.

PER SERVING 264 **Cal** | 22 g **Fat** (14 g **Sat**) | 3 g **Pro** | 13 g **Carb** | 9 g **Sugars** | 0 g **Fiber** | 79 mg **Sodium**

CHUNKY AVOCADO-CITRUS DIP, PAGE 123

B + T GUAC, PAGE 123

CHORIZO QUESO, PAGE 131

CHERRY TOMATO SALSA, PAGE 129

CILANTRO-SCALLION DIP, PAGE 127

BASIC GUACAMOLE, PAGE 123

AVOCADO MOUSSE, PAGE 123

SOUTHERN CAVIAR WITH HOMINY, PAGE 125

AVOCADO-CORN SALSA, PAGE 123

May

115

129

132

FAMILY DINNERS
Fettuccine with Fresh Tomato
 Sauce, 111
BBQ Bacon Cheddar Burgers, 112
Chicken and Apple Slaw, 115
Grilled Shrimp Caesar, 116
Pork with Blueberry Balsamic
 Sauce, 119

5X5 FOR 5/5
Basic Guacamole, 123
Avocado-Corn Salsa, 123
Avocado Mousse, 123
B + T Guac, 123

Chunky Avocado-Citrus Dip, 123
Smoky Beet and Bean Dip, 125
Roasted Red Pepper Hummus, 125
Edamame Dip, 125
Southern Caviar with Hominy, 125
White Bean Dip, 125
Cilantro-Scallion Dip, 127
Turmeric-Yogurt Dip, 127
Whipped Feta Dip, 127
Sour Cream and Leek Dip, 127
Caramelized Onion Dip, 127
Green Pea Dip, 129
Olive Tapenade, 129
Cherry Tomato Salsa, 129

Mushroom and Cheese
 Fondue, 129
Warm Spinach-Artichoke Dip, 129
Warm Anchovy Dip, 131
Chorizo Queso, 131
Warm Crab Dip, 131
Pepperoni Pizza Dip, 131
Buffalo Chicken Dip, 131

DESSERT
Lemon Tart, 132

FETTUCCINE WITH FRESH TOMATO SAUCE

FAMILY DINNERS

Because you've gotta get food on the table. Fast weeknight meals!

Fettuccine with Fresh Tomato Sauce

Serves 6 **Prep** 10 min **Cook** 20 min

- 1 **pkg (16 oz) dry fettuccine**
- ¼ **cup extra virgin olive oil**
- 1 **pint red cherry tomatoes**
- 1 **pint yellow cherry tomatoes**
- 2 **cloves garlic, sliced**
- ½ **tsp salt**
- ¼ **tsp black pepper**
- ½ **cup packed basil leaves, chopped**
- ½ **cup grated Asiago cheese**

1 Bring a pot of salted water to a boil. Add fettuccine and cook according to pkg directions. Drain, reserving 1 cup pasta water.

2 While pasta cooks, heat oil in a large skillet over medium-high. Add tomatoes. Cook, stirring, 4 minutes. Add garlic, salt and pepper. Cook 4 more minutes, until tomatoes soften. Remove from heat.

3 Stir in basil. Add pasta and reserved pasta water. Toss and top with Asiago.

PER SERVING 410 **Cal** | 14 g **Fat** (3 g **Sat**) | 12 g **Pro** | 59 g **Carb** | 4 g **Sugars** | 4 g **Fiber** | 391 mg **Sodium**

YOU SAY TOMATO...

The main difference between cherry and grape tomatoes is their shape. Grape tomatoes are oblong, like their namesakes, while cherry tomatoes are round. Also, grape tomatoes have thicker skin and are slightly less sweet; cherry tomatoes are juicier. Either type would work well in the fettuccine.

Make it meaty: Stir cooked sausage into fettuccine—a flavored chicken one—or fully cooked mini meatballs would be delicious.

Brioche buns are made with butter, eggs, milk and a pinch of sugar. It's no wonder they have so much flavor and a tender crumb. Toasting takes them over the top.

TURKEY BURGER TIPS

Grated zucchini adds moistness to often-dry ground turkey. A cup of grated or finely chopped mushrooms also works well.

Skip the mess Wet your hands when shaping the patties.

Ditch the bun and wrap this burger in a few lettuce leaves instead or serve the cheese-topped patty on a salad.

BBQ Bacon Cheddar Burgers

Serves 6 **Prep** 20 min **Broil** 21 min

2	small zucchini, peeled and grated
2	lb ground turkey
⅔	cup barbecue sauce
¾	tsp salt
¼	tsp black pepper
6	slices cheddar
6	brioche rolls, split
12	slices cooked turkey bacon
	Hot cooked sweet potato fries, optional

1 Pat shredded zucchini dry and place in a large bowl. Add turkey, ¼ cup barbecue sauce, salt and pepper. Shape into 6 patties.

2 Heat broiler to high. Broil burgers, turning once, 14 to 18 minutes. Add a slice of cheddar to each burger and broil 1 to 2 minutes more.

3 Broil brioche rolls, split sides down, until toasted, about 1 minute. Place patties on roll bottoms and top with 2 slices turkey bacon, breaking slices in half to fit in bun. Spoon 2 tbsp barbecue sauce on roll tops. If desired, serve with sweet potato fries.

PER SERVING 563 **Cal** | 24 g **Fat** (9 g **Sat**) | 46 g **Pro** | 35 g **Carb** | 17 g **Sugars** | 2 g **Fiber** | 1,398 mg **Sodium**

BBQ BACON
CHEDDAR
BURGERS

CHICKEN AND
APPLE SLAW

The sweetness from the apple mellows the cabbage and kale in this colorful slaw.

Chicken and Apple Slaw

Serves 6 **Prep** 20 min

1	bag (14 oz) multicolor coleslaw mix
3	cups shredded cooked chicken
2	cups shredded kale
1	Gala apple, cored and cut into matchsticks
½	cup salted pumpkin seeds
1	tsp salt
⅓	cup cider vinegar
1	tbsp Dijon mustard
1	tsp sugar
½	tsp black pepper
½	cup extra virgin olive oil

1 In an extra-large bowl, combine coleslaw, chicken, kale, apple and pumpkin seeds. Toss with ½ tsp salt.

2 In a medium bowl, whisk vinegar, mustard, sugar, pepper and remaining ½ tsp salt. While whisking, add oil in a thin stream. Add to slaw and toss to combine.

PER SERVING 320 **Cal** | 24 g **Fat** (3 g **Sat**) | 15 g **Pro** | 11 g **Carb** | 4 g **Sugars** | 3 g **Fiber** | 634 mg **Sodium**

SHREDDED CHICKEN 3 WAYS

Pile into taco shells and top with salsa, cheese and shredded lettuce.

Stir into mac and cheese along with cooked broccoli.

Make chicken salad and stuff into centers of halved avocados.

Be a hero: For bigger appetites, make the Caesar into a sandwich—just layer the components on a hero or hoagie roll.

Grilled Shrimp Caesar

Serves 6 **Prep** 15 min **Grill** 10 min

1	**baguette**
1	**stick softened unsalted butter**
1	**tbsp chopped parsley**
1½	**tsp garlic paste**
½	**tsp salt**
1½	**lb raw shrimp**
¼	**tsp black pepper**
3	**hearts romaine lettuce, cut lengthwise**
	Bottled Caesar dressing
	Shaved Parmesan cheese

1 Heat grill to medium-high. Split the baguette lengthwise, then cut into thirds. In a small bowl, combine butter, parsley, garlic paste and ¼ tsp salt. Reserve 2 tbsp garlic butter and spread the rest on bread.

2 Toss shrimp with ¼ tsp each salt and pepper. Thread onto skewers. Grill bread, buttered sides down, 1 minute. Remove from grill. Grill romaine, cut sides down, 2 to 3 minutes. Remove from grill.

3 Melt reserved butter. Grill shrimp 2 to 3 minutes. Flip and brush with melted butter. Grill 2 to 3 minutes. Place 1 lettuce half on a plate and drizzle with bottled Caesar dressing. Top with shrimp and some shaved Parmesan. Serve with grilled bread.

PER SERVING 604 **Cal** | 36 g **Fat** (13 g **Sat**) | 38 g **Pro** | 36 g **Carb** | 6 g **Sugars** | 8 g **Fiber** | 1,141 mg **Sodium**

**GRILLED SHRIMP
CAESAR**

PORK WITH BLUEBERRY
BALSAMIC SAUCE

Pork with Blueberry Balsamic Sauce

Serves 4   Prep 15 min   Cook 6 min   Roast 15 min   Rest 5 min

- ½   **tsp salt**
- ½   **tsp onion powder**
- ¼   **tsp black pepper**
- 1½ **lb pork tenderloin**
- 2   **tbsp butter**
- 6   **oz blueberries**
- ¼   **cup balsamic vinegar**
- 1   **tsp chopped fresh oregano**
- 2   **tsp sugar**
- **Asparagus and cauliflower rice, optional**

1 Heat oven to 400°. In a small bowl, combine salt, onion powder and pepper. Rub over pork.

2 Melt butter in a large stainless skillet over medium-high. Sear tenderloin, 3 minutes per side. Move to a small rimmed baking pan lined with foil and transfer to oven. Roast 15 to 20 minutes, until temp reaches 140°. Let pork rest 5 minutes before slicing.

3 Meanwhile, reduce heat under skillet to medium. Add blueberries, vinegar, oregano and sugar. Cook 7 minutes, scraping up browned bits in pan, until berries have popped and mixture has reduced slightly. Slice pork and spoon sauce over slices. If desired, serve with asparagus and cauliflower rice.

PER SERVING 317 **Cal** | 11 g **Fat** (6 g **Sat**) | 38 g **Pro** | 17 g **Carb** | 9 g **Sugars** | 4 g **Fiber** | 400 mg **Sodium**

B + T GUAC, PAGE 123

CHERRY TOMATO SALSA, PAGE 129

CHORIZO QUESO, PAGE 131

CHUNKY AVOCADO-CITRUS DIP, PAGE 123

CILANTRO-SCALLION DIP, PAGE 127

BASIC GUACAMOLE, PAGE 123

AVOCADO MOUSSE, PAGE 123

SOUTHERN CAVIAR WITH HOMINY, PAGE 125

AVOCADO-CORN SALSA, PAGE 123

5X5 FOR 5/5

Twenty-five dips for Cinco de Mayo—or whatever other get-together you've got cooking. Salsas and guacs are well represented, but there are lots of others too—creamy, cheesy, meaty and everything in between.

Avocado

BASIC GUACAMOLE

B + T GUAC

AVOCADO-CORN SALSA

AVOCADO MOUSSE

CHUNKY AVOCADO-CITRUS DIP

Basic Guacamole

Serves 16 **Prep** 20 min

Stir 6 peeled, pitted and diced **avocados** with 2 finely diced **jalapeños**, ½ cup finely chopped **cilantro**, 6 tbsp finely diced **red onion**, ½ cup fresh **lime juice** and 1 to 1½ tsp **salt**, mashing if desired. Makes 4 cups.

PER SERVING 214 **Cal** | 19 g **Fat** (4 g **Sat**) | 4 g **Pro** | 13 g **Carb** | 1 g **Sugars** | 12 g **Fiber** | 437 mg **Sodium**

Avocado-Corn Salsa

Serves 10 **Prep** 20 min **Grill** 15 min

Stir 1 cup finely diced and seeded **tomato** with ¾ cup grilled or roasted **corn**, ¼ cup each finely diced **red onion** and **cilantro**, 3 tbsp fresh **lime juice**, 1 tbsp minced **jalapeño** (or to taste) and ½ tsp **salt**. Fold in 1 peeled, pitted and diced **avocado**. Makes 2½ cups.

PER SERVING 86 **Cal** | 5 g **Fat** (1 g **Sat**) | 2 g **Pro** | 10 g **Carb** | 3 g **Sugars** | 4 g **Fiber** | 238 mg **Sodium**

Avocado Mousse

Serves 6 **Prep** 15 min

In a food processor, combine 2 large **avocados**, peeled, pitted and cut into chunks; ⅓ cup **fat-free Greek yogurt**; 1 tbsp fresh **lime juice**; 1 clove **garlic**, grated; and ¾ tsp **salt**. Process until completely smooth, 1 to 2 minutes, occasionally scraping down sides. Transfer to a serving bowl and top with salted **pumpkin seeds**. Makes 1½ cups.

PER SERVING 108 **Cal** | 9 g **Fat** (2 g **Sat**) | 4 g **Pro** | 7 g **Carb** | 1 g **Sugars** | 5 g **Fiber** | 323 mg **Sodium**

B + T Guac

Serves 8 **Prep** 15 min **Cook** 8 min

Stir 8 pieces cooked **bacon**, chopped (save 2 tbsp for garnish), with 1 cup seeded and diced **tomato**; ½ cup minced **basil**; 3 tbsp fresh **lemon juice**; and ½ tsp **salt**. Fold in 3 peeled, pitted and diced **avocados**. Garnish with reserved **bacon**. Makes 2 cups.

PER SERVING 452 **Cal** | 41 g **Fat** (11 g **Sat**) | 11 g **Pro** | 15 g **Carb** | 2 g **Sugars** | 12 g **Fiber** | 955 mg **Sodium**

Chunky Avocado-Citrus Dip

Serves 8 **Prep** 30 min

Trim top and bottom from 1 **orange** and 1 ruby red **grapefruit**, then cut around fruit to remove peel. Working over a bowl to collect juice, cut between membranes to release flesh. Chop flesh into large pieces and transfer to a bowl. Stir in 2 tbsp **pomegranate seeds**, 1½ tbsp finely chopped **shallot**, ½ tbsp of the fruit juice and ½ tsp **salt**. Fold in 1 peeled, pitted and chopped **avocado**. Top with more **pomegranate** if desired. Makes 2 cups.

PER SERVING 79 **Cal** | 4 g **Fat** (1 g **Sat**) | 1 g **Pro** | 11 g **Carb** | 3 g **Sugars** | 4 g **Fiber** | 195 mg **Sodium**

Bean

SMOKY BEET AND BEAN DIP

EDAMAME DIP

ROASTED RED PEPPER HUMMUS

SOUTHERN CAVIAR WITH HOMINY

MAKE YOUR OWN PITA CHIPS

Split and quarter five 4½-inch whole wheat pitas. Place on a rimmed baking sheet and coat pieces with cooking spray. Bake at 350° 8 to 9 minutes, until crisp. Serves 6.

Smoky Beet and Bean Dip

Serves 12 **Prep** 15 min

In a food processor, process until smooth 2 cans (15.5 oz each) **pinto beans**, drained and rinsed; 1 can (15 oz) cut **beets**, drained; 2 small **chipotles in adobo** plus 2 tsp **adobo sauce**; 1 clove **garlic**; 3 tbsp fresh **lime juice**; 1 tsp **salt**; and ¼ tsp ground **cumin**. Makes 3 cups.

PER SERVING 196 **Cal** | 2 g **Fat** (0 g **Sat**) | 11 g **Pro** | 36 g **Carb** | 5 g **Sugars** | 10 g **Fiber** | 911 mg **Sodium**

Roasted Red Pepper Hummus

Serves 12 **Prep** 15 min

In a food processor, process until smooth 2 cans (15.5 oz each) **chickpeas**, drained and rinsed; 1 jar (12 oz) **roasted red peppers**, drained; 2 cloves **garlic**; 3 tbsp **tahini**; 2 tsp **fresh lemon zest** plus 2 tbsp **fresh lemon juice**; and 1 tsp **salt**. Makes 3 cups.

PER SERVING 270 **Cal** | 8 g **Fat** (1 g **Sat**) | 12 g **Pro** | 40 g **Carb** | 6 g **Sugars** | 12 g **Fiber** | 822s mg **Sodium**

Edamame Dip

Serves 10 **Prep** 10 min **Cook** 4 min

Cook 12 oz frozen shelled **edamame**, covered, in microwave 4 minutes. Let cool. Drain and add to a blender with 3 large **scallions**, roughly chopped; ¼ cup each **miso paste** and **rice vinegar**; 3 tbsp **vegetable oil**; 1 tbsp **toasted sesame oil**; and 3 tbsp **water**. Process until smooth. Makes 2½ cups.

PER SERVING 218 **Cal** | 14 g **Fat** (2 g **Sat**) | 9 g **Pro** | 13 g **Carb** | 2 g **Sugars** | 5 g **Fiber** | 542 mg **Sodium**

Southern Caviar with Hominy

Serves 24 **Prep** 20 min

In a large bowl, stir 2 cans (15.5 oz each) **black-eyed peas**, drained and rinsed, with 1 can (15.5 oz) **white hominy**, drained and rinsed; 1 can (10 oz) **mild tomatoes with green chiles** (such as Rotel); 5 **scallions**, sliced; 1 **orange bell pepper**, diced; 1 medium **jalapeño**, finely diced; ¼ cup **cilantro**, chopped; ¼ cup **red wine vinegar**; 2 tbsp **olive oil**; and 1 tsp **sugar**. Add **salt** and **cracked black pepper** to taste. Serve immediately or chill 2 hours to blend flavors. Makes 6 cups.

PER SERVING 134 **Cal** | 3 g **Fat** (0 g **Sat**) | 3 g **Pro** | 23 g **Carb** | 5 g **Sugars** | 6 g **Fiber** | 448 mg **Sodium**

White Bean Dip

Serves 10 **Prep** 20 min

In a food processor, combine 2 cans (15.5 oz each) **cannellini beans**, drained and rinsed, with 2 tsp **fresh lemon zest** plus juice from 2 **lemons** (5 tbsp); 1 tsp fresh **thyme** leaves; 1 tsp **hot sauce**; 1 clove **garlic**, crushed; and ¾ tsp **salt**. Process 30 seconds; scrape down sides of bowl. Replace lid and, with processor running, add ⅓ cup **olive oil** in a thin stream. Transfer to a bowl, drizzle with a little more **olive oil** and top with additional fresh **thyme**. Makes 2½ cups.

PER SERVING 279 **Cal** | 18 g **Fat** (2 g **Sat**) | 8 g **Pro** | 24 g **Carb** | 2 g **Sugars** | 7 g **Fiber** | 427 mg **Sodium**

WHITE BEAN DIP

Creamy

CILANTRO-
SCALLION DIP

TURMERIC-
YOGURT DIP

WHIPPED
FETA DIP

SOUR CREAM
AND LEEK DIP

Cilantro-Scallion Dip

Serves 8   **Prep** 15 min

In a mini chopper, combine 2 **scallions**, trimmed and cut into 1-inch pieces; ⅔ cup **cilantro**; and ½ cup **fresh parsley**. Pulse until finely chopped. Add ¾ cup **sour cream**, 3 tbsp **milk**, 1 tbsp each **fresh lemon juice** and **olive oil**, ¾ tsp **salt** and **hot sauce** to taste. Pulse until smooth. Makes 2 cups.

PER SERVING 65 **Cal** | 6 g **Fat** (3 g **Sat**) | 1 g **Pro** | 2 g **Carb** | 1 g **Sugars** | 0 g **Fiber** | 243 mg **Sodium**

Turmeric-Yogurt Dip

Serves 6   **Prep** 10 min

In a medium bowl, whisk ¾ cup each **plain low-fat yogurt** and **sour cream**; 2 tbsp chopped **cilantro**; 1 tbsp each **olive oil**, **fresh lemon juice** and **water**; 2 to 3 tsp ground **turmeric**; 1 tsp each **garlic powder** and **onion powder**; and ½ tsp **salt**. Makes 1½ cups.

PER SERVING 124 **Cal** | 10 g **Fat** (4 g **Sat**) | 3 g **Pro** | 6 g **Carb** | 4 g **Sugars** | 0 g **Fiber** | 270 mg **Sodium**

Whipped Feta Dip

Serves 4   **Prep** 10 min

In a mini chopper, combine 8 oz room-temp **feta** (not crumbles), ½ cup **sour cream** and 1 tbsp **fresh lemon juice**. Process until very smooth, stopping to scrape sides as needed. Transfer to a bowl and stir in 2 tbsp chopped **fresh dill** and ½ tsp **cracked black pepper**. Serve at room temp. Makes 1 cup.

PER SERVING 208 **Cal** | 18 g **Fat** (11 g **Sat**) | 9 g **Pro** | 4 g **Carb** | 3 g **Sugars** | 0 g **Fiber** | 529 mg **Sodium**

Sour Cream and Leek Dip

Serves 8   **Prep** 15 min   **Cook** 15 min **Refrigerate** 2 hr

Split, wash and thinly slice 1 lb **leeks** (white and light-green parts only). In a medium nonstick skillet over medium, heat 1 tbsp **unsalted butter** and 1 tbsp **olive oil**. Add leeks and ½ tsp **salt** and cook 5 minutes. Add 1 medium **shallot**, thinly sliced; 2 cloves **garlic**, sliced; and ¼ tsp **salt**. Cook until softened and just starting to brown, 6 minutes. Let cool completely. Stir ½ cup each **sour cream** and **light mayonnaise** with ½ tsp **onion powder** and ¼ tsp **salt**. Fold in leek mixture and **cracked black pepper** to taste. Chill 2 hours. Makes 2 cups.

PER SERVING 126 **Cal** | 11 g **Fat** (3 g **Sat**) | 1 g **Pro** | 7 g **Carb** | 2 g **Sugars** | 1 g **Fiber** | 396 mg **Sodium**

Caramelized Onion Dip

Serves 10   **Prep** 15 min   **Cook** 30 min

Heat a 10-inch cast-iron pan over medium-high. Add 4 center-cut slices **bacon**, chopped, and cook 8 to 10 minutes. Remove to a plate with a slotted spoon and reduce heat to medium. Add 1 **Vidalia onion**, thinly sliced, and season with ¼ tsp **salt**. Cook, stirring often, 12 to 15 minutes. Add 1 pkg (8 oz) **cream cheese**, cut up, and 2 cups (8 oz) shredded **Fontina cheese**. Whisk ½ cup **milk** with 1 tsp **cornstarch**. Stir into skillet and bring to a simmer; cook 2 minutes. Top with bacon and serve warm. Makes 2¾ cups.

PER SERVING 382 **Cal** | 32 g **Fat** (17 g **Sat**) | 15 g **Pro** | 8 g **Carb** | 6 g **Sugars** | 1 g **Fiber** | 640 mg **Sodium**

CARAMELIZED ONION DIP

Veggie

GREEN PEA DIP

OLIVE TAPENADE

CHERRY TOMATO SALSA

MUSHROOM AND CHEESE FONDUE

Green Pea Dip

Serves 6 **Prep** 10 min

In a blender, combine 1 bag (10 oz) **frozen peas**, thawed, with ¼ cup each grated **Parmesan** and **part-skim ricotta**, 3 tbsp **fresh mint**, 2 tbsp **fresh lemon juice** and ¾ tsp **salt**. Blend until smooth. Blend in **cracked black pepper** to taste. Top with more fresh **mint** if desired. Makes 1½ cups.

PER SERVING 77 **Cal** | 2 g **Fat** (1 g **Sat**) | 5 g **Pro** | 9 g **Carb** | 3 g **Sugars** | 2 g **Fiber** | 472 mg **Sodium**

Olive Tapenade

Serves 10 **Prep** 10 min

In a mini chopper, combine 8 oz pitted **Kalamata olives**, drained, and 2 tbsp **pimientos**, drained. Add 2 tbsp **olive oil**, 1 tbsp **capers** plus 1 tbsp **caper brine**, 1 clove **garlic** and 1 tsp each **fresh thyme** and **white wine vinegar**. Process until well combined but still slightly chunky. Season with ¼ tsp **cracked black pepper**. Makes 1⅓ cups.

PER SERVING 144 **Cal** | 15 g **Fat** (0 g **Sat**) | 0 g **Pro** | 3 g **Carb** | 0 g **Sugars** | 0 g **Fiber** | 673 mg **Sodium**

Cherry Tomato Salsa

Serves 9 **Prep** 15 min

Dice 3 cups **heirloom cherry tomatoes** and add to a bowl with ⅓ cup finely chopped **red onion**; 2 tbsp chopped **cilantro**; 1½ tbsp **fresh lime juice**; 1 large clove **garlic**, minced; 1 tbsp **olive oil**; 1 to 2 tsp **hot sauce**; and ¾ tsp **salt**. Serve, adding more **hot sauce** to taste. Makes 2¼ cups.

PER SERVING 47 **Cal** | 3 g **Fat** (0 g **Sat**) | 1 g **Pro** | 5 g **Carb** | 3 g **Sugars** | 1 g **Fiber** | 404 mg **Sodium**

Mushroom and Cheese Fondue

Serves 8 **Prep** 15 min **Cook** 15 min

Heat 2 tbsp **unsalted butter** in a medium saucepan or fondue pot over medium. Add 1 pkg (8 oz) **baby bella mushrooms**, trimmed, halved and thinly sliced. Cook 5 minutes, stirring often. Add ½ tsp **fresh thyme leaves**, chopped if desired. Sprinkle with ¼ tsp **salt**. Stir in 1 cup **dry white wine** and bring to a simmer, 3 to 4 minutes. Grate 12 oz **Jarlsberg** or **Gruyère cheese** into a large bowl. Toss with 2 tsp **cornstarch**. Add cheese to saucepan, one handful at a time, stirring with a wooden spoon until melted and smooth. Stir in ½ tsp **salt** and ¼ tsp **garlic powder**. Top with **fresh thyme sprigs** if desired. Makes 2 cups.

PER SERVING 226 **Cal** | 16 g **Fat** (9 g **Sat**) | 12 g **Pro** | 3 g **Carb** | 1 g **Sugars** | 0 g **Fiber** | 301 mg **Sodium**

Warm Spinach-Artichoke Dip

Serves 16 **Prep** 20 min **Bake** 35 min

Heat oven to 375°. Drain 1 can (14 oz) **artichoke hearts** and add to a food processor. Pulse to slightly chop artichokes. Add 1 box (10 oz) **frozen chopped spinach**, thawed and squeezed dry; 1 pkg (8 oz) **cream cheese**, cut up; 1½ cups shredded **mozzarella**; ½ cup **light mayonnaise**; ¼ cup grated **Parmesan**; 1 tsp **garlic salt**; ¼ tsp **black pepper**; and a pinch of **cayenne**. Process until mixture is blended and uniform. Transfer to a 1½-qt baking dish. Top with ½ cup shredded **mozzarella** and ¼ cup grated **Parmesan**. Bake 35 minutes, until browned and bubbly. Makes 4 cups.

PER SERVING 278 **Cal** | 21 g **Fat** (10 g **Sat**) | 14 g **Pro** | 11 g **Carb** | 2 g **Sugars** | 2 g **Fiber** | 1,059 mg **Sodium**

WARM SPINACH-ARTICHOKE DIP

Meaty

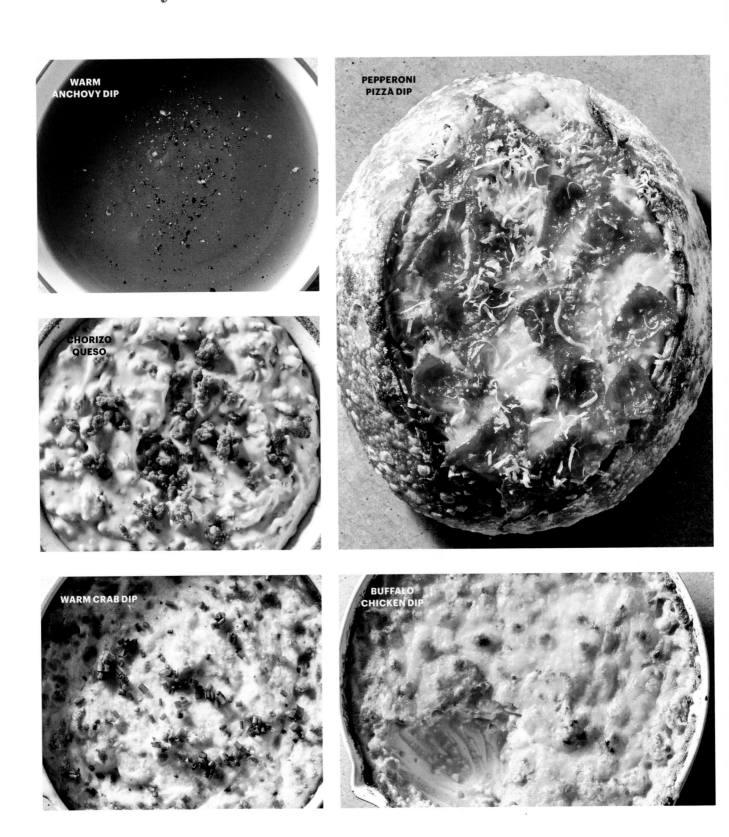

WARM
ANCHOVY DIP

PEPPERONI
PIZZA DIP

CHORIZO
QUESO

WARM CRAB DIP

BUFFALO
CHICKEN DIP

Warm Anchovy Dip

Serves 4   **Prep** 15 min   **Cook** 5 min

Very finely mince 2 oz drained **anchovy fillets**, then mash with a knife to make a paste. Add to a medium saucepan with ½ cup **olive oil** and 4 cloves **garlic**, grated. Bring to a simmer over medium-low and cook 5 minutes, until garlic is fragrant and anchovies melt a bit. Remove from heat and whisk in 4 tbsp cold **unsalted butter**, cubed, and **cracked black pepper** to taste. Dip will separate upon standing; if desired, use an immersion blender to emulsify. Makes 1 cup.

PER SERVING 250 **Cal** | 27 g **Fat** (7 g **Sat**) | 3 g **Pro** | 1 g **Carb** | 0 g **Sugars** | 0 g **Fiber** | 348 mg **Sodium**

Chorizo Queso

Serves 16   **Prep** 15 min   **Cook** 10 min

In a medium saucepan, combine 1½ cups **milk** with 8 oz **Velveeta**, cubed. Cook over medium until cheese is melted, 6 minutes. Toss 8 oz shredded **Mexican cheese blend** with 2 tsp **cornstarch** and stir into pot until melted, 1 minute. Remove from heat and stir in 1¾ cups cooked **chorizo crumbles** and ¼ cup finely chopped **pickled jalapeños** plus 2 tbsp **pickled jalapeño brine**. Keep warm in a small slow cooker and serve topped with ¼ cup cooked **chorizo crumbles**. Makes 4 cups.

PER SERVING 369 **Cal** | 27 g **Fat** (14 g **Sat**) | 22 g **Pro** | 6 g **Carb** | 5 g **Sugars** | 0 g **Fiber** | 1,023 mg **Sodium**

Warm Crab Dip

Serves 10   **Prep** 15 min   **Bake** 25 min   **Broil** 1 min

Heat oven to 350°. In a large bowl, beat 1 pkg (8 oz) softened **cream cheese** with ½ cup **light mayonnaise**, ½ tsp **onion powder**, ¼ tsp **salt**, ⅛ tsp **cayenne** and a few grinds of **black pepper**. Fold in 1 can (6 oz) **fancy white lump crab meat**, drained; ¼ cup grated **Parmesan**; and 1 tbsp minced **fresh chives**. Spread into a greased 2½- to 3-cup baking dish and top with 1 tbsp grated **Parmesan**. Bake 25 minutes. Broil 1 to 2 minutes to brown top. Season with **black pepper**. Makes 2¼ cups.

PER SERVING 176 **Cal** | 16 g **Fat** (7 g **Sat**) | 6 g **Pro** | 3 g **Carb** | 2 g **Sugars** | 0 g **Fiber** | 401 mg **Sodium**

Pepperoni Pizza Dip

Serves 10   **Prep** 15 min   **Bake** 30 min   **Stand** 10 min

Heat oven to 350°. In a medium bowl, combine 8 oz small-curd, **low-fat cottage cheese**, 8 oz **low-fat ricotta**, 1¼ cups jarred **marinara**, ¾ cup finely shredded **mozzarella**, 1 tsp **dried oregano** and ¼ tsp **crushed red pepper**. Add 4 oz **sun-dried tomatoes**, diced, and one 6.5 oz **stick pepperoni** or soppressata, diced; stir well. Pour into a hollowed-out 1 lb **loaf of bread**; top with ¼ cup finely shredded **mozzarella** and 2 tbsp grated **Parmesan**. Bake 30 minutes. Let stand 10 minutes; serve warm. Makes 2½ cups.

PER SERVING 323 **Cal** | 17 g **Fat** (6 g **Sat**) | 15 g **Pro** | 28 g **Carb** | 7 g **Sugars** | 3 g **Fiber** | 790 mg **Sodium**

Buffalo Chicken Dip

Serves 6   **Prep** 20 min   **Cook** 20 min   **Bake** 25 min   **Broil** 3 min

Heat broiler. In a mini chopper, pulse 1 medium **carrot**, chopped; 1 stalk **celery**, chopped; and 1 medium **shallot** until finely chopped. Melt 2 tbsp **unsalted butter** in a medium broiler-safe skillet over medium-high. Add carrot, celery, shallot and ¼ tsp **salt**; cook 5 minutes. Add 1½ lb **ground chicken** and ½ tsp **salt**; cook until vegetables are tender and chicken is cooked through, 7 minutes. Stir in ¾ cup **buffalo hot sauce**, 1 pkg (8 oz) **cream cheese**, cubed and at room temp, and 2 oz **blue cheese**, crumbled. Cook until cheese is melted, 3 minutes. Stir in 2 tsp **cornstarch** and cook until mixture thickens, 1 to 2 minutes. Remove from heat; top with 1 cup shredded **Monterey Jack**. Broil until bubbly, 3 minutes. Makes 1½ cups.

PER SERVING 449 **Cal** | 35 g **Fat** (18 g **Sat**) | 29 g **Pro** | 7 g **Carb** | 3 g **Sugars** | 1 g **Fiber** | 1,221 mg **Sodium**

DESSERT

Roll lemons between your palm and the counter before juicing. This helps to break apart the pulp, maximizing the amount of juice you'll get.

PREBAKED CRUST

1. Heat oven to 425°. Fit a refrigerated pie crust into a 10-inch removable-bottom tart pan or 9-inch pie plate.

2. Line crust with foil and fill with pie weights (or try dry beans or rice).

3. Bake 10 minutes. Remove foil and weights; bake 7 to 10 minutes more.

Lemon Tart

Serves 8 **Prep** 15 min **Cook** 10min
Bake 15 min **Refrigerate** 5 hr

3   **lemons, zested and juiced**

1¼ **cups sugar**

1   **stick unsalted butter**

4   **large eggs and 4 egg yolks**

   **Prebaked Pie Crust
   (recipe at left)**

   Whipped cream, optional

1 Heat oven to 325°. In a saucepan, combine 4 tsp lemon zest and ¾ cup lemon juice with sugar and butter. Cook over medium, stirring occasionally, until butter melts and sugar dissolves.

2 Combine eggs and yolks in a blender. With blender running on low, carefully add hot lemon mixture. Pour mixture from blender into saucepan and cook over medium-low to medium until thickened, 5 to 7 minutes, stirring constantly. Pour into Prebaked Pie Crust and smooth top.

3 Bake 15 minutes, until set but still shiny. Refrigerate 5 hours or until chilled and firm. Top with whipped cream if desired.

PER SERVING 392 **Cal** | 22 g **Fat** (11 g **Sat**) | 6 g **Pro** | 46 g **Carb** | 32 g **Sugars** | 0g **Fiber** | 172 mg **Sodium**

LEMON TART

**BABY BACK
RIBS, PAGE 153**

**PEPPERY
COLESLAW,
PAGE 153**

June

139

140

157

BREAKFAST
Hobo Packs, 137

FAMILY DINNERS
Chicken and Veggie Skillet, 139
Greek Steak and Salad, 140
Halfway Healthy Spaghetti
   Pesto, 143
Tuscan Chicken Cobb, 144
Ground Pork Banh Mi, 147

AMERICAN GRILL
Grilled Maine Lobster, 149
Corn and Crab Salad, 149
Chicago-Style Burger, 150
Warm German Potato Salad, 150
Baby Back Ribs, 153
Peppery Coleslaw, 153
Smoked Brisket, 154
Texas-Style Beans, 154
Grilled Salmon, 157
Apple and Fennel Salad, 157

BREAKFAST

Make these flavorful pouches with chorizo and potato for backwoods or backyard—no cleanup required.

Hobo Packs

Serves 6 **Prep** 25 min **Grill** 30 min

- **1 lb Idaho potatoes, scrubbed and diced**
- **1 lb sweet potatoes, scrubbed and diced**
- **1 large red bell pepper, seeded and sliced**
- **1 small yellow onion, diced**
- **½ tbsp vegetable oil**
- **1¼ tsp salt**
- **1 tsp chopped fresh oregano, plus more for serving**
- **1 lb fresh chorizo, casings removed**

1 Heat grill to 475°. In a large bowl, toss potatoes, sweet potatoes, bell pepper and onion with vegetable oil, salt and oregano.

2 Create 6 large rectangles of 2 layers of heavy-duty aluminum foil. Divide mixture (about 1⅓ cups per packet) among foil rectangles. Break chorizo into small pieces and sprinkle evenly over mixture. Fold packets to seal well.

3 Cook on covered grill, turning over halfway through, until sausage is cooked through and potatoes are tender, 28 to 30 minutes. Open packets very carefully. Sprinkle with additional oregano.

PER SERVING 470 **Cal** | 30 g **Fat** (11 g **Sat**) | 21 g **Pro** | 29 g **Carb** | 3 g **Sugars** | 3 g **Fiber** | 1,449 mg **Sodium**

NUTRITION BOOST

Stir salt and black pepper into plain Greek yogurt and add a dollop for some probiotic-packed creaminess.

SWAP IT

Try andouille or spicy Italian sausage in place of the chorizo.

Don't peek! Resist the urge to open the foil during cooking. Let the (extremely hot) steam do its job in the packets.

CHICKEN AND
VEGGIE SKILLET

FAMILY DINNERS

Because you've gotta get food on the table. Fast weeknight meals!

Chicken and Veggie Skillet

Serves 4 **Prep** 20 min **Cook** 25 min

- **2** tbsp butter
- **4** (4 to 5 oz) boneless, skinless chicken breasts
- **¾** tsp salt
- **½** tsp black pepper
- **1** pkg (10 oz) yellow rice
- **½** lb small carrots
- **½** lb thin green beans (haricots verts)
- **1** tbsp extra virgin olive oil
- **1½** tsp chopped fresh thyme
- Salsa verde, optional

1 Melt butter in a large lidded skillet over medium-high. Sprinkle chicken breasts with ½ tsp salt and ¼ tsp pepper. Add to skillet and brown 2 minutes per side. Remove to a plate.

2 Add 3 cups water to skillet, cover and bring to a boil. Stir in yellow rice. Cover tightly, reduce heat to medium-low and cook 10 minutes. Meanwhile, trim carrots and green beans. Place carrots and green beans in 2 separate bowls and toss each with ½ tbsp oil, ½ tsp chopped fresh thyme and ⅛ tsp each salt and pepper.

3 Uncover skillet and add carrots. Cover and cook 5 minutes. Uncover and add green beans and chicken. Sprinkle with ½ tsp thyme. Cover and cook until chicken is cooked through, about 5 minutes. Serve with salsa verde on the side if desired.

PER SERVING 538 **Cal** | 14 g **Fat** (5 g **Sat**) | 39 g **Pro** | 63 g **Carb** | 7 g **Sugars** | 4 g **Fiber** | 1,315 mg **Sodium**

Swap it: Try large bone-in thighs instead of breasts and cook 5 to 10 minutes more.

It's easy to overcook a great cut of steak, and there's no fixing it! Remember, the meat keeps cooking after you take it off the grill—that's why you let it rest 10 minutes.

Greek Steak and Salad

Serves 6 **Prep** 15 min **Grill** 12 min **Stand** 10 min

2	**lb sirloin steak**
1¼	**tsp salt**
¾	**tsp black pepper**
2	**cups assorted cherry tomatoes**
½	**English cucumber**
¼	**cup fresh dill, chopped**
2	**chopped scallions**
3	**tbsp red wine vinegar**
3	**tbsp extra virgin olive oil**
¾	**cup crumbled feta**
	Plain Greek yogurt
	Toasted pitas

1 Season steak with 1 tsp salt and ½ tsp pepper. Heat grill or grill pan to high. Grill steak 10 to 12 minutes, turning once, until temp reaches 130°. Remove from grill and let rest 10 minutes.

2 While steak rests, quarter cherry tomatoes and dice cucumber. Toss in a bowl along with dill, scallions, red wine vinegar, oil and ¼ tsp each salt and pepper. Gently fold in feta. Place steak on a platter and spoon salad on top. Serve with plain Greek yogurt and pitas.

PER SERVING 489 **Cal** | 29 g **Fat** (10 g **Sat**) | 36 g **Pro** | 22 g **Carb** | 4 g **Sugars** | 1 g **Fiber** | 917 mg **Sodium**

GREEK STEAK
AND SALAD

**HALFWAY HEALTHY
SPAGHETTI PESTO**

Halfway Healthy Spaghetti Pesto

Serves 4 **Prep** 20 min **Cook** 6 min
Stand 10 min

1	**lb zucchini noodles (from 2 large zucchini)**
¾	**tsp salt**
½	**lb dry spaghetti**
1	**tbsp extra virgin olive oil**
4	**cups broccoli florets**
1	**cup green peas, thawed**
¼	**tsp red pepper flakes**
1	**pkg (7 oz) refrigerated pesto**
¼	**cup grated Parmesan**

1 Place zucchini noodles in a colander in the sink and sprinkle with ¼ tsp salt. Let stand 10 minutes. Rinse zucchini noodles.

2 Bring a large pot of salted water to a boil. Add spaghetti and cook to al dente, about 10 minutes, then drain spaghetti over zucchini.

3 Meanwhile, heat oil in a large lidded skillet over medium-high. Add broccoli, ¼ cup water and ¼ tsp salt. Cover and cook 4 minutes. Uncover and add peas and red pepper flakes. Cook 2 minutes.

4 Add spaghetti mixture to skillet, along with pesto, Parmesan and ¼ tsp salt. Toss to combine.

PER SERVING 542 **Cal** | 27 g **Fat** (6 g **Sat**) | 19 g **Pro** | 58 g **Carb** | 9 g **Sugars** | 7 g **Fiber** | 886 mg **Sodium**

Tuscan Chicken Cobb

Serves 4   **Prep** 20 min   **Cook** 5 min   **Grill** 12 min

⅓   cup balsamic vinegar

1   tsp Dijon mustard

1   tsp sugar

¼   tsp black pepper

½   tsp plus ⅛ tsp salt

⅓   cup extra virgin olive oil

1¼ lb skinless, boneless chicken breasts

3   to 4 oz soppressata or prosciutto

1   bag (5 oz) baby kale

4   hard-boiled eggs, halved

2   medium tomatoes, cut into wedges

1   cup small marinated mozzarella balls, halved

1 In a small bowl, whisk vinegar, mustard, sugar, pepper and ½ tsp salt. While whisking, add oil in a thin stream. Place chicken breasts in a dish and add 3 tbsp dressing, turning to coat.

2 Heat grill or grill pan to medium-high. While grill heats, cut soppressata into thin strips and cook in a small skillet until crisp, 5 minutes. Add chicken to grill and cover. Grill 9 to 12 minutes, until cooked through, turning once. Remove to a cutting board and cut into cubes.

3 On a large platter, toss kale with ¼ cup dressing. Scatter eggs, tomato wedges and mozzarella over kale. Sprinkle tomatoes and eggs with ⅛ tsp salt and serve salad with remaining dressing.

PER SERVING 541 **Cal** | 34 g **Fat** (9 g **Sat**) | 50 g **Pro** | 7 g **Carb** | 2 g **Sugars** | 2 g **Fiber** | 971 mg **Sodium**

TUSCAN CHICKEN
COBB

GROUND PORK
BANH MI

A great banh mi sandwich has the perfect interplay between juicy pork, a smear of sriracha, crunchy veggies and soft yet chewy bread.

Ground Pork Banh Mi

Serves 6 **Prep** 15 min **Cook** 10 min

- ¼ **cup packed dark brown sugar**
- 3 **tbsp low-sodium soy sauce**
- 2 **tbsp Asian fish sauce**
- 1 **tbsp honey**
- 2 **tsp cornstarch**
- 1½ **lb ground pork**
- 2 **baguettes**
- ¾ **cup sriracha mayo**
- ¾ **cup cilantro leaves**
- ¾ **cup sliced or matchstick-cut seedless cucumber**
- ¾ **cup sliced or matchstick-cut carrots**
- ¾ **cup sliced or matchstick-cut radishes**

1 In a small bowl, whisk brown sugar, soy sauce, fish sauce, honey and cornstarch.

2 In a large nonstick skillet, cook ground pork 7 minutes over medium-high, breaking apart with a spoon. Drain off most of the fat and add sauce mixture. Cook, stirring, 3 minutes.

3 Slice baguettes crosswise into thirds, then split each piece lengthwise. Spread 2 tbsp sriracha mayo on cut sides of bread. Fill each sandwich with ½ cup pork mixture, 2 tbsp cilantro leaves and 2 tbsp each cucumber, carrots and radishes.

PER SERVING 611 **Cal** | 25 g **Fat** (4 g **Sat**) | 34 g **Pro** | 61 g **Carb** | 14 g **Sugars** | 2 g **Fiber** | 1,268 mg **Sodium**

BANH MI BASICS

For a hit of tangy crunch, quickly pickle your veggies. Mix ¾ cup white vinegar with 1 tbsp sugar and ½ tsp salt. Add sliced veggies and let stand 15 minutes.

DIY spicy mayo Combine ½ cup light mayo with 1 tbsp sriracha or your favorite hot sauce.

GRILLED MAINE
LOBSTER

CORN AND CRAB
SALAD

AMERICAN GRILL

Taste your way across the USA without leaving your backyard.

Northeast

Grilled Maine Lobster

Serves 4 **Cook** 8 min **Grill** 4 min

- **2** **live Maine lobsters (1½ lb each)**
  Salt
- **1** **tbsp vegetable oil**
  Shallot-Chive Butter (recipe at right)

1 Heat grill over medium-high. Meanwhile, bring a large pot of water to a boil over high.

2 Add 1 lobster to pot and cook, covered, about 4 minutes. (Lobsters should be red but not fully cooked.) Transfer lobster to a cutting board. Return water to a boil and repeat with remaining lobster.

3 Remove rubber bands from claws. Cut lobsters in half lengthwise and, if desired, remove any tomalley or roe. Rinse inside with water and pat dry. Sprinkle with salt and drizzle with oil. Place lobsters cut sides down on grill rack and grill, covered, until tail meat temp reaches 135°. Season with salt to taste and serve with Shallot-Chive Butter.

Shallot-Chive Butter Stir 1 stick unsalted butter, softened, with 1 tbsp each finely diced shallot and thinly sliced chives and ⅛ tsp salt. Use immediately or wrap in parchment and store in refrigerator up to 2 weeks. Makes ½ cup.

PER SERVING 210 **Cal** | 16 g **Fat** (8 g **Sat**) | 17 g **Pro** | 0 g **Carb** | 0 g **Sugars** | 0 g **Fiber** | 755 mg **Sodium**

Corn and Crab Salad

Serves 8 **Prep** 15 min

- **6** **tbsp lemon juice**
- **3** **tbsp vegetable oil**
- **2** **tbsp whole-grain mustard**
- **½** **tsp salt**
- **¼** **tsp black pepper**
- **¼** **tsp cayenne pepper**
- **4** **cups cooked corn kernels**
- **½** **large red bell pepper, quartered and sliced**
- **⅓** **cup parsley, finely chopped**
- **8** **oz jumbo lump crabmeat, picked over for shells**
- **1** **cup oyster crackers, slightly crushed**

1 In a large bowl, whisk first 6 ingredients. Stir in corn, bell pepper and parsley. Fold in crab.

2 Top with crushed oyster crackers.

PER SERVING 162 **Cal** | 7 g **Fat** (1 g **Sat**) | 8 g **Pro** | 20 g **Carb** | 5 g **Sugars** | 2 g **Fiber** | 382 mg **Sodium**

Every tourist knows to eat lobster up North. But the locals also stock up on peekytoe crab—and plenty of oyster crackers.

Where's the beef? In the Midwest! This juicy burger has flavors reminiscent of Chicago's famed hot dog.

Midwest

Chicago-Style Burger

Serves 4 **Prep** 15 min **Grill** 10 min

- 1½ **lb ground beef**
- 2 **tbsp yellow mustard, plus more for serving**
- 1½ **tsp celery salt, plus more for serving**
- 4 **poppy seed buns**
- 4 **dill pickle sandwich slices, halved**
- 4 **slices tomato, halved**
- ¼ **cup sweet pickle relish**
- 4 **sport peppers or pepperoncini, quartered**

1 Heat grill over medium-high. Mix beef with mustard and celery salt until well combined. Form into four 4-inch-wide 6 oz patties.

2 Place patties on grill and cook 4 to 5 minutes per side for medium-rare or to desired doneness.

3 Meanwhile, split buns and grill cut sides 1 to 2 minutes. Place burgers on bottom buns and top with a sprinkle of celery salt plus mustard, pickle, tomato, relish and sport peppers. Top with remaining buns.

PER SERVING 477 **Cal** | 21 g **Fat** (8 g **Sat**) | 32 g **Pro** | 36 g **Carb** | 7 g **Sugars** | 2 g **Fiber** | 1,419 mg **Sodium**

Warm German Potato Salad

Serves 10 **Prep** 15 min **Cook** 31 min

- 3 **lb red potatoes, unpeeled and cut into 1½-inch pieces**
- 8 **cups unsalted beef broth**
- 2½ **tsp salt**
- ½ **lb bacon, chopped**
- 1 **small yellow onion, diced**
- ⅔ **cup apple cider vinegar**
- 2½ **tsp sugar**
- 1 **tsp black pepper**
- ¼ **cup parsley, roughly chopped**

1 Place potatoes in a large pot and cover with broth and 2 cups water. Stir in 2 tsp salt and bring to a boil over high. Reduce heat to medium and simmer until tender, 20 to 25 minutes. Drain.

2 Meanwhile, cook bacon in a large stainless skillet over medium until crisp, about 10 minutes, stirring occasionally. With a slotted spoon, transfer bacon to a paper-towel-lined plate. Pour off and reserve all bacon fat.

3 Add onion to skillet with ¼ cup bacon fat; cook over medium until softened, 5 to 6 minutes. Remove skillet from heat and whisk in vinegar, sugar, pepper and ½ tsp salt. Pour vinegar mixture over warm potatoes. Add bacon and parsley and stir to coat well. Serve warm.

PER SERVING 219 **Cal** | 9 g **Fat** (3 g **Sat**) | 9 g **Pro** | 26 g **Carb** | 3 g **Sugars** | 3 g **Fiber** | 1,088 mg **Sodium**

WARM GERMAN
POTATO SALAD

CHICAGO-STYLE
BURGER

BABY BACK RIBS

PEPPERY COLESLAW

In the South, locals definitely have an opinion on tomato-based or mustard sauce—or just dry rub. Some prefer the sweetness of the tomato-based sauce; others go for the tangy mustard sauce.

South

Baby Back Ribs

Serves 6 **Prep** 15 min **Refrigerate** 12 to 24 hr **Grill** 2 hr, 10 min **Let rest** 15 min

2 **racks baby back ribs (1½ lb each), membranes removed**

2 **tbsp kosher salt**

5 **tbsp Dry Rub (recipe at right)**

Tomato-Based Rib Sauce or Mustard-Based Rib Sauce (recipes at right)

1 Place each rack of ribs on 4 layers of heavy-duty aluminum foil. Sprinkle meaty side of each with 1 tbsp kosher salt. Rub each all over (including bone side) with 2½ tbsp Dry Rub. Fold foil to seal well in packets and refrigerate 12 to 24 hr.

2 Prepare grill for indirect heat over medium-high (400°). Grill packets over indirect heat, with lid closed, until meat pulls away from bones, 1 hour, 45 minutes to 2 hours (Or grill about 1 hour over direct heat.) Let ribs rest in packets 10 minutes, then open very carefully.

3 Brush meaty sides of ribs with ½ cup Rib Sauce. Discard foil and drippings and place ribs meaty sides down over direct heat on grill. Cook 5 minutes per side, until well marked. Let rest 5 minutes. Serve with additional Rib Sauce if desired.

PER SERVING 551 **Cal** | 34 g **Fat** (12 g **Sat**) | 40 g **Pro** | 21 g **Carb** | 15 g **Sugars** | 1 g **Fiber** | 3,062 mg **Sodium**

Dry Rub Stir 3 tbsp packed dark brown sugar with 3 tsp hot paprika, 1 tbsp each black pepper, garlic powder and cumin and 1 tsp dry mustard powder. Makes ½ cup.

PER SERVING 26 **Cal** | 0 g **Fat** (0 g **Sat**) | 0 g **Pro** | 6 g **Carb** | 5 g **Sugars** | 1 g **Fiber** | 2 mg **Sodium**

Tomato-Based Rib Sauce In a small saucepan, whisk 1 cup ketchup with ¼ cup spicy brown mustard, 2 tbsp each molasses and Worcestershire sauce and 1 tbsp each apple cider vinegar and Dry Rub. Cover and simmer 5 minutes over medium. Makes 1¼ cups.

PER SERVING 101 **Cal** | 0 g **Fat** (0 g **Sat**) | 1 g **Pro** | 23 g **Carb** | 19 g **Sugars** | 0 g **Fiber** | 683 mg **Sodium**

Mustard-Based Rib Sauce In a small saucepan, whisk ¾ cup yellow mustard with 5 tbsp packed light brown sugar and 1 tbsp each apple cider vinegar, Worcestershire sauce and Dry Rub. Cover and simmer 5 minutes over medium. Makes 1 cup.

PER SERVING 66 **Cal** | 0 g **Fat** (0 g **Sat**) | 0 g **Pro** | 26 g **Carb** | 17 g **Sugars** | 0 g **Fiber** | 537 mg **Sodium**

Peppery Coleslaw

Serves 10 **Prep** 20 min

7 **cups thinly sliced green cabbage (from 1 medium)**

4 **cups thinly sliced purple cabbage (from 1 small)**

1½ **cups shredded carrot**

3 **scallions, thinly sliced**

½ **cup light mayonnaise**

3 **tbsp white wine vinegar**

2 **tbsp milk**

2 **tsp sugar**

1 **tsp salt**

1 **tsp coarsely ground black pepper**

¼ **tsp celery seeds**

1 Toss green and purple cabbages in a large bowl with carrot and scallions.

2 Whisk remaining ingredients and toss with cabbage mixture. Makes 8 cups.

PER SERVING 145 **Cal** | 11 g **Fat** (3 g **Sat**) | 2 g **Pro** | 11 g **Carb** | 6 g **Sugars** | 4 g **Fiber** | 619 mg **Sodium**

In Texas, brisket is practically a religion—that's how much people love the cut. And they pride themselves on meat so good it doesn't even need sauce.

Southwest

SMOKE 'EM IF YOU GOT 'EM

If you cook out all the time, consider adding a smoker to your backyard lineup. Smokers specialize in indirect heat, which lets you cook low and slow. Most have adjustable vents that help you control the temperature for large items, like turkeys, as well as for more-delicate items, like salmon. Look for models that have easy access to the fuel box (to load charcoal or wood) and are easy to clean.

Smoked Brisket

Serves 20 **Prep** 20 min
Smoke 10 hr **Rest** 30 min

- **12 cups hickory wood or applewood chunks, soaked in water 1 hour and drained**
- **6 tbsp kosher salt**
- **4 tbsp black pepper**
- **3 tbsp paprika**
- **1 tbsp hot paprika**
- **12 lb whole packer-cut beef brisket, trimmed**

1 Prepare smoker according to manufacturer's instructions. Place 2 cups wood chunks on coals. Maintain temp of 275° to 300° 15 to 20 minutes.

2 Stir together spices and rub evenly over brisket, pressing so it adheres. Place brisket fatty side up in smoker. Close lid and smoke until a "bark" starts to form on meat surface, 4 to 6 hours, adding wood chips 2 cups at a time as necessary. (The meat's surface will be very dark and shift from looking moist to appearing drier.)

3 Carefully remove brisket from smoker, wrap loosely in parchment and return to smoker. Smoke until temp in center of brisket reaches 200° to 205°, 3 to 4 hours (check temp every hour).

4 Transfer brisket to a cutting board; let rest 20 to 30 minutes. Thinly slice across the grain.

PER SERVING 863 **Cal** | 65 g **Fat** (26 g **Sat**) | 63 g **Pro** | 2 g **Carb** | 0 g **Sugars** | 1 g **Fiber** | 2,396 mg **Sodium**

Texas-Style Beans

Serves 8 **Prep** 15 min **Cook** 25 min
Stand 3 min

- **8 slices bacon, chopped**
- **1 small yellow onion, diced**
- **3 large cloves garlic, minced**
- **1 tbsp chili powder**
- **¼ tsp salt**
- **12 oz light beer**
- **½ cup packed dark brown sugar**
- **¼ cup ketchup**
- **2 cans (15 oz each) pinto beans, drained and rinsed**

1 In a large heavy pot over medium, cook bacon until crispy, about 10 minutes, stirring occasionally. Remove pot from heat and transfer bacon to a paper-towel-lined plate with a slotted spoon. Pour off all but 2 tbsp bacon fat. Return pot to heat and add onion; cook, stirring, until starting to soften, 3 to 4 minutes.

2 Add garlic, chili powder and salt to pot; cook 1 minute, stirring constantly. Add beer and stir to scrape up browned bits. Add brown sugar and ketchup.

3 Stir beans and bacon into pot. Simmer 10 minutes, until sauce has thickened. Let stand 3 minutes. Serve warm.

PER SERVING 315 **Cal** | 12 g **Fat** (4 g **Sat**) | 11 g **Pro** | 39 g **Carb** | 15 g **Sugars** | 6 g **Fiber** | 621 mg **Sodium**

TEXAS-STYLE
BEANS

SMOKED
BRISKET

PINOT GRIS
OREGON GROWN
UND
ERW
OOD

APPLE AND
FENNEL SALAD

GRILLED
SALMON

The silver lining to all those cool, rainy days? Rivers filled with salmon, and loads of crisp apples and tart berries.

Pacific Northwest

Grilled Salmon

Serves 4 **Prep** 10 min **Grill** 10 min

- **4** center-cut skinless salmon fillets (6 oz each)
- **½** tsp salt
- **1** tbsp Dijon mustard
- **1** tbsp vegetable oil
- **2** scallions, thinly sliced on the bias
- **2** lemons, halved

1 Heat grill over medium-high. Pat salmon dry and sprinkle all over with ¼ tsp salt.

2 Whisk mustard with oil and ¼ tsp salt. Brush tops of fish with half the mustard mixture and grill, tops down, until well marked, 3 to 5 minutes.

3 Brush second side of salmon with remaining mustard mixture. Flip and cook until temp reaches 120°, 3 to 5 minutes more. Top salmon with scallions and serve with lemon halves.

PER SERVING 321 **Cal** | 16 g **Fat** (2 g **Sat**) | 39 g **Pro** | 3 g **Carb** | 1 g **Sugars** | 1 g **Fiber** | 467 mg **Sodium**

Apple and Fennel Salad

Serves 6 **Prep** 20 min

- **1½** tbsp Dijon mustard
- **1½** tbsp lemon juice
- **1½** tbsp honey
- **1½** tbsp vegetable oil
- **½** tsp salt
- **1½** cups thinly sliced fennel bulb (about 12 oz), fronds reserved
- **2** stalks celery, thinly sliced, leaves reserved
- **1** Granny Smith apple, thinly sliced
- **¾** cup toasted hazelnuts, roughly chopped
- **¼** cup mint, roughly chopped
- **6** oz blackberries

1 In a small bowl, whisk mustard, lemon juice, honey, oil and salt.

2 Add fennel, celery and apple to a large bowl with ½ cup hazelnuts; ¼ cup fennel fronds, chopped; ¼ cup celery leaves, chopped; and mint. Toss to combine. Pour dressing over salad and toss to coat.

3 Transfer to a serving dish and top with remaining hazelnuts and the blackberries.

PER SERVING 193 **Cal** | 13 g **Fat** (1 g **Sat**) | 3 g **Pro** | 17 g **Carb** | 10 g **Sugars** | 6 g **Fiber** | 310 mg **Sodium**

RED, WHITE AND
BLUEBERRY
POPS, 170

July

166

176

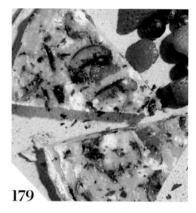

179

FAMILY DINNERS
Blackened Zucchini and Corn
    Tacos, 161
Lemon-Thyme Chicken Burgers, 162
Pork with Peaches and
    Pecans, 165
Tuna Kebabs, 166
Tomato and Cheddar Slab Tart, 168

A WEDGE WITH AN EDGE
Watermelon Toppings, 169

FOUR FOR JULY
Red, White and Blueberry Pops, 170
No-Bake Fireworks Cheesecake
    Bars, 172
Swirled Meringue Sorbet
    Sandwiches, 175
Rocking Berry Roll, 176

POWER UP
Vegetable Frittata, 179
Cherry Cooler, 179
Salmon Pasta, 180
Turmeric Chicken Salad, 181

**BLACKENED ZUCCHINI
AND CORN TACOS**

FAMILY DINNERS

Because you've gotta get food on the table. Fast weeknight meals!

Blackened Zucchini and Corn Tacos

Serves 4 **Prep** 20 min **Grill** 16 min

2 **lb small zucchini, quartered, seeds removed**

2 **tbsp vegetable oil**

2 **to 3 tbsp Cajun seasoning**

2 **medium ears fresh sweet corn, husks removed**

  Salt

8 **warm corn tortillas**

  Chopped cilantro, crumbled queso fresco and salsa

  Lime wedges

1 In a medium bowl, toss zucchini with 1 tbsp oil and 1 to 2 tbsp Cajun seasoning. Coat corn with 1 tbsp vegetable oil and 1 tbsp Cajun seasoning. Grill zucchini over medium-high until well marked and just tender, 6 to 7 minutes per side. Cut in half crosswise. Grill corn, turning occasionally, 10 minutes or until charred in spots. Use a sharp knife to cut kernels from cobs.

2 Season zucchini and corn with salt to taste. Divide evenly among warm corn tortillas and top with cilantro, queso fresco and salsa. Serve with lime wedges.

PER SERVING 267 **Cal** | 13 g **Fat** (3 g **Sat**) | 8 g **Pro** | 34 g **Carb** | 9 g **Sugars** | 6 g **Fiber** | 654 mg **Sodium**

TACOS CON CARNE

If you want to add steak, shrimp or chicken to our veggie tacos, brush with oil before grilling and use the same Cajun seasoning blend to taste.

MAKE YOUR OWN CAJUN SEASONING

All the components of this spice blend are probably in your pantry. According to your taste—and tolerance for spicy food!—stir together:

• **paprika**

• **onion powder**

• **garlic powder**

• **dried thyme**

• **dried oregano**

• **cayenne pepper**

Leave out the salt to make it more versatile and then just salt your meat or vegetables to taste.

Summer squash secret:
If you get young zucchini or yellow squash, the seed bed will be smaller, and you won't need to scrape out the seeds before grilling.

Easy does it when it comes to forming the patties. Use clean hands to gently mix the ground chicken, lemon zest, thyme, salt and pepper.

Lemon-Thyme Chicken Burgers

Serves 4   **Prep** 15 min   **Bake** 18 min

- **1½** **lb ground chicken**
- **1** **lemon, zested and juiced**
- **2** **tsp chopped fresh thyme leaves**
- **1** **tsp salt**
-   **Freshly ground black pepper**
- **4** **brioche buns, split**
- **2** **cups lightly packed arugula**
- **2½** **oz garlic and fine herb cheese spread (such as Boursin)**

1 In a medium bowl, combine ground chicken with lemon zest, thyme, salt and a few grinds of pepper. Form into four-inch patties and grill over medium-high 15 to 18 minutes or until temp reaches 165°, turning once halfway through. Grill buns, cut sides down, 1 minute.

2 In a medium bowl, toss arugula with 1 tbsp lemon juice and a pinch of salt. Divide arugula evenly among bottom halves and top with patties. Spread cheese spread on top halves.

PER SERVING 603 **Cal** | 30 g **Fat** (13 g **Sat**) | 37 g **Pro** | 46 g **Carb** | 6 g **Sugars** | 4 g **Fiber** | 1,236 mg **Sodium**

LEMON-THYME
CHICKEN BURGERS

**PORK WITH PEACHES
AND PECANS**

Pork with Peaches and Pecans

Serves 4 **Prep** 15 min **Grill** 14 min
Rest 5 min

- **2** **medium peaches, pitted and diced**
- **1** **cup toasted pecans, chopped**
- **3** **tbsp fresh lemon juice**
- **3** **tbsp extra virgin olive oil**
- **1¼** **tsp salt**
- **4** **bone-in center-cut pork chops (about 2 lb)**
- **Freshly ground black pepper**
- **½** **cup packed fresh basil, finely chopped**

1 In a medium bowl, stir peaches with pecans, lemon juice, 1 tbsp oil and ¼ tsp salt.

2 Brush pork chops all over with remaining 2 tbsp oil and sprinkle with 1 tsp salt and a few grinds of pepper. Grill over medium-high until temp reaches 140°, 6 to 7 minutes per side depending on thickness. Let meat rest 5 minutes.

3 Stir basil into peach mixture and serve over chops.

PER SERVING 519 **Cal** | 34 g **Fat** (5 g **Sat**) | 32 g **Pro** | 13 g **Carb** | 8 g **Sugars** | 4 g **Fiber** | 814 mg **Sodium**

Don't toss any juice that accumulates from your chopped pineapple. Stir it into the chili-teriyaki sauce.

KEBABS: OTHER LINEUPS

Use swordfish, chicken, pork or shrimp in place of tuna.

Try orange or mango instead of pineapple.

Go with snow peas, mushrooms or cubed Japanese eggplant rather than bell peppers.

Tuna Kebabs

Serves 4 Prep 20 min Grill 10 min

1¼	lb tuna steak
¼	tsp salt
½	red onion, cut into chunks
2	red bell peppers, cut into chunks
½	cored pineapple, cut into chunks
1	cup sweet chili sauce
½	cup teriyaki sauce
2	cups hot cooked rice

1 Sprinkle tuna with salt; cut into 1½-inch cubes. Thread onto 4 metal skewers. Thread onion, bell peppers and pineapple onto 4 more metal skewers. Stir sweet chili sauce with teriyaki sauce. Brush half the sauce over kebabs, then spray with cooking spray.

2 Grill over medium-high until tuna reaches 120°, 4 to 5 minutes, and vegetables are tender, 8 to 10 minutes, turning kebabs once halfway through.

3 Serve kebabs with rice and remaining sauce on the side for dipping or drizzling.

PER SERVING 526 **Cal** | 1 g **Fat** (0 g **Sat**) | 40 g **Pro** | 71 g **Carb** | 37 g **Sugars** | 2 g **Fiber** | 1,202 mg **Sodium**

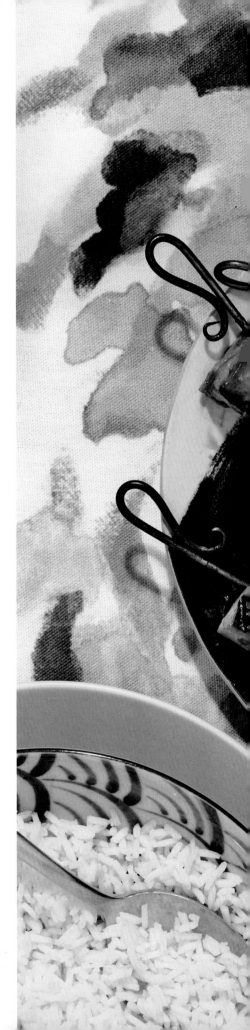

TUNA KEBABS

Tomato and Cheddar Slab Tart

Serves 4 **Prep** 10 min **Bake** 40 min

Cornmeal

1 **lb refrigerated pizza dough**

1 **medium shallot, sliced**

1½ **tsp chopped fresh thyme, plus
more for serving**

¼ **tsp salt**

8 **oz shredded extra-sharp white
cheddar**

**Tomatoes (a mix of colors and
sizes), thinly sliced**

Freshly ground black pepper

1 Heat oven to 400°. Lightly coat a
10 x 15-inch rimmed baking sheet
with cooking spray, then sprinkle
with cornmeal. Spread dough
in pan so it fits with a slight lip.
Sprinkle dough with shallot, thyme
and ⅛ tsp salt. Top with cheddar.

2 Pat tomato slices dry and
arrange over cheese. Sprinkle
tomatoes with ⅛ tsp salt. Bake
35 to 40 minutes. Top with pepper
and more thyme, if desired.

PER SERVING 541 **Cal** | 23 g **Fat** (11 g **Sat**) |
24 g **Pro** | 61 g **Carb** | 5 g **Sugars** | 4 g **Fiber** |
801 mg **Sodium**

A WEDGE WITH AN EDGE

Plain old watermelon has been a regular guest at cookouts for years. It turns into a party animal when topped and sprinkled with some surprisingly simple pantry staples.

SPICY HONEY + CHOPPED PISTACHIOS

SMOKED PAPRIKA + HAWAIIAN BLACK SEA SALT

RICOTTA CHEESE + ALEPPO PEPPER FLAKES + BASIL + EVOO

FOUR FOR JULY

Stay cool with these red-white-and-blue redos of summer favorites—
all made in the fridge or freezer.

Red, White and Blueberry Pops

Serves 6 **Prep** 15 min **Cook** 4 min **Freeze** 2 hr, plus overnight

- **2** **containers (6 oz each) blueberries**
- **¼** **cup plus 1 tbsp granulated sugar**
- **1** **tbsp lime juice**
- **½** **cup plain yogurt (not fat-free)**
- **6** **tbsp heavy cream**
- **1** **tbsp vanilla extract**
- **½** **cup freeze-dried raspberries, crushed**

1 Combine blueberries, ¼ cup sugar and ¼ cup water in a small saucepan. Bring to a boil and cook, covered, over medium-high until berries release their liquid but still hold some shape, 4 minutes. Add lime juice. Cool completely.

2 Pour into a 2-cup liquid measuring cup and add enough water to reach 1¾ cups. Divide evenly among 6 pop molds (scant ⅓ cup each) and freeze. After 1 to 2 hours, insert ice pop sticks. Freeze overnight.

3 Place a parchment-lined baking sheet in freezer to chill. Remove pops from molds, lay on chilled baking sheet and return to freezer.

4 In a small bowl, stir yogurt with cream, 1 tbsp sugar and vanilla. Dip each pop into yogurt mixture, covering a third of the pop. Sprinkle with raspberries and return to baking sheet in freezer. When firm, transfer to a resealable plastic bag until ready to serve.

PER SERVING 187 **Cal** | 7 g **Fat** (4 g **Sat**) | 4 g **Pro** | 28 g **Carb** | 22 g **Sugars** | 3 g **Fiber** | 14 mg **Sodium**

POP TIPS

We like the look of classic molds, but you could use Dixie or small plastic cups instead.

For an equally fun finish, swap in freeze-dried strawberries or mango for the raspberries. Or try toasted coconut, colored sprinkles or chopped almonds.

Vary the flavor of yogurt. Lemon would be a perfect contrast to the blueberries, while tart cherry would offer a tangy yet sweet hit.

If your pop molds don't come with covers, use foil or plastic wrap to help hold the sticks in place.

These pops are more red, white and blue in vibe than visuals, but guests won't complain once they taste them! The yogurt and berries make them refreshingly tart; if you want something sweeter, up the sugar in the blueberry mixture to ⅓ cup.

**RED, WHITE AND
BLUEBERRY POPS**

If you plan to eat these out of hand, bake crust at 350° 8 to 10 minutes. Cool completely before topping with filling.

No-Bake Fireworks Cheesecake Bars

Serves 12 **Prep** 30 min **Refrigerate** 5 hr **Cook** 3 min

CRUST

Butter, for the pan

1¾ **cups graham cracker crumbs (13 whole crackers, ground)**

8 **tbsp unsalted butter, melted**

¼ **cup granulated sugar**

Pinch of salt

FILLING

1 **pkg (8 oz) cream cheese, softened**

½ **cup granulated sugar**

1 **cup 2% Greek yogurt**

1 **tbsp lemon juice**

1 **tsp vanilla extract**

⅔ **cup heavy cream**

GLAZE AND TOPPING

2 **tbsp plus 1 tsp cornstarch**

1 **cup pomegranate juice**

1 **cup fresh raspberries**

¼ **cup granulated sugar**

Fresh raspberries and pomegranate seeds, for garnish

1 Butter bottom of a 13 x 9 x 2-inch pan and line with parchment, leaving overhang on long sides. Make crust: Combine graham cracker crumbs, butter, sugar and salt; mix thoroughly. Press mixture into bottom of pan and freeze.

2 Make filling: In a stand mixer fitted with paddle attachment, beat cream cheese and sugar on medium speed until smooth and fluffy, scraping down bowl once or twice. Add yogurt, lemon juice and vanilla and beat until smooth. Switch to whisk attachment, add cream and whip, starting at medium-low and gradually increasing to high, until thick and fluffy, 2 to 3 minutes.

3 Transfer filling to crust and use an offset spatula to spread evenly, smoothing as level as possible. Cover pan with foil (don't let it touch filling) and chill at least 4 hours or overnight.

4 Make glaze: In a small saucepan, whisk cornstarch and pomegranate juice until smooth. Add raspberries and sugar and bring to a boil, stirring occasionally. Cook 2 to 3 minutes, stirring occasionally, until raspberries have completely fallen apart. Pour through a fine-mesh strainer into a small metal bowl. Place bowl in a slightly larger bowl of ice and stir occasionally until cool but still pourable.

5 Score cake into 12 almost-square bars. Pour cooled glaze over pan, tipping as needed to coat evenly. Decorate center of each bar with a few raspberries and some pomegranate seeds. Chill until firm, about 1 hour. Lift parchment to remove bars from pan and carefully cut along score marks, wiping knife as needed. Transfer to a serving platter. Keep chilled until serving.

PER SERVING 350 **Cal** | 21 g **Fat** (12 g **Sat**) | 5 g **Pro** | 37 g **Carb** | 25 g **Sugars** | 2 g **Fiber** | 195 mg **Sodium**

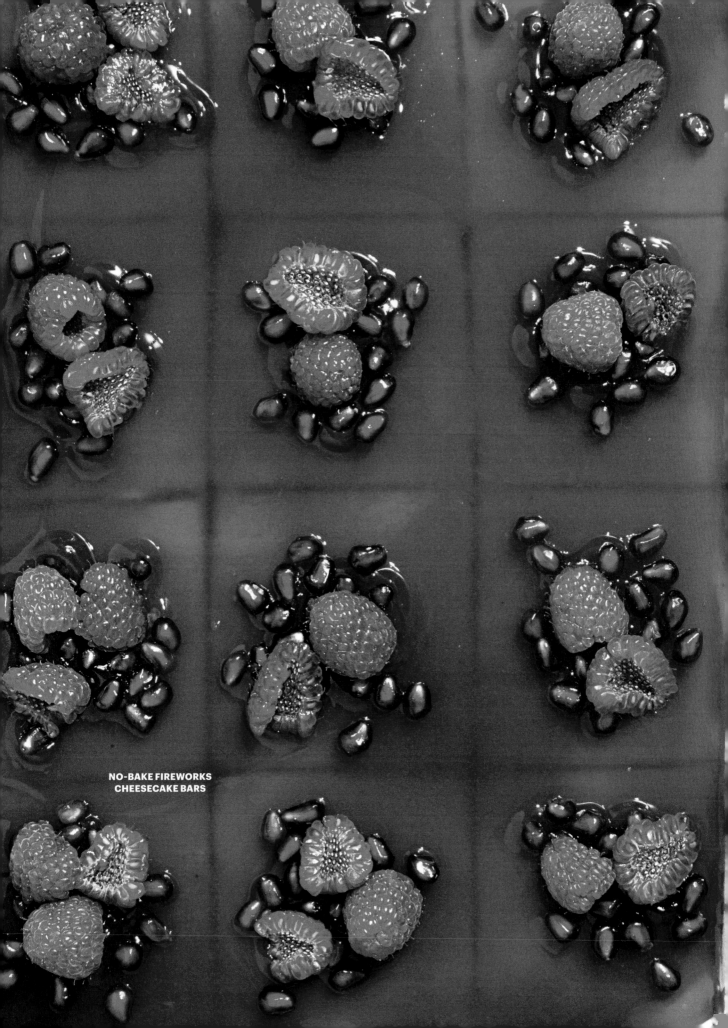

NO-BAKE FIREWORKS
CHEESECAKE BARS

SWIRLED MERINGUE
SORBET SANDWICHES

Swirled Meringue Sorbet Sandwiches

Serves 6 **Prep** 30 min **Bake** 2 hr **Freeze** at least 1 hr

8	**egg whites (1 cup)**
2	**cups granulated sugar**
1	**tsp vanilla extract**
	Blue food coloring
2	**pints raspberry sorbet**

1 Heat oven to 200°. Line 2 baking sheets with parchment. Trace six 3-inch circles on each piece of parchment; flip over (pencil side down).

2 Bring 1 inch of water to a simmer in a large saucepan. Whisk egg whites and sugar in a stand mixer bowl. Set over simmering water, whisking constantly, until mixture is hot to the touch and sugar is dissolved (feel a bit between your fingers), about 2 minutes. Transfer bowl to mixer fitted with whisk attachment, add vanilla and beat on medium-high speed, until stiff peaks form, about 4 minutes.

3 Remove bowl from mixer. Scatter 4 or 5 drops food coloring over meringue. Fold 2 or 3 times with a large rubber spatula. (Don't overstir; you want to leave streaks in meringue.)

4 With a serving spoon, scoop ½ cup meringue and use another spoon to scrape it onto one of the circles. Gently spread meringue with back of spoon to fill circle. Repeat with all circles. Bake 2 hours, rotating pans halfway through. Turn off oven and let meringues cool.

5 When cool, set aside the 6 prettiest meringues. Place the remaining meringues, flat sides up, on a baking sheet. With a serving spoon, scoop about ½ cup sorbet (in a couple of flat layers, not one big scoop) onto each meringue on baking sheet. Gently press a prettier meringue on each (sorbet will help them adhere). Cover baking sheet with plastic wrap and freeze at least 1 hour or until serving.

PER SERVING 405 **Cal** | 0 g **Fat** (0 g **Sat**) | 5 g **Pro** | 97 g **Carb** | 92 g **Sugars** | 0 g **Fiber** | 74 mg **Sodium**

MERINGUE TIPS

Don't use liquid egg whites (from a carton). They won't whip up.

Be careful when separating eggs: Even a drop of yolk will cause them to fall flat.

A dab of meringue on the underside of each corner of parchment will keep the paper from sliding around.

You can prepare meringues in advance, especially if the weather is dry. Once cool, store in an airtight container. Form sandwiches up to a day ahead and serve straight from freezer.

For variety, make a red-swirled batch of meringues and fill with coconut sorbet.

Rocking Berry Roll

Serves 8 to 10 **Prep** 20 min **Bake** 17 min **Microwave** 30 sec

CAKE

Butter, for pan

6 large eggs

1 cup granulated sugar

2 tsp vanilla extract

¾ cup all-purpose flour

¾ cup cornstarch

Pinch of salt

Red food coloring

Confectioners' sugar, for dusting

FILLING AND FROSTING

1 tsp powdered unflavored gelatin

1 container (7 or 8 oz) crème frâiche

2 cups heavy cream

3 tbsp confectioners' sugar

1 tsp vanilla extract

1 container (6 oz) each raspberries, blueberries and blackberries

1 container (16 oz) strawberries

1 Heat oven to 350°. Make cake: Butter an 11 x 17-inch rimmed baking sheet, line with parchment and butter parchment.

2 In metal bowl of a stand mixer, combine eggs, sugar and vanilla and whisk well. Set over a saucepan of simmering water, whisking constantly, until warm and sugar dissolves, about 2 minutes. Return bowl to mixer and, using whisk attachment, beat egg mixture until very fluffy and pale yellow, starting at medium speed and gradually increasing to high as it thickens, about 4 minutes.

3 Sift together flour and cornstarch twice. Sift this over egg mixture in 3 additions along with salt, folding in thoroughly each time, until no flour is visible. Fold in food coloring.

4 Transfer to prepared pan. Bake in center of oven, rotating halfway through, 15 to 17 minutes, until golden brown and top springs back.

5 Immediately run a knife around edge of cake to release. Spread out a clean thin dish towel and generously dust with confectioners' sugar. Invert cake onto towel and remove pan. Carefully peel off parchment. Sift more sugar over exposed cake.

Starting from a short side, roll cake into a tight spiral, rolling towel with it. Transfer to a rack, seam side down, to cool.

6 Make filling and frosting: Sprinkle gelatin over 1½ tbsp water in a small microwave-safe bowl. Let sit 5 minutes. Microwave in a few 10-second bursts until mixture is very warm and gelatin dissolves completely. Cool slightly.

7 Combine crème frâiche, cream, confectioners' sugar and vanilla in bowl of a stand mixer. Using whisk attachment, whip mixture on medium-low speed until it starts to thicken. Drizzle in gelatin mixture and gradually increase speed to medium-high and then high until cream holds soft peaks.

8 Carefully unroll cake and spread a little more than half the cream on top, leaving about a 1-inch border at one short end. Roll cake back up without the towel. Transfer to a serving platter, seam side down. Spread remaining cream all over cake and decorate with berries. Serve remaining berries on the side.

PER SERVING 470 **Cal** | 28 g **Fat** (17 g **Sat**) | 7 g **Pro** | 46 g **Carb** | 28 g **Sugars** | 3 g **Fiber** | 100 mg **Sodium**

ROCKING
BERRY ROLL

VEGETABLE
FRITTATA

POWER UP

These recipes will keep you fully charged whether you work out morning, noon or night.

Vegetable Frittata

Serves 4 **Prep** 10 min **Cook** 16 min
Bake 15 min

- **2 tbsp unsalted butter**
- **4 oz sliced mushrooms**
- **¾ cup halved cherry tomatoes**
- **1 cup riced cauliflower, prepared per pkg directions**
- **½ tsp plus ⅛ tsp salt**
- **¼ tsp black pepper**
- **6 large eggs**
- **½ cup milk**
- **¾ cup crumbled goat cheese**
- **2 tbsp chopped parsley**

1 Heat oven to 350°. Melt 1 tbsp butter in a 10-inch oven-safe nonstick skillet over medium-high. Add mushrooms and cook 8 minutes. Add tomatoes and cook 3 minutes. Stir in cauliflower and 1 tbsp butter. Season with ⅛ tsp each salt and pepper. Remove from heat.

2 Whisk eggs, milk, ½ tsp salt and ⅛ tsp pepper in a medium bowl. Sprinkle half the cheese into skillet, then pour in egg mixture.

3 Return to medium heat and cook 5 minutes, gently stirring occasionally, until starting to set. Top with remaining cheese and transfer to oven.

4 Bake 10 to 15 minutes, until puffed and set. Sprinkle with chopped parsley.

PER SERVING 255 **Cal** | 19 g **Fat** (10 g **Sat**) | 16 g **Pro** | 6 g **Carb** | 3 g **Sugars** | 2 g **Fiber** | 741 mg **Sodium**

Cherry Cooler

Serves 2 **Prep** 5 min

- **1 cup tart cherry juice**
- **¾ cup banana-almond milk or ½ cup plain almond milk and ½ frozen banana**
- **½ cup frozen dark cherries (not thawed)**
- **2 to 3 tbsp plain Greek yogurt**
- **2 tbsp white or black chia seeds**
- **1 tbsp honey, optional**

1 Combine juice, banana-almond milk, cherries, yogurt, chia seeds and honey (if using) in a blender and blend until smooth and slightly thickened.

PER SERVING 249 **Cal** | 7 g **Fat** (1 g **Sat**) | 7 g **Pro** | 44 g **Carb** | 29 g **Sugars** | 8 g **Fiber** | 110 mg **Sodium**

Cherries help boost circulation, chia adds protein and the potassium in the banana aids muscle recovery and endurance.

FOOD PHILOSOPHY

"We all want energy that lasts, but most people go for the quick fix, a boost of energy that's often loaded with sugar. Your body will then spike and crash, leaving you feeling more tired than when you started. The perfect trifecta is a combo of carbs, protein and healthy fats that offers sustained energy." —Bonnie Taub-Dix, RDN

Salmon Pasta

Serves 4 **Prep** 15 min **Cook** 7 min

1	box (8.8 oz) chickpea pasta
¾	lb skinless salmon, cut into small chunks
1	tsp salt
¼	tsp Italian seasoning
½	tsp cracked black pepper
2	tbsp extra virgin olive oil
2	cups packed baby spinach
1	cup cherry tomatoes, halved
2	tbsp fresh lemon juice
½	cup crumbled feta cheese

1 Bring a large pot of salted water to a boil. Add pasta and cook 7 minutes. Meanwhile, toss salmon with ½ tsp salt, the Italian seasoning and ¼ tsp black pepper.

2 Heat oil in a large stainless skillet or sauté pan over medium-high to high. When oil is hot, add salmon and cook, stirring occasionally, 2 minutes.

3 Add spinach and tomatoes and cook until spinach is wilted, about 2 minutes. Add lemon juice; cook 1 minutes.

4 Drain pasta and add to pan. Season with ½ tsp salt and ¼ tsp pepper and sprinkle with feta. Toss to combine and serve warm.

PER SERVING 474 **Cal** | 21 g **Fat** (5 g **Sat**) | 35 g **Pro** | 42 g **Carb** | 4 g **Sugars** | 10 g **Fiber** | 819 mg **Sodium**

SALMON PASTA

Turmeric Chicken Salad

Serves 3   **Prep** 15 min   **Cook** 11 min

- ½   **cup dry whole wheat pearl couscous**
- 1   **tsp ground turmeric**
- ½   **tsp salt, plus to taste**
- ½   **lb boneless, skinless chicken breast**
- 1   **tbsp vegetable oil**
- 2   **tbsp lemon juice**
- 1   **tbsp chopped cilantro**
- 1   **tsp honey**
- 3   **tbsp extra virgin olive oil**
- ½   **yellow bell pepper, diced**
- ¾   **cup chickpeas, drained and rinsed**
- ⅓   **cup golden raisins**
- ¼   **cup toasted sliced almonds**

1 Bring a medium pot of lightly salted water to a boil. Add couscous; cook 10 minutes. Drain and rinse in cool water; transfer to a medium bowl.

2 While couscous cooks, combine turmeric with ¼ tsp salt and rub all over chicken.

3 Heat vegetable oil in a large stainless skillet over medium-high. Sear chicken 3 minutes on each side, reduce heat to medium and cook 3 to 5 minutes, until cooked through. Remove to a cutting board and let cool.

4 Make dressing: In a small bowl, whisk lemon juice, cilantro, honey and ¼ tsp salt. While whisking, add olive oil in a thin stream.

5 Cut chicken into ½-inch pieces. Combine in a bowl with couscous, bell pepper, chickpeas, raisins and half the almonds. Toss with half the dressing and salt to taste. Just before serving, drizzle with remaining dressing and top with almonds.

PER SERVING 539 **Cal** | 25 g **Fat** (3 g **Sat**) | 26 g **Pro** | 53 g **Carb** | 17 g **Sugars** | 6 g **Fiber** | 702 mg **Sodium**

TURMERIC
CHICKEN SALAD

CHOCOLATE CHIP
COOKIE ICEBOX
CAKE, PAGE 196

August

187

189

195

BREAKFAST
Zucchini Muffins, 185

FAMILY DINNERS
Turkey Taco Salad, 187
Pho-Style Beef Salad, 189
Salmon Veggie Bowls, 190
Grilled Halloumi Salad, 190
Spinach and Tortellini Salad, 192

BETTER BUTTERS
Greek Butter, 193
Chimichurri Butter, 193
Red Curry Butter, 193

CAT KNOWS SNACKS
Greek Nachos, 195

DESSERT
Chocolate Chip Cookie Icebox
    Cake, 196

ZUCCHINI
MUFFINS

BREAKFAST

Freezer-friendly grab-and-go muffins your family will love.

Zucchini Muffins

Serves 12 **Prep** 15 min **Bake** 23 min

- **2** cups all-purpose flour
- **¾** tsp baking soda
- **¾** tsp baking powder
- **½** tsp salt
- **½** tsp ground cinnamon
- **¾** cup sugar
- **⅔** cup vegetable oil
- **2** large eggs
- **1½** cups shredded zucchini

1 Heat oven to 350°. Coat a standard-size muffin pan with cooking spray. In a large bowl, whisk together flour, baking soda, baking powder, salt and cinnamon.

2 In a medium bowl, combine sugar, oil and eggs. Whisk 30 seconds to dissolve sugar. Fold in zucchini, then stir into flour mixture.

3 Divide batter among muffin cups, a slightly heaping ¼ cup in each. Bake 20 to 23 minutes, until crowned and lightly browned. Remove muffins from pan and cool on a rack.

PER SERVING 249 **Cal** | 13 g **Fat** (1 g **Sat**) | 4 g **Pro** | 30 g **Carb** | 14 g **Sugars** | 1 g **Fiber** | 221 mg **Sodium**

FREEZER-FRIENDLY

Pop leftover muffins in the freezer for an anytime grab-and-go breakfast or snack. To thaw, microwave 10 to 15 seconds.

NO SKIN IN THE GAME

Get sneaky with it—peel zucchini to remove all remnants of green before grating, and your kids won't even know it's in there.

These moist and tender zucchini muffins couldn't get much easier: one bowl and everyday ingredients and no mixer required!

TURKEY TACO
SALAD

FAMILY DINNERS

Because you've gotta get food on the table. Fast weeknight meals!

Turkey Taco Salad

Serves 4 **Prep** 15 min **Cook** 8 min

1	**lb ground turkey**
1	**packet taco seasoning**
1	**head butter lettuce**
5	**oz spring mix greens**
2	**oz extra-sharp cheddar, crumbled**
2	**or 3 thinly sliced radishes**
	Grape tomatoes, halved
1	**avocado, pitted, peeled and sliced**
3	**tbsp fresh lime juice**
¼	**cup vegetable oil**
¼	**tsp salt**
	Tortilla chips

1 In a medium skillet, cook turkey, taco seasoning and ¼ cup water over medium-high until cooked through, 7 to 8 minutes. Set aside to cool.

2 Wash, dry and tear butter lettuce; toss with spring mix. Top with turkey, cheddar, radishes, tomatoes and avocado. In a small bowl, whisk lime juice with oil and salt. Drizzle dressing over salad; serve with tortilla chips.

PER SERVING 421 **Cal** | 26 g **Fat** (5 g **Sat**) | 32 g **Pro** | 14 g **Carb** | 3 g **Sugars** | 6 g **Fiber** | 969 mg **Sodium**

TACO SALAD TAKES

Make the dressing creamy by whisking in a little sour cream, or spicy by adding hot sauce. Or use salsa instead.

Swap the greens for baby spinach and kale or try a cruciferous mix.

Skip the chips: Serve the whole thing in DIY taco shell bowls, like Ortega bakeable tortilla bowls.

This salad is easy to make your own with simple substitutions. Not a fan of ground turkey? Swap lean ground beef or chicken. Matchstick carrots can replace the radishes, and mild Monterey Jack cheese subs for the sharp cheddar.

Pho-Style Beef Salad

Serves 4 **Prep** 20 min
Cook 12 min **Rest** 5 min

- **7** oz rice vermicelli
- **1¾** tsp salt
- **3** scallions, sliced
- **3** cups thinly sliced napa cabbage
- **2** cups shredded carrot
- **¾** cup torn basil leaves
- **¾** cup torn mint
- **¼** cup unsalted peanuts, chopped
- **1** lb flank steak
- **2** tsp Chinese five-spice powder
- **6** tbsp vegetable oil
- **5** tbsp lime juice
- **4** tsp sambal oelek (Indonesian hot chile paste)

1 Cook vermicelli in salted water per pkg directions. Drain and rinse with cold water. Add to a large bowl and toss with ½ tsp salt. Toss with scallions, cabbage, carrot, basil, mint, peanuts and ¼ tsp salt.

2 Meanwhile, pat steak dry. Sprinkle all over with ½ tsp salt and 1 tsp five-spice powder. Heat a medium stainless skillet over high; add 2 tbsp oil. Cook steak until temp reaches 125°, about 5 minutes per side. Let rest 5 minutes, then slice against grain.

3 Whisk lime juice with sambal oelek, 1 tsp five-spice powder, ¼ tsp salt and remaining oil. Pour three-fourths of the dressing over noodle mixture and toss well. Top with steak and drizzle meat with a little dressing. Garnish with more scallions, peanut and sambal oelek, if desired; serve with remaining dressing.

PER SERVING 610 **Cal** | 32 g **Fat** (5 g **Sat**) | 32 g **Pro** | 49 g **Carb** | 3 g **Sugars** | 4 g **Fiber** | 1,286 mg **Sodium**

Salmon Veggie Bowls

Serves 4 **Prep** 15 min **Cook** 10 min
Rest 5 min

- **4** skinless salmon fillets (5 to 6 oz each)
- **½** tsp salt
- **2** tbsp Asian sesame dressing
- **2** tbsp vegetable oil
- **4** cups cooked and chilled cauliflower rice
- **1** cup shredded carrot
- **¼** cup drained pickled ginger
  Sliced English cucumber
  Roasted, salted seaweed snacks

1 Pat salmon dry and sprinkle all over with salt. Brush with sesame dressing. Heat a large stainless skillet over medium-high; add oil. Cook salmon until temp reaches 120°, turning halfway through, 8 to 10 minutes. Remove from skillet; rest 5 minutes.

2 Divide cauliflower rice among 4 bowls. Top each evenly with shredded carrot, pickled ginger and cucumber to taste. Add a fillet to each bowl and garnish with torn seaweed snacks. Serve with additional dressing, if desired.

PER SERVING 387 **Cal** | 22 g **Fat** (2 g **Sat**) | 38 g **Pro** | 11 g **Carb** | 5 g **Sugars** | 4 g **Fiber** | 631 mg **Sodium**

> Canned salmon or mackerel is an easy swap for the seared salmon.

SALMON VEGGIE BOWLS

Grilled Halloumi Salad

Serves 4 **Prep** 15 min **Grill** 8 min

- Vegetable oil
- **½** lb sourdough bread, sliced 1 inch thick
- **1** lb sliced Halloumi cheese (if not presliced, cut ¼ inch thick)
- **2** medium heirloom tomatoes
- **½** tsp salt
- **5** oz arugula
- **3** tbsp red wine vinegar
- **2** tbsp extra virgin olive oil

1 Heat grill to high and brush with vegetable oil. Grill bread 2 to 3 minutes per side. Let slices cool; cut into 1-inch cubes. Rinse, dry and grill Halloumi until well marked on one side, 1½ to 2 minutes. (You'll have to work quickly with the cheese. Test a slice first to see how long to grill it.)

2 Cut the tomatoes into wedges; place in a large bowl and sprinkle with ¼ tsp salt. Add arugula to tomatoes. Toss with vinegar, olive oil and ¼ tsp salt. Add bread and Halloumi; toss to combine.

PER SERVING 594 **Cal** | 41 g **Fat** (22 g **Sat**) | 28 g **Pro** | 26 g **Carb** | 3 g **Sugars** | 3 g **Fiber** | 1,274 mg **Sodium**

3 ROUTES TO CAULIFLOWER RICE

Freezer aisle Grab bags from the frozen-foods section. Cook per package directions.

Produce section Find a bag or plastic container with the refrigerated vegetables. Cook per package directions.

Make your own Break a 2-lb head of cauliflower into florets. Pulse in batches in a food processor until they resemble rice. Cook in a large nonstick skillet over medium with 2 tbsp vegetable oil and 1 tsp salt about 15 minutes, stirring occasionally. You want it tender but not browned.

GRILLED
HALLOUMI
SALAD

SPINACH AND TORTELLINI SALAD

Spinach and Tortellini Salad

Serves 6 **Prep** 15 min **Cook** 5 min

20 oz refrigerated cheese tortellini

5 oz baby spinach

2 cups fully cooked chicken strips, cubed

1 jar (12 oz) marinated artichoke hearts, drained and sliced

1 cup roasted red pepper, drained and chopped

½ small red onion, very thinly sliced

1 container (7 oz) refrigerated pesto

3 tbsp balsamic vinegar

1 Cook tortellini per pkg directions; drain. Rinse with cold water and place in a large bowl. Add spinach, chicken, artichoke hearts, roasted red pepper and onion.

2 Whisk pesto with vinegar. Drizzle salad with dressing to taste; toss well.

PER SERVING 578 Cal | 27 g **Fat** (8 g **Sat**) | 31 g **Pro** | 53 g **Carb** | 5 g **Sugars** | 6 g **Fiber** | 1,177 mg **Sodium**

BETTER BUTTERS

Grilling goes over-the-top delicious with these flavored spreads.
Try them on corn or these proteins (and if you sneak a bit straight
off a spoon, your secret's safe with us).

Greek Butter

Use on shrimp

In a small bowl, combine 1 stick softened unsalted butter with 3 tbsp finely crumbled feta cheese; 2 tsp each grated lemon peel and fresh oregano, chopped; 1/2 tsp grated garlic; 1/4 to 1/2 tsp red pepper flakes; and 1/4 tsp salt. Stir until blended.

Chimichurri Butter

Use on steak

Add 1 cup packed parsley leaves and stems, 1 tbsp fresh oregano or cilantro leaves, 1 tbsp red wine vinegar, 1/2 tsp grated garlic, 1/2 tsp salt and 1/4 tsp red pepper flakes to a mini chopper. Pulse until herbs are finely chopped. Add 1 stick softened unsalted butter and process until blended.

Red Curry Butter

Use on chicken

In a small bowl, combine 1 stick softened unsalted butter; 2 tbsp red curry paste; 2 tbsp cilantro leaves, minced; 1 tbsp fresh lime juice; 1 tsp fresh lime zest; and 1/4 tsp salt. Stir until blended.

Other Flavors

Stir into 1 stick softened unsalted butter:

HONEY-CARDAMOM spread on biscuits
2 tbsp honey + 1 tsp lemon zest + 1/2 tsp cardamom + 1/8 tsp salt

SRIRACHA-SCALLION use to sauté fresh broccoli
1/3 cup thinly sliced scallions + 4 tsp sriracha + 1/4 tsp salt

BLUEBERRY-MAPLE slather on pancakes
1/4 cup frozen wild blueberries, thawed + 2 tbsp maple syrup + 1 tbsp blueberry preserves + 1/8 tsp salt

STORAGE

Log Spread a sheet of plastic wrap on countertop and spoon butter onto center. Fold one end over butter and roll into a log. Wrap ends under log.

Scoops Spoon tablespoonfuls of butter onto small pieces of plastic wrap, fold to close and freeze. Toss still-frozen scoops into your skillet or add to hot drained pasta.

Refrigerate butter up to two weeks or freeze up to three months.

GREEK NACHOS

CAT KNOWS SNACKS

The chef and "Family Food Fight" judge lives with six hungry boys.
So of course she swears by stocking up on snacks.

Greek Nachos

Serves 6 **Prep** 20 min **Bake** 10 min

- **1**   **batch Roasted Pepper Salsa**
- **12**   **oz pita chips**
- **2**   **cups shredded pepper Jack**
- **8**   **oz crumbled mild feta cheese**
- **½**   **cup sliced pepperoncini**
- **½**   **cup sliced green Greek olives**
- **¼**   **cup sliced Kalamata olives**
- **½**   **cup quartered cherry tomatoes**
- **½**   **cup nonfat Greek yogurt**

1 Prepare salsa. Heat oven to 350°. Remove salsa from refrigerator.

2 Spread pita chips in a single layer on a baking sheet or a large heatproof platter. Sprinkle both cheeses evenly over chips. Scatter pepperoncini over cheese.

3 Bake chips just until cheese is melted, about 7 to 10 minutes. Remove from oven and scatter olives and cherry tomatoes over nachos.

4 Spoon some salsa over nachos and top with small dollops of yogurt. Place remaining salsa in a bowl so folks can dip while they eat. Serve immediately.

Roasted Pepper Salsa Dice 1 cup jarred roasted red peppers and combine in a bowl with 1 tbsp minced fresh oregano, 2 tsp minced garlic and ⅛ tsp kosher salt. Stir in 1 tbsp extra virgin olive oil. Taste and add more salt, if necessary. Refrigerate 30 minutes to let flavors meld. Makes 1 cup.

PER SERVING 408 **Cal** | 24 g **Fat** (9 g **Sat**) | 16 g **Pro** | 34 g **Carb** | 3 g **Sugars** | 3 g **Fiber** | 1,241 mg **Sodium**

SKIP THE CHOPPING

For a smooth salsa, combine all ingredients except the extra virgin olive oil in a mini chopper. Pulse until puréed. With motor running, pour in extra virgin olive oil; purée until smooth.

"My sons and stepsons range in age from 9 to 15, so I keep our fridge stocked with healthy snacks like cheese, fruit and yogurt the boys can grab when they get hungry—and that's often! In the pantry, I stash protein bars, nuts, pretzels or baked chips. Healthy dry cereal also gets a thumbs-up."

DESSERT

Enjoy this make-ahead layered cake any time of year.

Chocolate Chip Cookie Icebox Cake

Serves 10 | **Prep** 20 min | **Cook** 3 min | **Rest** 5 min | **Chill** 10 hr

CHOCOLATE CREAM

- **2** cups heavy cream
- **3** tbsp sugar
- **6** oz finely chopped bittersweet chocolate
- **1** tsp vanilla extract

CAKE

- **21** thin chocolate chip cookies, such as Tate's Bake Shop

  Brewed coffee
- **1** cup heavy cream

  Block of bittersweet chocolate, for shaving

1 Make Chocolate Cream: Combine heavy cream and sugar in a small saucepan over medium. Heat just until steaming. Add chocolate and let sit 5 minutes, then whisk until smooth. Transfer to a metal bowl and place bowl in an ice bath. Stir occasionally until cold (or refrigerate overnight). Add vanilla and whip until soft peaks form (tips curl). Keep cold until ready to use.

2 Make Cake: Line an 8½ x 4½-inch loaf pan with plastic wrap, leaving an overhang at short ends. Stand 3 cookies along each long side of pan. Lay 3 cookies flat on bottom of pan and brush with a little coffee.

3 With a spatula, spread ½ cup Chocolate Cream in pan. Repeat twice, layering cookies and ½ cup cream; then layer 3 cookies and remaining cream (brushing all cookies with coffee). Top with 3 more cookies and wrap tightly with plastic. Refrigerate overnight.

4 Unwrap and invert onto a platter. Whip the heavy cream until soft peaks form and spread onto cake. Shave bittersweet chocolate over cake and chill until serving. Slice carefully with a serrated knife.

PER SERVING 513 **Cal** | 40 g **Fat** (25 g **Sat**) | 5 g **Pro** | 34 g **Carb** | 24 g **Sugars** | 3 g **Fiber** | 177 mg **Sodium**

A THIN LINE

We recommend using Tate's cookies because they're nice and thin—so they'll soften better—and their diameter fits well in the pan. You'll need 21 cookies for this (from two 7-ounce bags).

Make chocolate curls with a chunk of chocolate and a vegetable peeler or use a knife to finely sliver a thinner bar.

CHOCOLATE
CHIP COOKIE
ICEBOX CAKE

RASPBERRY
CRUMB BARS,
PAGE 211

September

202

206

215

DINNER TONIGHT, LUNCH TOMORROW
Sheet Pan Sausage and Broccoli Rabe, 201
Sausage and Broccoli Rabe Hoagie, 201
Fontina, Basil and Bacon Grilled Cheese, 202
Grilled Cheese Salad, 202

Tomato and Spinach Mini Ravioli, 205
Pasta and White Bean Soup, 205
Chicken Ramen, 206
Spicy Chicken Lettuce Wraps, 206
Chipotle Corn Chili, 209
Chili, Rice and Spinach Burrito, 209

BAR CODE
Salted Caramel Bars, 211
Raspberry Crumb Bars, 211
Birthday Cake Cookie Bars, 212
Coconut-Almond Brownies, 215

SHEET PAN
SAUSAGE AND
BROCCOLI RABE

DINNER TONIGHT, LUNCH TOMORROW

September means back to busy. So thank goodness for these double-duty recipes that get dinner on the table— and bust you out of your sad-desk-lunch rut.

The Dinner

Sheet Pan Sausage and Broccoli Rabe

Serves 4 **Prep** 15 min **Cook** 5 min
Bake 20 min

- **2**   **bunches trimmed broccoli rabe (about 1½ lb)**
- **¼**   **cup extra virgin olive oil**
- **2**   **tsp dried oregano**
- **1½**   **tsp salt**
- **½**   **tsp crushed red pepper**
- **4**   **bell peppers, seeded and sliced**
- **4**   **small shallots, sliced**
- **1**   **lb hot Italian sausage links**
- **1**   **box (8.8 oz) quick-cooking polenta**
-     **Unsalted butter**

1 Heat oven to 450°. On a rimmed baking sheet, toss broccoli rabe with 2 tbsp oil, 1 tsp dried oregano, ¾ tsp salt and ¼ tsp crushed red pepper. On a second rimmed baking sheet, toss bell peppers and shallot with 2 tbsp olive oil, 1 tsp dried oregano, ¾ tsp salt and ¼ tsp crushed red pepper. Slide peppers over and add sausage, turning in coat with oil. Place both pans to oven and roast 20 minutes, tossing everything halfway through.

2 Meanwhile, prepare polenta according to pkg directions, adding butter and salt to taste. Spoon some polenta onto 4 plates. Slice sausage into coins and serve with polenta and vegetables.

PER SERVING 530 **Cal** | 25 g **Fat** (9 g **Sat**) | 25 g **Pro** | 54 g **Carb** | 7 g **Sugars** | 10 g **Fiber** | 1,413 mg **Sodium**

The Lunch

Sausage and Broccoli Rabe Hoagie

Serves 1 **Prep** 10 min

-     **Leftovers from Sheet Pan Sausage and Broccoli Rabe (recipe, left)**
-     **Hoagie bun, hinge-cut and toasted**
-     **Pesto, garlic mayo, red pepper hummus or tapenade**
-     **Sliced provolone, fresh mozzarella or crumbled feta**

1 In a small skillet, heat leftover sausage and vegetables from Sheet Pan Sausage and Broccoli Rabe. Spread pesto, garlic mayo, red pepper hummus or tapenade on toasted hoagie. Layer sausage and vegetables into the center of hoagie and top with provolone, mozzarella or feta.

PER SERVING 551 **Cal** | 21 g **Fat** (8 g **Sat**) | 28 g **Pro** | 62 g **Carb** | 11 g **Sugars** | 5 g **Fiber** | 1,403 mg **Sodium**

POLENTA ALL DAY

Make that leftover polenta work even harder and try it for breakfast. (Remember, it's just cornmeal.) Top with a fried egg, or drizzle with maple syrup.

SAUSAGE AND BROCCOLI RABE HOAGIE

Fully loaded grilled cheese sandwiches are a legit (and irresistible) dinner. Make a few extra, chop them into croutons—and take your green salad over the top.

CRUNCHIER CROUTONS

For extra-crisp croutons, toast the leftover sandwiches for a few minutes. Let cool and then cut.

GRILLED CHEESE SALAD

The Dinner

Fontina, Basil and Bacon Grilled Cheese

Serves 4 **Prep** 15 min **Cook** 6 min **Bake** 20 min

12 **slices bacon**

12 **oz fontina cheese**

12 **slices sandwich bread of choice**

Fresh basil

Extra virgin olive oil, optional

1 Arrange bacon on a rack over a foil-lined rimmed sheet pan. Roast at 400° about 20 minutes; cool. Meanwhile, shred fontina. Over 6 slices of bread, sprinkle half the shredded cheese. Break cooled bacon in half and place 4 halves on each slice. Top bacon with torn basil to taste. Sprinkle with remaining cheese.

2 Pour bacon fat from pan into a small measuring cup and, if needed, add enough oil to equal ¼ cup. Brush 1 side of 6 more slices of bread with half the bacon fat and place on cheese, fat sides up. Place sandwiches, fat sides down, on a large hot electric griddle (or work in batches in a skillet). Brush top of each sandwich with remaining bacon fat. Cook until crispy, 2 to 3 minutes per side. Serve warm.

PER SERVING 482 **Cal** | 32 g **Fat** (15 g **Sat**) | 23 g **Pro** | 21 g **Carb** | 4 g **Sugars** | 1 g **Fiber** | 899 mg **Sodium**

The Lunch

Grilled Cheese Salad

Serves 2 **Prep** 10 min

Cooked grilled cheese sandwich, such as Fontina, Basil and Bacon Grilled Cheese (recipe, left)

Chopped romaine

Tomato wedges

Green Goddess Dressing (recipe page 67)

1 Cut grilled cheese sandwich into cubes and toss with romaine and tomato. Serve with Green Goddess Dressing.

PER SERVING 371 **Cal** | 27 g **Fat** (8 g **Sat**) | 13 g **Pro** | 18 g **Carb** | 7 g **Sugars** | 3 g **Fiber** | 729 mg **Sodium**

FONTINA, BASIL
AND BACON
GRILLED CHEESE

TOMATO AND SPINACH MINI RAVIOLI

A go-pack of broth and a zap in the break room's microwave transforms a hearty dinner into a lighter (but still filling) soup.

The Dinner

Tomato and Spinach Mini Ravioli

Serves 4 **Prep** 15 min **Cook** 10 min

2	lb refrigerated cheese ravioletti
2	tbsp extra virgin olive oil
4	cloves garlic, thinly sliced
2	pt grape tomatoes, halved
¾	tsp salt
10	oz baby spinach, chopped
1	cup parsley, chopped
1	cup shaved Parmesan
	Cracked black pepper

1 Bring a large pot of salted water to a boil over high. Add ravioletti; cook 1 minute less than pkg instructions. Reserve ½ cup pasta cooking water, then drain.

2 Meanwhile, in a large skillet, heat oil over medium-high. Add garlic; cook 30 seconds. Add tomatoes and ½ tsp salt; cook 5 minutes. Working in batches, stir in spinach and ¼ tsp salt; cook 2 minutes. Remove from heat and stir in ravioletti, parsley, Parmesan, ¼ cup reserved pasta water and cracked pepper to taste. Stir well. Add more salt and pasta water as needed. Serve with additional Parmesan, parsley and pepper, if desired.

PER SERVING 604 **Cal** | 20 g **Fat** (8 g **Sat**) | 29 g **Pro** | 85 g **Carb** | 6 g **Sugars** | 6 g **Fiber** | 1,197 mg **Sodium**

The Lunch

Pasta and White Bean Soup

Serves 1 **Prep** 5 min **Microwave** 3 min

	Leftover Tomato and Spinach Mini Ravioli (recipe, left)
	Handful baby spinach, torn
	Cannellini, navy or Great Northern beans, drained and rinsed
1	container (8.25 oz) vegetable broth
	Shaved Parmesan
	Cracked black pepper

1 In a microwave-safe container with a lid, pack leftovers with spinach and beans.

2 When you're ready to eat, add broth to container and stir to combine. Heat in microwave 3 minutes. Sprinkle with shaved Parmesan and cracked black pepper, if desired.

PER SERVING 239 **Cal** | 7 g **Fat** (3 g **Sat**) | 12 g **Pro** | 35 g **Carb** | 4 g **Sugars** | 4 g **Fiber** | 1,161 mg **Sodium**

PASTA AND WHITE BEAN SOUP

When you're done with dinner, just drain off the broth, and then everything— including the noodles—is ready for a wrap.

PERFECT RAMEN EGGS

In a medium saucepan, bring 3 inches of water to a boil; reduce heat to medium for a strong simmer. Add 4 cold large eggs and cook 7 minutes. Transfer to a bowl of ice water 1 minute. Peel and cut in half.

SPICY CHICKEN LETTUCE WRAPS

The Dinner

Chicken Ramen

Serves 4   Prep 15 min   Cook 13 min

2	**qt unsalted chicken broth**
1	**tbsp sliced ginger**
3	**cloves garlic, sliced**
¾	**tsp salt**
1¼	**lb boneless, skinless chicken breasts**
2	**tbsp reduced-sodium soy sauce**
1	**tbsp rice vinegar**
2	**pkg (3 oz each) chicken ramen noodles**
	Shredded carrot
	Thinly sliced radish and scallion
	Perfect Ramen Eggs, halved (recipe, left), optional

1 In a medium saucepan, bring broth, ginger, garlic and salt to a boil. Reduce heat to medium-low and add chicken; simmer, covered, until cooked through, about 10 minutes. Transfer to a cutting board, let cool slightly, then shred. Stir soy sauce and vinegar into broth.

2 Meanwhile, bring a pot of salted water to a boil. Cook noodles (reserve seasoning packet) 3 minutes; drain. Divide noodles and chicken among 4 bowls and ladle in hot broth. Top with carrot, radish and scallion; add Perfect Ramen Eggs, if desired.

PER SERVING 367 **Cal** | 4 g **Fat** (1 g **Sat**) | 45 g **Pro** | 38 g **Carb** | 3 g **Sugars** | 1 g **Fiber** | 1,380 mg **Sodium**

The Lunch

Spicy Chicken Lettuce Wraps

Serves 1   Prep 5 min

- **Chicken Ramen (recipe, left) or other ramen**
- **Sriracha mayonnaise**
- **Rice vinegar**
- **Ramen seasoning packet**
- **Butter lettuce leaves**

1 Drain broth from Chicken Ramen and toss leftover chicken, vegetables and noodles with sriracha mayonnaise to taste. Add a splash of rice vinegar and season with the ramen seasoning packet to taste. Pack clean butter lettuce leaves separately and fill with chicken salad when you're ready to eat.

PER SERVING 213 **Cal** | 11 g **Fat** (1 g **Sat**) | 15 g **Pro** | 13 g **Carb** | 1 g **Sugars** | 0 g **Fiber** | 561 mg **Sodium**

CHIPOTLE CORN CHILI

Heated rice absorbs the chili's delicious flavors and excess liquid, making it burrito-ready.

The Dinner

Chipotle Corn Chili

Serves 4 **Prep** 15 min **Cook** 25 min

- **2** tbsp vegetable oil
- **1** medium red onion, diced
- **4** cloves garlic, chopped
- **¼** cup chili powder
- **1½** lb ground beef
- **1½** tsp salt
- **1** can (28 oz) crushed tomatoes
- **1** can (15.5 oz) red kidney beans, drained and rinsed
- **1** can (15.5 oz) pinto beans, drained and rinsed
- **1** cup frozen corn
- **1** or 2 chipotles in adobo, finely minced
- **Chopped scallions**
- **Shredded cheddar cheese**

1 In a large heavy pot, heat oil over medium-high. Add onion and cook 4 minutes. Add garlic and cook 1 minute. Stir in chili powder and cook 30 seconds. Add beef and ¾ tsp salt. Cook, stirring to break up meat, until cooked through, about 5 minutes.

2 Stir in tomatoes, beans, corn, chipotle and ¾ tsp salt. Reduce heat to low; cover and simmer 15 minutes. Top servings with scallions and cheese.

PER SERVING 638 **Cal** | 26 g **Fat** (8 g **Sat**) | 48 g **Pro** | 56 g **Carb** | 9 g **Sugars** | 9 g **Fiber** | 1,402 mg **Sodium**

The Lunch

Chili, Rice and Spinach Burrito

Serves 1 **Prep** 5 min

- **⅔** cup prepared chili, such as Chipotle Corn Chili (recipe, left)
- **⅓** cup cooked white or brown rice
- **Chopped baby spinach**
- **Shredded extra-sharp cheddar**
- **1** burrito-size multigrain tortilla

1 Combine prepared chili with cooked white or brown rice, a handful of chopped baby spinach and some shredded extra-sharp cheddar. Wrap in tortilla and heat when you're ready to eat.

PER SERVING 557 **Cal** | 22 g **Fat** (8 g **Sat**) | 26 g **Pro** | 62 g **Carb** | 5 g **Sugars** | 10 g **Fiber** | 1,212 mg **Sodium**

CHILI, RICE AND SPINACH BURRITO

SALTED
CARAMEL
BARS

BAR CODE

In the time it takes to make a basic brownie, you could whip up one of these next-level bars (which your kids would call "extra"—and mean that as high praise).

Salted Caramel Bars

Serves 24 **Prep** 25 min
Microwave 1 min **Bake** 32 min

1½ **sticks unsalted butter**

1 **bag (11 oz) caramels (such as Kraft), unwrapped**

2½ **cups all-purpose flour**

¾ **tsp baking soda**

½ **tsp salt**

1¾ **cups packed dark brown sugar**

3 **large eggs**

1 **tsp vanilla extract**

¼ **cup heavy cream**

Flaky sea salt (such as Maldon)

1 Heat oven to 375°. Coat a 13 x 9 x 2-inch baking pan with cooking spray and line with parchment, leaving a 2-inch overhang on long sides.

2 Combine butter and 14 caramels (about ½ cup) in a medium saucepan. Heat over medium-low, whisking until caramels soften and start to melt. Meanwhile, whisk flour, baking soda and salt.

3 Once caramels are soft, remove from heat and whisk in brown sugar. Whisk in eggs, one at a time, until blended. Whisk in flour mixture and vanilla.

4 Pour a little less than half the batter into prepared pan and bake 10 to 12 minutes, until set. Meanwhile, combine remaining caramels with cream in a glass bowl and microwave 1 minute. Stir until smooth.

5 Once base layer is done, pour caramel mixture over top, followed by remaining batter. Bake 20 minutes, until set. Remove from oven and sprinkle with sea salt. Cool completely, then cut into bars.

PER SERVING 227 **Cal** | 8 g **Fat** (5 g **Sat**) | 3 g **Pro** | 36 g **Carb** | 24 g **Sugars** | 0 g **Fiber** | 135 mg **Sodium**

Raspberry Crumb Bars

Serves 24 **Prep** 20 min **Bake** 35 min

2 **sticks unsalted butter, at room temp**

¾ **cup packed light brown sugar**

1 **tsp vanilla extract**

2 **cups all-purpose flour**

½ **cup plus 2 tbsp old-fashioned oats**

½ **tsp salt**

¼ **cup chopped walnuts (optional)**

1 **container (6 oz) fresh raspberries**

¾ **cup seeded raspberry preserves**

Confectioners' sugar, for dusting (optional)

1 Heat oven to 375°. Line a 13 x 9 x 2-inch baking pan with foil or parchment, leaving a 2-inch overhang on long sides.

2 In a stand mixer, beat butter and brown sugar until smooth. Beat in vanilla, scraping down sides of bowl. On low speed, beat in flour, ½ cup oats and salt until dough comes together.

3 Press 2 cups dough into bottom of prepared pan in a thin layer. Bake 10 minutes. Meanwhile, with your hands, mix 2 tbsp oats and the walnuts (if using) into remaining dough, crumbling into small pieces. In a medium bowl, stir together raspberries and raspberry preserves.

4 Remove pan from oven, spread raspberry mixture over crust and sprinkle with crumbs. Return to oven and bake 25 minutes. Cool slightly and dust with confectioners' sugar, if using. Cut into bars.

PER SERVING 177 **Cal** | 9 g **Fat** (5 g **Sat**) | 2 g **Pro** | 24 g **Carb** | 13 g **Sugars** | 1 g **Fiber** | 52 mg **Sodium**

RASPBERRY CRUMB BARS

Vary the sprinkles in and on top of these birthday cake bars for different events.

Birthday Cake Cookie Bars

Serves 24   **Prep** 20 min   **Bake** 25 min

BARS

2	sticks unsalted butter, at room temp
1¼	cups granulated sugar
½	tsp baking powder
½	tsp salt
2	large eggs
1	tsp vanilla extract
2½	cups all-purpose flour
3	tbsp disco sprinkles (see "Over the Top," left)

FROSTING

1	stick unsalted butter, at room temp
¼	cup vegetable shortening
2	cups confectioners' sugar
1	tbsp milk
½	tsp vanilla extract
3	to 4 tbsp disco sprinkles

1 Heat oven to 350°. Line a 13 x 9 x 2-inch baking pan with foil.

2 In a stand mixer, beat butter on medium speed until smooth. Beat in sugar, baking powder and salt.

3 Beat in eggs, one at a time, scraping down sides of bowl after each. Beat in vanilla.

4 Beat in flour just until blended, then stir in sprinkles. Spread into prepared pan.

5 Bake until browned at edges and firm, 25 minutes. Cool completely.

6 Make the frosting: In a medium bowl, beat butter, shortening, confectioners' sugar, milk, vanilla and salt with an electric mixer on medium-high speed until smooth. Spread over cooled bars. Top with sprinkles and cut into bars.

PER SERVING 269 **Cal** | 15 g **Fat** (8 g **Sat**) | 2 g **Pro** | 33 g **Carb** | 22 g **Sugars** | 0 g **Fiber** | 79 mg **Sodium**

BIRTHDAY CAKE
COOKIE BARS

COCONUT-
ALMOND
BROWNIES

Be sure to use cream of coconut—not coconut cream—in these indulgent brownies. It is a sweeter version of coconut cream and is often found with cocktail mixers in the grocery store.

Coconut-Almond Brownies

Serves 24 **Prep** 25 min **Microwave** 1½ min **Bake** 35 min

1½ **sticks unsalted butter**

4 **oz unsweetened chocolate, broken apart**

2 **cups sugar**

4 **large eggs**

1¼ **cups all-purpose flour**

½ **tsp plus ⅛ tsp salt**

1 **cup mini semisweet chocolate chips**

2 **tsp vanilla extract**

4 **cups sweetened flake coconut**

1 **cup cream of coconut**

1 **large egg white**

½ **tsp almond extract**

Toasted sliced almonds

1 Heat oven to 350°. Line a 13 x 9 x 2-inch baking pan with foil.

2 Combine butter and chocolate in a large glass bowl. Microwave 1½ minutes, then whisk until smooth. Whisk in sugar until blended, then whisk in eggs, one at a time.

3 With a wooden spoon, stir in flour and ½ tsp salt, then stir in mini chips and vanilla. Pour into prepared pan, spreading to edges.

4 Bake 25 minutes. Meanwhile, stir together coconut, cream of coconut, egg white, almond extract and ⅛ tsp salt.

5 Remove brownie from oven and spread coconut mixture on top. Return to oven and bake 10 minutes. Cool completely, then cut into bars, topping each with a few toasted almond slices.

PER SERVING 373 **Cal** | 20 g **Fat** (14 g **Sat**) | 9 g **Pro** | 42 g **Carb** | 33 g **Sugars** | 3 g **Fiber** | 211 mg **Sodium**

BROWNIE VARIATIONS

Three twists to fit your tastes or dietary needs:

Not into nuts? Trade in vanilla for almond extract and skip the almonds on top.

Change up the coconut For a less sweet but fluffier topping, sub in 3½ cups unsweetened shredded coconut and use the whole 15-oz can of cream of coconut.

Make it gluten-free Swap in ¾ cup almond flour plus ½ cup cocoa powder for the all-purpose flour.

**SLOW COOKER
CURRIED LENTIL SOUP,
PAGE 225**

October

219

221

232

BREAKFAST
Cheddar, Bacon and Scallion
    Bread, 219

FAMILY DINNERS
Sheet Pan Pork, Butternut Squash
    and Potato, 221
Shrimp Fra Diavolo, 222
Slow Cooker Curried Lentil
    Soup, 225
Crispy Tofu with Peanut Sauce, 226
Chicken with Garlic and Sage
    Sauce, 229

**STRANGER THINGS
HALLOWEEN PARTY**
Mini Eggo Sliders, 231
Salted Caramel Dip, 231
The Upside-Down Cake, 232
Mr. Clarke's Chemistry Punch, 232

CHEDDAR, BACON AND SCALLION BREAD

BREAKFAST

This savory pull-apart loaf has layers of flavor. Pair with eggs for a complete breakfast or serve as a side with lunch or dinner.

Cheddar, Bacon and Scallion Bread

Serves 8 **Prep** 25 min **Let rise** 1½ hr plus overnight **Bake** 40 min

- ½ stick unsalted butter, cubed, plus more for pan
- 1½ cups all-purpose flour
- 1 cup bread flour
- 1½ tbsp sugar
- 1 tsp active dry yeast
- 1 tsp salt
- 2 large eggs
- 17 thin slices cheddar cheese (from deli dept; about ½ lb)
- 8 oz thick-cut bacon, cooked and chopped or crumbled
- 3 large scallions, trimmed and sliced

1 Combine cubed butter and ⅓ cup water in a small saucepan. Heat until butter melts. Remove from heat and cool to 120° to 130°. Meanwhile, in a large bowl combine ½ cup each of both flours with sugar, yeast and salt.

2 Once butter mixture has cooled, add to flour mixture; stir vigorously with a wooden spoon until combined.

3 Whisk eggs, then beat into flour mixture. Slowly add remaining flours until dough starts to pull away from bowl.

4 Transfer to countertop and knead in any flour remaining in bowl. Knead 5 minutes, until smooth and elastic. Place in a well-greased bowl, turning to coat. Cover with a clean kitchen towel and let rise in a warm place until doubled, 1½ hours.

5 Gently punch dough down and roll to a 20 x 9-inch rectangle. Cut long side into 6 strips and cut each strip crosswise into 3 pieces, for a total of 18 pieces.

6 Grease an 8½ x 5½-inch loaf pan with butter and stand it on a short end. Begin layering: Start with 1 piece of dough followed by a slice of cheese and about 1 tsp each bacon and scallions. Repeat with all the dough, cheese, bacon and scallions, ending with a piece of dough.

7 Turn pan right side up and shake gently so that layers spread out slightly. Cover with foil and let rise in the fridge overnight (or let rise in a warm place 1 hour).

8 Remove loaf from fridge and heat oven to 350°. Uncover loaf and bake 35 to 40 minutes, until browned and bread sounds hollow when tapped. Remove from pan and let cool 10 minutes.

PER SERVING 370 **Cal** | 20 g **Fat** (11 g **Sat**) | 17 g **Pro** | 33 g **Carb** | 3 g **Sugars** | 1 g **Fiber** | 606 mg **Sodium**

3 OTHER COMBOS

Sliced pepper Jack
+
crumbled bacon
+
pickled jalapeños

Gruyère cheese
+
shaved shallots

Grated Parmesan
+
chopped parsley
+
minced garlic

To make a sweet pull-apart loaf, skip the cheese, bacon and scallions. Brush dough with melted butter, then sprinkle liberally with cinnamon-sugar before cutting and stacking.

SHEET PAN PORK, BUTTERNUT SQUASH AND POTATO

FAMILY DINNERS

Because you've gotta get food on the table.
Fast weeknight meals!

Sheet Pan Pork, Butternut Squash and Potato

Serves 4 **Prep** 15 min **Roast** 41 min **Cook** 5 min

- **2 tbsp balsamic vinegar**
- **½ tbsp finely chopped rosemary**
- **2 medium cloves garlic, grated**
- **1½ tsp salt**
- **3½ tbsp extra virgin olive oil**
- **1 lb butternut squash, peeled and cut into ½-inch cubes**
- **1 lb tricolor potatoes, cut into ½-inch slices**
- **1 lb pork tenderloin**
- **Cracked black pepper**

1 In a small bowl, whisk together vinegar, rosemary, garlic, ½ tsp salt and 1½ tbsp oil. On a rimmed baking sheet, toss squash with 1½ tbsp vinegar mixture, sprinkle with ¼ tsp salt and roast at 425° 8 minutes. Toss potatoes with 1½ tbsp vinegar mixture and ¼ tsp salt add to sheet with squash and roast 15 minutes.

2 Meanwhile, sprinkle pork all over with ¼ tsp salt and a few grinds of pepper. Heat 2 tbsp oil in a large skillet over high; add pork and brown all over, about 5 minutes. Remove veggies from oven, sprinkle with ¼ tsp salt and top with pork. Drizzle remaining vinegar mixture all over pork. Roast until temp reaches 140° and veggies are tender, 15 to 18 minutes. Rest pork 5 minutes.

PER SERVING 352 **Cal** | 14 g **Fat** (2 g **Sat**) | 26 g **Pro** | 31 g **Carb** | 4 g **Sugars** | 5 g **Fiber** | 939 mg **Sodium**

SHRIMP SWAPS

Stir in cooked lobster meat with the tomatoes to heat through.

Nestle cleaned mussels in the sauce, cover pan and cook until shells open, about 8 minutes.

Pick through jumbo lump crab for shells, then add at the end with some of the juices.

Shrimp Fra Diavolo

Serves 4 **Prep** 10 min **Cook** 18 min

12	oz pipette pasta
1	lb peeled, deveined large shrimp
3	tbsp extra virgin olive oil
¾	tsp salt
3	large cloves garlic, sliced
¼	to ½ tsp crushed red pepper
½	cup dry white wine
1	can (28 oz) diced tomatoes
½	tsp dried oregano
¼	cup parsley, finely chopped

1 Bring a large pot of salted water to a boil. Add pasta and cook to al dente, about 8 minutes. Drain.

2 Meanwhile, toss shrimp with 1 tbsp oil and ¼ tsp salt. Heat a large stainless skillet over medium-high. Add shrimp and cook until opaque, about 2 minutes per side. Transfer to a plate.

3 Reduce heat to medium. Add 2 tbsp oil, garlic and crushed red pepper; cook 1 minute. Remove from heat; carefully add wine and stir, scraping up browned bits. Return to heat and cook until reduced to ⅓ cup, about 3 minutes. Add tomatoes, oregano and ½ tsp salt; simmer until slightly thickened, 3 minutes. Return shrimp and any juices to pan and heat through, 1 minute. Toss pasta with sauce and parsley.

PER SERVING 562 **Cal** | 12 g **Fat** (2 g **Sat**) | 35 g **Pro** | 70 g **Carb** | 7 g **Sugars** | 5 g **Fiber** | 780 mg **Sodium**

SLOW COOKER CURRIED LENTIL SOUP

Slow Cooker Curried Lentil Soup

Serves 8 Prep 15 min Cook 1 min
Slow cook 8 hr on LOW or 6 hr on HIGH

- ¼ cup unsalted butter
- 4 cloves garlic, grated
- 1 tbsp grated ginger
- 2 to 3 tbsp curry powder
- ½ tsp ground cinnamon
- ⅛ tsp cayenne
- 2 cups red lentils
- 1 small yellow onion, diced
- 1 large carrot, diced
- 2 ribs celery, diced
- 2 tsp salt
- ½ cup light coconut milk
- 3 to 4 tbsp lemon juice
- Plain yogurt and cilantro leaves

1 Melt butter in a medium skillet over medium. Stir in garlic, ginger, curry powder, cinnamon and cayenne; cook 1 minute. Stir in lentils until well coated. Spoon mixture into 3 ½- or 4-qt slow cooker. Stir in onion, carrot, celery, salt and 6 cups water. Cook 6 hours on HIGH or 8 hours on LOW. Stir in coconut milk and lemon juice. Blend with immersion blender until smooth and adjust seasoning to taste. Serve topped with yogurt and torn cilantro.

PER SERVING 266 **Cal** | 8 g **Fat** (5 g **Sat**) | 13 g **Pro** | 37 g **Carb** | 3 g **Sugars** | 7 g **Fiber** | 620 mg **Sodium**

MAKE THIS SOUP IN AN INSTANT POT

We adapted our slow cooker recipe for multicookers so you can speed up things.

Cook garlic, ginger, curry powder, cinnamon and cayenne in butter 30 seconds using the Sauté function. Stir in lentils and turn off pot.

Add onion, carrot and celery; try vegetable broth instead of water for a more long-simmered flavor. Seal the lid, set pot to Manual and cook 15 minutes.

Manually release steam and stir in coconut milk and lemon juice. Blend as directed.

Fast Flavor: Grab tubes of minced garlic and ginger in the produce aisle and just squeeze the equivalent amount into the pan.

Savor the Sauce: Make extra peanut sauce to use as a dip for veggies or a dressing for salad or cold noodles.

FRYING FACTS

We used cornstarch for dredging our tofu because it makes fried foods extra crispy. It's a pure starch, so it works even better than wheat flour, which contains gluten. Try it with fish, pork or vegetables. Or mix it with an equivalent amount of all-purpose flour and use for fried chicken.

Crispy Tofu with Peanut Sauce

Serves 4 **Prep** 15 min **Cook** 15 min

1   **pkg (14 oz) extra-firm tofu**

½   **cup cornstarch**

1¼   **tsp salt**

½   **tsp black pepper**

⅓   **cup vegetable oil**

3   **tbsp creamy peanut butter**

1½   **tbsp tamari or low-sodium soy sauce**

1   **tbsp rice vinegar**

1   **tbsp sriracha**

1   **bag (10 oz) frozen stir-fry veggies**

2   **cups hot cooked rice**

    Sliced scallions

1 Press tofu dry; slice in half lengthwise, then into ¼-inch-thick pieces. In a shallow dish, combine cornstarch, 1 tsp salt and ½ tsp pepper. Heat oil in a large stainless skillet over medium-high. Dredge tofu in seasoned cornstarch and add to pan in 2 batches. Cook until crispy, 2 to 3 minutes per side, adding oil as needed. Transfer to a paper-towel-lined plate to drain.

2 Meanwhile, whisk peanut butter, tamari, vinegar and sriracha; stir in 2½ to 3 tbsp water. Add veggies to a second skillet over medium-high. Cook until cooked through and crisp, about 3 minutes. Stir half the peanut sauce, rice and ¼ tsp salt into veggies. Top rice mixture with tofu, drizzle with peanut sauce and top with scallions.

PER SERVING 481 **Cal** | 26 g **Fat** (3 g **Sat**) | 16 g **Pro** | 46 g **Carb** | 4 g **Sugars** | 5 g **Fiber** | 1,127 mg **Sodium**

CRISPY TOFU WITH
PEANUT SAUCE

CHICKEN WITH GARLIC AND SAGE SAUCE

Chicken with Garlic and Sage Sauce

Serves 4 **Prep** 15 min **Cook** 9 min **Microwave** 6 min

3   **tbsp extra virgin olive oil**

4   **thin-cut boneless, skinless chicken breasts**

¾   **tsp salt**

¼   **tsp black pepper**

3   **cloves garlic, minced**

2   **tbsp chopped fresh sage**

2   **tbsp all-purpose flour**

1   **cup unsalted chicken broth**

12 **oz trimmed green beans**

1   **to 2 tbsp unsalted butter**

     Crusty bread

1 In a large skillet over medium-high, heat 2 tbsp oil. Pat chicken dry and sprinkle with ½ tsp salt and ¼ tsp pepper. Cook 6 to 7 minutes, until cooked through, turning at halfway point; transfer to a plate.

2 To skillet, add 1 tbsp oil. Add garlic and sage; cook 20 seconds. Sprinkle with flour and cook, whisking, until well incorporated, 30 seconds. Slowly whisk in chicken broth, scraping up browned bits, and cook to thicken slightly, about 1 minute. Whisk in ¼ tsp salt or to taste.

3 Meanwhile, place green beans in a glass pie plate. Cover with well-salted water, cover plate and microwave at 100% 5 to 6 minutes. Drain any water, toss with butter and season to taste. Serve chicken with sauce, beans and crusty bread.

PER SERVING 460 **Cal** | 21 g **Fat** (5 g **Sat**) | 36 g **Pro** | 31 g **Carb** | 3 g **Sugars** | 3 g **Fiber** | 738 mg **Sodium**

SAGE ADVICE

If you don't have fresh sage, use 2 tsp dried sage instead. If you don't have green beans, cook broccoli florets the same way, but 2 to 3 minutes.

Can't find thin-cut chicken breasts? Do it yourself! Remove the tender from the breast half and place the breast on a cutting board. Hold the chicken flat with one hand and, using a sharp knife, slice the breast horizontally into two even pieces.

HAPPY HALLOWE EN RUN!

MINI EGGO SLIDERS

SALTED
CARAMEL DIP

STRANGER THINGS HALLOWEEN PARTY

It's the show you and your teens actually agree on and equally love to binge-watch: you for a hit of 1980s nostalgia and flashbacks of your own undersupervised youth; your kids because Mom jeans and Barb glasses are cool again. (Plus: Teens being a force for good in a dire, threatening world? They'll take it!) So this year, make your Halloween party one you'll both want to throw and get ready for some spooky synthesizer music!

BUILD AN EGGO BAR

Mini Eggo Sliders

Serves 8 **Prep** 15 min **Cook** 10 min

1 lb ground beef

2 tsp Worcestershire sauce

½ tsp onion powder

½ tsp salt

Cracked black pepper

Toasted mini Eggo waffles

Pickles, cheese and assorted condiments

1 In a bowl, combine beef, Worcestershire, onion powder, salt and a few grinds of pepper. Shape into 16 small patties.

2 Heat a large cast-iron skillet over medium-high. Add half the patties and cook 3 minutes. Flip over and cook 2 minutes more. Repeat with remaining patties; keep warm in a slow cooker on WARM setting.

3 Serve patties on waffles with pickles, cheese and assorted condiments.

PER SERVING 176 **Cal** | 8 g **Fat** (3 g **Sat**) | 12 g **Pro** | 13 g **Carb** | 1 g **Sugars** | 0 g **Fiber** | 376 mg **Sodium**

Salted Caramel Dip

Serves 16 **Prep** 10 min **Cook** 14 min

2 cups sugar

1 tsp salt

1¼ cups heavy cream

2 tbsp unsalted butter

Apple slices and toasted mini Eggo waffles

1 In a saucepan, stir sugar and ½ cup water. Bring to a boil over medium-high and cook 14 minutes without stirring, until dark amber.

2 Remove from heat and add salt. Gradually stir in heavy cream. Add butter and whisk until incorporated.

3 Serve with apple slices and toasted mini Eggo waffles for dipping. Store leftover dip in an airtight container in the refrigerator. Reheat and drizzle over ice cream, French toast or pancakes.

PER SERVING 174 **Cal** | 8 g **Fat** (5 g **Sat**) | 1 g **Pro** | 26 g **Carb** | 26 g **Sugars** | 0 g **Fiber** | 151 mg **Sodium**

DIY WAFFLE TOPPINGS

Whip up Mini Eggo Sliders (left) and top with the works.

Bake store-bought chicken tenders—cut them small for mini waffles—and drizzle with maple syrup.

Fan out sliced pears and Brie, then add honey or balsamic glaze.

Dunk the waffles and apple wedges in Salted Caramel Dip (left).

Spread on peanut butter and offer banana slices or bacon strips—or both.

Party in the Upside Down with an LED snowfall projector, black camouflage netting and slices of—what else?—upside-down cake.

The Upside-Down Cake

Serves 16 **Prep** 25 min **Bake** 1 hr, 12 min

- 1½ **sticks unsalted butter, softened**
- 1⅓ **cups sugar**
- 4 **cups black seedless grapes**
- 2 **cups all-purpose flour**
- 2 **tsp baking powder**
- ½ **tsp salt**
- 2 **large eggs**
- ½ **cup orange juice**
- ½ **cup milk**
- 2 **tsp grated orange zest**
- 1 **tsp vanilla extract**
   Whipped cream, for serving, optional

1 Heat oven to 350°. Coat a 10-inch springform pan with nonstick spray. Wrap outside of pan with heavy-duty aluminum foil.

2 Melt ½ stick butter with ⅓ cup sugar in a medium saucepan over medium. Remove from heat, add grapes and stir to coat. Pour into prepared pan and transfer to oven. Bake 12 minutes. In a small bowl whisk together flour, baking powder and salt.

3 In a large bowl, beat 1 stick butter and 1 cup sugar until fluffy. Beat in eggs, one at a time. Add half the flour mixture and beat on low until combined. Beat in orange juice, milk and orange zest and beat until blended. Beat in remaining flour mixture and vanilla.

4 Carefully remove pan from oven and spread batter on top of grapes. Return to oven and bake 1 hour, until cake springs back when lightly touched.

5 Cool cake in pan 5 minutes. Run a thin knife around edge of cake. Place a plate over cake and turn it upside down. Release and remove side and bottom of pan. Replace any grapes that stick to pan. Serve with whipped cream, if desired.

PER SERVING 226 **Cal** | 10 g **Fat** (6 g **Sat**) | 3 g **Pro** | 33 g **Carb** | 20 g **Sugars** | 1 g **Fiber** | 148 mg **Sodium**

Mr. Clarke's Chemistry Punch

Serves 12 **Prep** 10 min

- 6 **cups Concord grape juice**
- 1 **bottle (16 oz) pomegranate juice**
- 1½ **cups lemon juice (from 6 lemons)**
- ¼ **cup superfine sugar**
   Ice cubes

In a large punchbowl or drink dispenser, combine juices and sugar with 1 to 2 cups water. Stir to dissolve sugar and add ice.

PER SERVING 120 **Cal** | 0 g **Fat** (0 g **Sat**) | 0 g **Pro** | 31 g **Carb** | 28 g **Sugars** | 0 g **Fiber** | 8 mg **Sodium**

MR. CLARKE'S
CHEMISTRY
PUNCH

THE
UPSIDE-DOWN
CAKE

November

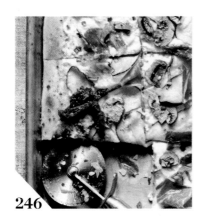
246

256

267

BREAKFAST
Potato Puff Casserole, 239

FAMILY DINNERS
Lemon Chicken with
    Artichokes, 241
Rigatoni with Meat Sauce, 242
New England Fish Dinner, 245
Shaved Vegetable and Prosciutto
    Pizza, 246
Tomato, Zucchini and Parmesan
    Fristrata, 249

THE FEAST
Citrus Herb Turkey, 250
Basic Gravy, 252
Wine and Herb Gravy, 252
Vegan Mushroom Gravy, 252
Green Beans Amandine, 256
Glazed Delicata Squash, 256
Chard and Sausage Stuffing, 256
Potatoes Anna, 257

PUMP UP THE GLAM
Pumpkin Flan, 259
Pumpkin Meringue Pie, 260
Swirled Pumpkin Spice
    Cheesecake Bars, 263
Pumpkin Mousse Parfaits, 264
Pumpkin Spice Layer Cake, 267

POTATO PUFF CASSEROLE

BREAKFAST

Satisfy every breakfast craving—cheesy, eggy, potatoey—in a single skillet.

Potato Puff Casserole

Serves 8 **Prep** 15 min **Bake** 45 min **Rest** 10 min

- **1**   **bag (28 oz) frozen potato puffs**
- **10**   **large eggs**
- **3**   **tbsp milk**
- **¼**   **tsp salt**
- **¼**   **tsp black pepper**
- **2**   **boxes (10 oz) frozen spinach, thawed and squeezed very dry**
- **1½** **cups shredded smoked Gouda**
- **3**   **tbsp diced shallot**

1 Thaw 2 cups potato puffs and press into a greased 11-inch cast-iron skillet. Beat eggs with milk, salt and pepper. Whisk in spinach, Gouda and shallot. Pour mixture over crust in skillet and top with remaining still-frozen potato puffs.

2 Bake at 425° until browned and bubbly, 40 to 45 minutes. Let rest 10 minutes; serve warm.

PER SERVING 437 **Cal** | 28 g **Fat** (11 g **Sat**) | 20 g **Pro** | 28 g **Carb** | 2 g **Sugars** | 3 g **Fiber** | 996 mg **Sodium**

QUICK TIP

Try frozen crinkle-cut fries for the crusts!

SWAP IT

Sub in broccoli and cheddar, or kale and Gruyère.

**LEMON CHICKEN
WITH ARTICHOKES**

FAMILY DINNERS

As parents of two grown kids, chef duo Marge Perry and David Bonom conservatively estimate that they've made 11,000 weeknight meals over the years. They've compiled a slew of them in their new cookbook, *Hero Dinners*. These five will give you a little taste.

Lemon Chicken with Artichokes

Serves 4 **Prep** 20 min **Cook** 10 min **Bake** 15 min

- **2** tbsp olive oil
- **1** pkg (9 oz) frozen artichoke hearts, thawed
- **¾** tsp salt
- **½** tsp black pepper
- **4** (6 oz each) boneless, skinless chicken breast halves
- **2** tbsp unsalted butter
- **1** medium onion, cut into ½-inch pieces
- **3** cloves garlic, minced
- **1½** cups dry orzo pasta
- **¼** cup fresh lemon juice
- **2½** cups unsalted chicken broth
- **2** tbsp chopped fresh parsley

1 Heat oven to 400°.

2 Heat 1 tbsp oil in a large ovenproof skillet over medium-high. Add artichoke hearts, ¼ tsp salt and ⅛ tsp pepper. Cook, stirring occasionally, until lightly browned, 3 to 4 minutes. Transfer to a bowl.

3 Season chicken with ½ tsp salt and ¼ tsp pepper. Add 1 tbsp oil to same skillet and reduce heat to medium. Add chicken to skillet and cook, turning once, until lightly browned on both sides, about 8 minutes. Transfer to a plate.

4 Melt butter in skillet over medium and add onion and garlic. Cook, stirring occasionally, until onion begins to soften, 1 to 2 minutes. Add orzo and cook until lightly toasted, 2 to 3 minutes. Add lemon juice and cook, stirring, 30 seconds. Return artichoke hearts to skillet and stir in broth, ¼ tsp salt and ⅛ tsp pepper. Bring mixture to a boil, nestle chicken breasts on top of orzo and transfer to oven.

5 Bake until chicken reaches 165° and orzo is cooked through, about 15 minutes. Stir in parsley just before serving.

PER SERVING 574 **Cal** | 18 g **Fat** (6 g **Sat**) | 49 g **Pro** | 52 g **Carb** | 4 g **Sugars** | 7 g **Fiber** | 738 mg **Sodium**

This soon-to-be family favorite is easy to make your own. Not a fan of artichoke hearts? Use halved Brussels sprouts. Fresh dill would be a nice change from parsley.

Rigatoni with Meat Sauce

Serves 4 **Prep** 20 min **Cook** 50 min

- 2 **tbsp olive oil**
- 1 **cup diced onion**
- 1 **medium carrot, peeled and finely chopped**
- 1 **stalk celery, finely chopped**
- 1 **tbsp chopped fresh oregano (or 1 tsp dried)**
- 12 **oz 85%-lean ground beef**
- 5 **cloves garlic, minced**
- ½ **cup dry red wine (such as Cabernet Sauvignon)**
- 1 **can (28 oz) crushed tomatoes with basil**
- 2 **tbsp tomato paste**
- 1 **medium zucchini, trimmed and cut into ½-inch dice**
- 12 **oz rigatoni**
- 1 **tsp salt**
- ¼ **tsp black pepper**
- ½ **cup grated Pecorino Romano**
- ⅓ **cup basil leaves, thinly sliced**

1 Heat oil in a large skillet over medium. Add onion, carrot, celery and oregano. Cook, stirring occasionally, until slightly softened, 4 to 5 minutes.

2 Add ground beef and garlic. Cook, breaking beef into smaller pieces with a wooden spoon, until onion and beef are lightly browned, 9 to 10 minutes. Pour in wine and cook until nearly evaporated, 1 to 2 minutes. Add crushed tomatoes, tomato paste and zucchini. Bring to a simmer and cook, stirring often, until slightly thickened, 2 minutes.

3 Stir in rigatoni, salt, pepper and 3 cups water. Bring to a simmer and cook, stirring often, until sauce is somewhat thickened, about 18 minutes. Add 1 cup water and continue cooking until pasta is tender, 9 to 10 minutes more.

4 Serve rigatoni topped with Pecorino Romano and basil.

PER SERVING 709 **Cal** | 21 g **Fat** (7 g **Sat**) | 36 g **Pro** | 87 g **Carb** | 18 g **Sugars** | 9 g **Fiber** | 1,451 mg **Sodium**

RIGATONI WITH
MEAT SAUCE

NEW ENGLAND FISH DINNER

New England Fish Dinner

Serves 4 **Prep** 20 min **Roast** 30 min

1	lb Yukon gold potatoes, cut into ¾-inch chunks
1	medium onion, chopped
2	tbsp olive oil
1	tsp fresh thyme
1	tsp salt
½	tsp black pepper
12	oz green beans, trimmed
4	(6 oz each) cod fillets
¾	cup panko breadcrumbs
2	tbsp melted unsalted butter
2	tbsp chopped fresh parsley
1	tsp lemon zest

1 Heat oven to 425°. Coat a sheet pan with cooking spray.

2 Combine potatoes and onion with 1 tbsp oil in a bowl. Toss with thyme, ¼ tsp salt and ¼ tsp pepper. Arrange on sheet pan in a single layer.

3 Combine green beans and 1 tbsp oil in the same bowl. Toss with ¼ tsp salt.

4 Roast potatoes until they just start to soften, about 10 minutes. Slide potatoes to one side, add green beans to pan and roast 5 minutes more.

5 Meanwhile, season cod with ½ tsp salt and ¼ tsp pepper. Combine panko, butter, parsley and lemon zest in a bowl. Firmly press mixture evenly over top of each fillet.

6 Slide green beans and potatoes over, coat exposed portion of pan with cooking spray and add cod. Roast until potatoes are browned and cod just flakes but is still moist, 14 to 15 minutes.

PER SERVING 413 **Cal** | 14 g **Fat** (5 g **Sat**) | 33 g **Pro** | 42 g **Carb** | 6 g **Sugars** | 6 g **Fiber** | 742 mg **Sodium**

We always make an extra batch of pizza dough for the freezer. It keeps for several months when wrapped tightly in plastic wrap and slid into a heavy-duty, freezer-worthy plastic zip-top bag.

Shaved Vegetable and Prosciutto Pizza

Serves 4 **Prep** 15 min **Bake** 17 min **Rest** 3 min

- **1** **lb pizza dough (recipe right; or store-bought)**
- **6** **oz part-skim mozzarella, shredded**
- **1** **cup part-skim ricotta**
- **1** **medium zucchini, trimmed and shaved with a vegetable peeler**
- **4** **white mushrooms, thinly sliced**
- **1** **tbsp olive oil**
- **⅓** **cup grated Pecorino Romano**
- **2** **oz thinly sliced prosciutto, torn into bite-size pieces**
- **½** **cup oil-packed sun-dried tomatoes, drained and sliced**

1 Heat oven to 500°. Coat a sheet pan with cooking spray.

2 Place pizza dough on the pan and stretch to fit. (Work from the center outward so you don't get skinny, torn edges and a thick crust in the middle.)

3 Combine mozzarella and ricotta in a bowl. Spread top of dough with ricotta mixture, leaving a ½-inch border around edge. Toss zucchini and mushrooms with oil and arrange over cheese in an even layer. Sprinkle Pecorino Romano over top.

4 Bake pizza until edges of dough are lightly browned and vegetables are tender, 14 to 15 minutes. Top with prosciutto and sun-dried tomatoes. Bake until heated through, about 2 minutes. Remove from oven and let rest about 3 minutes before slicing.

David's No-Fail Homemade Pizza Dough Combine ¾ cup plus 2 tbsp warm water (100° to 110°), 1 packet (.25 oz) active dry yeast, 2 tsp sugar and 1 tbsp plus 2 tsp extra virgin olive oil in a small bowl; let stand 5 minutes or until mixture is bubbly. Combine 2 cups all-purpose flour, ¼ cup cornmeal and ½ tsp salt in a large bowl and stir in yeast mixture until a rough dough forms. Knead dough in bowl with your hands once or twice or until it comes together. Turn dough out onto a lightly floured surface and knead it with heels of your hands until smooth and elastic, 5 to 7 minutes.

Place dough in a large bowl and drizzle with 2 tsp oil, turning to coat. Cover bowl with plastic wrap and let rise in a warm place (85° to 100°) 1 hour or until doubled in size. (Press 2 fingers into dough. If an indentation remains, dough has risen enough.) Press down on dough to deflate it and let rest 5 minutes.

PER SERVING 600 **Cal** | 25 g **Fat** (11 g **Sat**) | 33 g **Pro** | 58 g **Carb** | 4 g **Sugars** | 3 g **Fiber** | 1,652 mg **Sodium**

**TOMATO, ZUCCHINI
AND PARMESAN
FRISTRATA**

This is the love child of a frittata and a strata. We're talking about layers of bread soaked in a custardy egg-milk mixture and layered with sliced tomatoes and little nuggets of zucchini. Oh yes, and let's top it with a heavy-handed sprinkling of Parmesan.

Tomato, Zucchini and Parmesan Fristrata

Serves 6 **Prep** 15 min **Bake** 40 min **Stand** 10 min

1	**tbsp olive oil**
12	**large eggs**
¾	**cup milk**
½	**tsp salt**
½	**cup fresh basil leaves, chopped**
4	**plum tomatoes, sliced lengthwise into ¼-inch-thick slices**
1	**medium zucchini, cut into ½-inch dice**
10	**(½ inch thick) slices of French baguette**
½	**cup shredded Parmesan**

1 Heat oven to 375°. Brush bottom and sides of a large ovenproof skillet with oil.

2 Whisk eggs, milk and salt in a bowl until fairly smooth. Stir in basil.

3 Place half the tomato slices in bottom of skillet and top with zucchini. Pour in egg mixture. Place baguette slices in skillet in a decorative pattern, turning each slice over once to completely coat it with egg mixture. Arrange remaining tomato slices over top and bake 20 minutes. Remove from oven, sprinkle with Parmesan and bake until egg is set (a toothpick inserted into center will come out clean) and cheese is golden, about 20 minutes more.

4 Let stand 10 minutes before cutting into wedges to serve.

PER SERVING 296 **Cal** | 15 g **Fat** (5 g **Sat**) | 20 g **Pro** | 20 g **Carb** | 5 g **Sugars** | 2 g **Fiber** | 604 mg **Sodium**

THE FEAST

Call it task-giving. You'll handle the main event—then nominate your family members, friends and relatives to pitch in on the rest. (It takes a village.)

Citrus Herb Turkey

Serves 12 **Prep** 15 min **Cook** 1 min **Roast** 2 hr 35 min **Rest** 20 min

- 1 **(12 to 16 lb) frozen turkey, thawed**
- 3 **medium onions, cut into wedges**
- 3 **medium carrots, cut into 2-inch pieces on the bias**
- 2 **ribs celery, cut into 2-inch pieces on the bias**
- 1 **orange, cut into wedges, plus more for garnish**
- 2¼ **tsp salt**
- 1¼ **tsp black pepper**
- 3 **tbsp unsalted butter**
- 3 **tbsp honey**
- 2 **tsp chopped fresh thyme**
  Fresh herbs and assorted fall fruit

1 Heat oven to 425°. Remove giblets, tuck wings under and dry with paper towels. Toss 2 of the onions with the carrots and celery. Place in a large roasting pan. Set turkey on top of vegetables in pan.

Place remaining onion wedges and orange wedges inside turkey cavity. Tie legs together with cooking twine. Season turkey with 2 tsp salt and 1 tsp pepper, including under skin and in cavity.

2 Combine butter, honey, thyme and ¼ tsp each salt and pepper in a small saucepan. Cook over medium 1 minute. Brush glaze over turkey and under breast skin. Roast 35 minutes. Baste with any remaining glaze.

3 Lower oven temp to 350°. Cover with foil and continue to roast 1½ to 2 hours, until temp reaches 165° in thickest part of thigh. Place turkey on a platter, tent with foil and let rest 20 minutes before carving. Garnish with fresh herbs, additional orange wedges and assorted fall fruit.

PER SERVING 538 **Cal** | 19 g **Fat** (7 g **Sat**) | 81 g **Pro** | 5 g **Carb** | 5 g **Sugars** | 0 g **Fiber** | 626 mg **Sodium**

GET ORGANIZED

"The key to a successful Thanksgiving potluck is a shared Google doc," says Emily Stephenson, author of **The Friendsgiving Handbook.** Divide it into categories—starters, starchy sides, veggies, desserts—and send the link along with your evite. (This way, you can avoid a dinner of, say, six kale salads.) Include how many portions you're looking for. And when it comes to getting your own household to pitch in? "I write out a list of everything that needs to be done and ask my kids to pick three things," says L.A.-based cookbook author Pamela Salzman. "It's more pleasant for all of us than having me order them around."

Lean into the idea of asking for help preparing this year's Thanksgiving feast. If you focus solely on the turkey and gravy—and your family and friends handle everything else— you'll feel truly thankful. And isn't that what this celebration is all about?

CITRUS HERB
TURKEY

WINE AND HERB GRAVY

VEGAN MUSHROOM GRAVY

BASIC GRAVY

MAKE THE GRAVY

If your family wants classic, the Basic won't disappoint. For more complexity, try the Wine and Herb. And if there are herbivores in the house, the Vegan has you covered.

Basic Gravy

Serves 6   **Prep** 5 min   **Cook** 8 min

½   **stick unsalted butter**

¼   **cup all-purpose flour**

1¾   **cups low-sodium turkey or chicken stock**

½   **tsp salt**

¼   **tsp black pepper**

1 In a large stainless skillet over medium-high, melt butter, about 30 seconds. Whisk in flour and cook, whisking, until mixture darkens, about 2 minutes.

2 Slowly stream in stock and, whisking constantly to prevent lumps, cook to desired consistency, 4 to 5 minutes.

3 Whisk in salt and pepper. Adjust seasoning to taste.

PER SERVING 92 **Cal** | 8 g **Fat** (5 g **Sat**) | 2 g **Pro** | 4 g **Carb** | 0 g **Sugars** | 0 g **Fiber** | 380 mg **Sodium**

Wine and Herb Gravy

Serves 6   **Prep** 15 min   **Cook** 9 min

½   **stick unsalted butter**

¼   **cup all-purpose flour**

¼   **cup dry white wine**

1½   **cups low-sodium turkey or chicken stock**

2   **tsp finely chopped parsley**

1   **tsp finely chopped sage**

1   **tsp finely chopped thyme**

½   **tsp salt**

1 In a large stainless skillet over medium-high, melt butter, about 30 seconds. Cook 2 to 3 minutes or until starting to brown and become fragrant. Add flour and cook, whisking constantly, 2 minutes.

2 Whisking vigorously, slowly add wine and cook until alcohol has evaporated, 20 seconds. Slowly stream in stock and, whisking constantly to prevent lumps, cook to desired consistency, 4 to 5 minutes.

3 Whisk in herbs and salt. Adjust seasoning to taste.

PER SERVING 99 **Cal** | 8 g **Fat** (5 g **Sat**) | 1 g **Pro** | 4 g **Carb** | 0 g **Sugars** | 0 g **Fiber** | 334 mg **Sodium**

Vegan Mushroom Gravy

Serves 6   **Prep** 15 min   **Soak** 20 min   **Cook** 14 min

1¾   **oz dried porcini mushrooms**

1   **small shallot**

8   **oz cremini mushrooms**

3   **tbsp vegetable oil**

½   **tsp salt**

2   **tbsp all-purpose flour**

1   **tsp chopped thyme**

Black pepper

1 Rinse and drain porcini, cover with 2 cups hot water and soak 20 minutes. Drain again, reserving soaking liquid and soaked mushrooms separately. While porcini soak, mince shallot and clean, trim and chop cremini.

2 In a large stainless skillet over medium-high, heat oil. Add shallot and cook about 30 seconds. Add cremini and ¼ tsp salt; cook until well browned, 7 to 8 minutes.

3 Whisk flour into mushroom mixture and cook well, at least 1 minute. Slowly whisk in 1½ cups porcini soaking liquid. Add ½ cup soaked porcini (reserve remaining for another purpose, such as pasta sauce). Whisk in thyme, ¼ tsp salt and pepper to taste. Cook to desired thickness, 3 to 4 minutes. Adjust seasoning to taste.

PER SERVING 113 **Cal** | 7 g **Fat** (1 g **Sat**) | 4 g **Pro** | 9 g **Carb** | 1 g **Sugars** | 2 g **Fiber** | 200 mg **Sodium**

INSTA-PERFECT CHEESE BOARD IN SIX EASY STEPS

1. The Cheese "You want variety—a soft, a hard and a funky cheese," says Marissa Mullen, the creative force behind **@thatcheeseplate**, an Insta feed for fromage fans. That could mean a Brie, a sharp cheddar or Gruyère, and a blue.

2. The Meat "I like to make a 'salami river,'" Mullen says. Not only does this make the board look cool, but the folded pieces are also easier for guests to pick up. Fold a slice of Genoa in half, fold it again—then bunch up several of the little wedges and snake them across the board.

3. The Produce "Create 'produce ponds'—circular piles—throughout." Blueberries, pomegranates and dried apricots are all good for color and sweetness.

4. Crunchy Items "Put in a handful of crackers to get people started, then fill in gaps with candied walnuts, pistachios and almonds." Pro tip: Have an extra cracker plate or bowl on the side.

5. The Dip "Fig jam is easy to find in a grocery store and goes really well with any cheese." Same with honey.

6. The Garnish "Stores sell poultry herbs around the holiday: sage, rosemary and thyme—my herb trifecta. They smell great and tie into Thanksgiving."

GLAZED DELICATA SQUASH, PAGE 256

GREEN BEANS AMANDINE, PAGE 256

POTATOES ANNA,
PAGE 257

CHARD AND
SAUSAGE STUFFING,
PAGE 256

Green Beans Amandine

Serves 6 **Prep** 15 min **Bake** 5 min
Cook 5 min

¼ **cup sliced almonds**
1 **small shallot, thinly sliced**
1½ **tbsp lemon juice**
1 **tbsp plus ⅛ tsp salt**
1 **lb green beans, trimmed**
1 **tsp Dijon mustard**
¼ **tsp black pepper**
2 **tbsp extra virgin olive oil**

1 Heat oven to 350°. Spread almonds on a rimmed baking sheet and bake 4 to 5 minutes, until lightly browned. Transfer to a small bowl to cool. Place shallot and lemon juice in a medium bowl. Fill a large bowl with ice and cold water.

2 Meanwhile, in a medium pot, bring 8 cups water and 1 tbsp salt to a boil. Add green beans and cook until bright green, 4 to 5 minutes.

3 Drain beans, transfer to ice water to stop cooking, then drain again and pat dry.

4 Whisk mustard, ⅛ tsp salt and the pepper into shallot-lemon mixture. Whisk in olive oil.

5 Add beans to dressing and toss to coat. Transfer to a serving platter and top with toasted almonds.

PER SERVING 118 **Cal** | 9 g **Fat** (1 g **Sat**) | 3 g **Pro** | 9 g **Carb** | 28 g **Sugars** | 3 g **Fiber** | 100 mg **Sodium**

Glazed Delicata Squash

Serves 8 **Prep** 20 min
Roast 25 min **Cook** 5 min

2 **lb delicata squash**
2 **tbsp vegetable oil**
½ **tsp salt plus a pinch**
½ **cup honey**
½ **cup apple cider vinegar**
1 **tsp grated fresh ginger**
   Cracked black pepper

1 Heat oven to 450°. Trim ends from each squash and scrape out seeds. Cut into ½-inch-thick slices.

2 Toss slices with oil and ½ tsp salt. Divide between 2 rimmed baking sheets and roast until dark brown on bottom, 20 to 25 minutes, rotating pans between top and bottom racks halfway through.

3 Meanwhile, heat honey, vinegar and ginger in a large stainless skillet over medium-high until boiling. Reduce heat and let simmer until it reduces to a glaze, about 5 minutes. Remove skillet from heat. Add a pinch of salt and cracked black pepper to taste.

4 Transfer squash to platter and drizzle with glaze. Serve warm.

PER SERVING 151 **Cal** | 4 g **Fat** (1 g **Sat**) | 1 g **Pro** | 32 g **Carb** | 17 g **Sugars** | 4 g **Fiber** | 151 mg **Sodium**

Chard and Sausage Stuffing

Serves 8 **Prep** 30 min **Bake** 50 min
Cook 12 min **Stand** 10 min

8 **cups cubed French bread**
1 **lb sweet Italian sausage (casings removed)**
1 **tbsp vegetable oil**
2 **ribs celery, sliced**
2 **cloves garlic, sliced**
1 **small onion, chopped**
¾ **tsp salt**
½ **cup finely chopped parsley**
½ **tsp dried oregano**
4 **cups chopped chard leaves**
2 **cups unsalted chicken broth**

1 Heat oven to 425°. Grease a 13 x 9-inch baking dish. Place bread cubes on a rimmed baking sheet and bake 10 minutes.

2 Meanwhile, in a large heavy pot over medium-high, cook sausage, breaking up with a wooden spoon, 6 to 8 minutes. Transfer to a plate with a slotted spoon. Reduce heat to medium.

3 Add oil, celery, garlic, onion and ¼ tsp salt to drippings in pot. Cook until just starting to soften, about 4 minutes, scraping up browned bits. Remove pot from heat and stir in sausage, bread, parsley and oregano.

4 Fold in chard leaves; transfer mixture to prepared baking dish and spread evenly. Stir ½ tsp salt into broth and pour over mixture. Bake 20 minutes covered with foil and 15 to 20 minutes uncovered. Let stand 10 minutes.

PER SERVING 221 **Cal** | 6 g **Fat** (2 g **Sat**) | 16 g **Pro** | 26 g **Carb** | 3 g **Sugars** | 2 g **Fiber** | 864 mg **Sodium**

Potatoes Anna

Serves 8 **Prep** 35 min
Microwave 40 sec **Bake** 1 hr
Stand 10 min

½ **stick unsalted butter**

1 **tsp finely chopped thyme**

2 **lb russet potatoes**

Salt

1 Heat oven to 425°. Place butter in a microwave-safe cup and melt in two 20 second-intervals. Stir until completely melted.

2 Brush a well-seasoned 10-inch cast-iron skillet liberally with some butter. Stir thyme into remaining butter.

3 Peel potatoes and cut in half crosswise. Set a mandoline slicer to ⅛-inch slices. Using the mandoline's hand guard, thinly slice potatoes.

4 Working quickly and starting in center of skillet, overlap slices in concentric circles to create 1 layer. Sprinkle with scant ¼ tsp salt and drizzle with about 2 tsp butter mixture. Top with another layer of potatoes and use your hands to press gently; sprinkle with salt and drizzle with butter. Repeat, pressing layers gently, until all potatoes and butter are used. Coat a sheet of foil with baking spray and cover pan.

5 Bake 30 minutes covered with foil and 30 minutes uncovered. Let stand 10 minutes, then run a spatula around edge and under bottom. Turn out onto a cutting board.

PER SERVING 135 **Cal** | 6 g **Fat** (4 g **Sat**) | 2 g **Pro** | 20 g **Carb** | 1 g **Sugars** | 2 g **Fiber** | 437 mg **Sodium**

DELEGATE THE WINE

First, tap the die-hard wine buff in your crew. "We wine nerds looove that kind of thing," says Elizabeth Schneider, author of *Wine for Normal People*. But it's also fine to arm one or two guests with basic shopping clues: Rather than specify brand, which can turn into a wild goose chase at the store, request a wine from a particular region. Here are Schneider's top budget-friendly picks.

Spanish Cava "is proof that good sparkling wine doesn't have to be expensive; they sell a $10 bottle at my Whole Foods that's lovely." Plus, "the bubbles and acidity cut through all the butter."

French Demi-Sec If there are a lot of sweet things on the table (yams!), go for a demi-sec Vouvray from France's Loire Valley, which is a touch sweet and follows the golden rule dictating that the wine should be at least as sweet as the food. Good vintages include 2010, 2016 and 2017.

Spätlese Riesling, from the Mosel or Rheingau in Germany, is another sweet white. For a dry style that can stand up to savory food, try a dry Riesling from the Pfalz region of Germany or the Alsace region of France. Great German vintages are 2012, 2015 and 2016.

Beaujolais "A wonderful option for red wine—but stay away from Beaujolais nouveau, which can taste like bubble gum." Try Beaujolais-Villages from 2011, 2015 or 2017.

American Zinfandel can handle a lot of flavor. Look for one from the Dry Creek Valley of Sonoma or from Amador County. Great years are 2015 and 2016.

PASS OFF THE BAR

Teri Turner, of the *No Crumbs Left* blog and cookbook, has adapted the catering concept of "beverage manager" for her feast. "This person must text all the guests, figure out what they like to drink and get it. They can subcontract different parts—ask someone to get the ice or buy the beer, but the manager is the boss of the beverages, which also means setting up the self-serve bar."

OUTSOURCE THE PIE

Dessert is the perfect category to hand off to noncooks because there are so many good store-bought options. It pays to do a little research at your local bakeries up front, says Turner. "Then, when someone asks, 'What can I bring?' you can say, for example, 'An apple pie from Bittersweet Bakery. You need to order it by this date.'"

Word to the wise: "people want two things for Thanksgiving dessert: pie and finger foods like cookies, bars or brownies," says Annie Campbell, an event planner in Los Angeles. "If someone brings cake, it plays second fiddle." And don't forget the go-withs! "Ask someone to bring whipped cream and ice cream," she says.

PUMPKIN FLAN

PUMP UP THE GLAM

Good ol' canned pumpkin is the star of these
five showstopping desserts.

Pumpkin Flan

Serves 12 **Prep** 15 min **Cook** 7 min **Bake** 50 min **Refrigerate** 2 hr or overnight

1	**cup sugar**
3	**large eggs**
2	**large egg yolks**
1	**cup canned pumpkin**
1	**can (12 oz) evaporated milk**
½	**tsp vanilla extract**

1 Heat oven to 325°. Place a 9-inch pie plate in oven to heat up.

2 Meanwhile, place ½ cup sugar in a small saucepan over medium-high. Tilting pan, cook 7 minutes, until sugar dissolves and turns dark amber.

3 Remove pan from heat and pie plate from oven. Carefully pour caramel into pie plate and, with oven mitts on, tilt plate so that caramel coats bottom and slightly up sides.

4 In a large bowl, whisk eggs, egg yolks and ½ cup sugar. Whisk in pumpkin, then evaporated milk and vanilla, trying to keep bubbles to a minimum. Pour into pie plate and place in a large roasting pan. Add enough hot water to come halfway up side of pie plate. Bake 50 minutes or until knife inserted in center comes out clean.

5 Run a knife around edge of flan. Cool completely in pan, then refrigerate 2 hours or overnight.

6 To serve, place a large serving plate over pie plate and hold both tightly while flipping over. Cut into wedges.

PER SERVING 123 **Cal** | 2 g **Fat** (1 g **Sat**) | 4 g **Pro** | 21 g **Carb** | 20 g **Sugars** | 0 g **Fiber** | 51 mg **Sodium**

Words matter! Look for 100% pure pumpkin or pumpkin puree—not pumpkin pie filling—when grocery shopping for these dessert recipes.

Weeping is the most common complaint about homemade meringue. The fix? Spread the meringue on the HOT filling— this heats and seals the meringue.

MAKE AHEAD

Meringue tastes best if you eat it the same day. To make things easier, bake the pie a day or two in advance. The day of, pop pie into a cold oven and heat to 350°. Then whip your meringue; spread it on top of the warm pie. Bake 10 to 12 minutes or until the meringue is golden and registers 160° when an instant-read thermometer is inserted in the center.

Pumpkin Meringue Pie

Serves 12 **Prep** 20 min **Bake** 1 hr, 12 min **Cool** at least 4 hr

1	**refrigerated pie crust or pecan or walnut pie crust (look for Diamond of California crusts in baking aisle)**
1	**can (15 oz) pumpkin**
1½	**cups sugar**
4	**large eggs, separated**
1	**tsp ground cinnamon**
½	**tsp ground ginger**
½	**tsp plus a pinch of salt**
1	**cup half-and-half**
¼	**tsp cream of tartar**

1 Heat oven to 375°. Place refrigerated pie crust in a 9-inch pie dish or use nut crust in its own pan. In a medium bowl, whisk pumpkin, ¾ cup sugar, egg yolks, cinnamon, ginger and ½ tsp salt. Whisk in half-and-half and pour into prepared crust. (There may be about ¼ to ½ cup mixture left over; pour into a small ramekin.)

2 Bake pie 50 minutes, until center is set.

3 About 10 minutes before pie is done, pulse ¾ cup sugar in a food processor or blender to make superfine sugar.

4 Combine egg whites with a pinch of salt and the cream of tartar in a large bowl. Beat until frothy. Gradually beat in superfine sugar until stiff peaks form.

5 Remove pie from oven and immediately spoon meringue on top, spreading to edge of crust. Return to oven; bake 10 to 12 minutes until, golden and meringue reaches 160°.

6 Cool at least 4 hours before slicing.

PER SERVING 241 **Cal** | 9 g **Fat** (4 g **Sat**) | 4 g **Pro** | 35 g **Carb** | 30 g **Sugars** | 0 g **Fiber** | 212 mg **Sodium**

PUMPKIN MERINGUE PIE

**SWIRLED PUMPKIN
SPICE CHEESECAKE
BARS**

Swirled Pumpkin Spice Cheesecake Bars

Makes 24 bars **Prep** 30 min
Bake 35 min **Refrigerate** at least 2 hr

- **64** **gingersnap cookies (1 lb box)**
- **3** **tbsp plus ⅔ cup sugar**
- **1** **stick unsalted butter, melted**
- **3** **pkg (8 oz each) cream cheese, softened**
- **2** **tbsp cornstarch**
- **3** **large eggs**
- **1** **tsp vanilla extract**
- **¾** **cup canned pumpkin**
- **1¼** **tsp pumpkin pie spice**

1 Heat oven to 325°. Line a 13 x 9 x 2-inch baking pan with foil.

2 Combine cookies and 3 tbsp sugar in a food processor and process until fine crumbs form. Add melted butter and pulse until all crumbs are moistened. Transfer to prepared pan and press into bottom of pan. Refrigerate while making filling.

3 In a stand mixer, beat cream cheese until smooth. In a small bowl, whisk ⅔ cup sugar and the cornstarch, then beat into cream cheese. Beat in eggs, one at a time, occasionally scraping down sides of bowl. Beat in vanilla.

4 Spoon 1½ cups filling into a medium bowl. Stir in pumpkin and pumpkin pie spice. Alternately dollop spoonfuls of plain batter and pumpkin spice batter over crust. Swirl together with a skewer or paring knife. Bake 30 to 35 minutes, until set but still jiggly in center. Cool to room temperature, then refrigerate at least 2 hours or until serving. Cut into bars with a wet knife.

PER SERVING 254 **Cal** | 16 g **Fat** (9 g **Sat**) | 4 g **Pro** | 24 g **Carb** | 12 g **Sugars** | 0 g **Fiber** | 192 mg **Sodium**

CRUSHING YOUR CRUST

For a level bottom layer of cookie crust, use a flat metal measuring cup to press crumbs into the bottom of the pan.

These creamy parfaits make a pretty presentation and come together in less than 30 minutes. Serve in a variety of glassware you have on hand.

Pumpkin Mousse Parfaits

Serves 12 **Prep** 15 min **Cook** 6 min

2½   **cups milk**

½   **cup plus 2 tbsp maple syrup**

⅓   **cup cornstarch**

2   **large eggs**

1   **can (15 oz) pumpkin**

½   **tsp pumpkin pie spice**

¼   **tsp plus ⅛ tsp salt**

1   **cup heavy cream**

1 In a medium saucepan, whisk milk, ½ cup maple syrup and the cornstarch. Place over medium and bring to a simmer. Whisk once, then stir constantly with a wooden spoon, cooking 3 minutes. (Mixture will be the consistency of yogurt.) Remove from heat.

2 Whisk eggs in a large bowl. Gradually add warm milk mixture to eggs, whisking constantly. Return mixture to saucepan and cook 3 minutes over medium, until thickened, stirring constantly. Remove from heat. Fold in pumpkin, pumpkin pie spice and salt.

3 Make an ice bath: Combine equal parts ice and cold water in a large bowl. Place saucepan in ice bath and cool, stirring occasionally, until mixture is cool to the touch.

4 Beat cream and 2 tbsp maple syrup until moderately stiff. Fold pumpkin mixture into whipped cream. Serve one of three ways: topped with additional whipped cream and a sprinkle of pumpkin pie spice, mounded into a graham cracker pie crust or layered with whipped cream and crushed gingersnap cookies.

PER SERVING 182 **Cal** | 10 g **Fat** (6 g **Sat**) | 4 g **Pro** | 20 g **Carb** | 15 g **Sugars** | 0 g **Fiber** | 115 mg **Sodium**

PUMPKIN MOUSSE
PARFAITS

Pumpkin Spice Layer Cake

Serves 12 **Prep** 25 min **Bake** 35 min

- 2½ **cups cake flour (not self-rising)**
- 2 **tsp baking powder**
- 2 **tsp pumpkin pie spice**
- ½ **tsp salt**
- 1½ **sticks unsalted butter, at room temp**
- 1½ **cups packed dark brown sugar**
- 4 **large eggs**
- 1 **cup canned pumpkin**
- ¾ **cup milk**
- 1 **tsp vanilla extract**
- 1 **batch Cream Cheese Frosting (recipe follows)**
- 1 **batch Pumpkin Seed Brittle, optional (recipe follows)**

1 Heat oven to 350°. Coat two 9-inch round baking pans with nonstick baking spray.

2 In a medium bowl, whisk flour, baking powder, pumpkin pie spice and salt.

3 In a large bowl, beat butter until smooth, then beat in brown sugar until fluffy. Beat in eggs, one at a time, then pumpkin. On low, beat in half the flour mixture, then the milk, followed by remaining flour mixture. Stir in vanilla.

4 Divide batter between prepared pans and bake 35 minutes, until top springs back lightly when pressed.

5 Cool in pans 10 minutes, then turn out and cool completely.

6 Carefully cut each layer in half horizontally to create 4 layers. Place one layer, cut side down, on a cake stand and spread top only with ½ cup Cream Cheese Frosting. Repeat with a second layer (place layer cut side down to keep crumbs to a minimum) and ½ cup frosting. Sprinkle with some chopped Pumpkin Seed Brittle, if using. Repeat with remaining layers and frosting, and top with brittle, if using.

Cream Cheese Frosting In a large bowl, beat 1 pkg softened cream cheese and ½ stick unsalted butter (at room temp). Beat in 1 cup confectioners' sugar until smooth. While beating, add ½ cup heavy cream until fluffy. Makes 2 cups.

PER SERVING 559 **Cal** | 29 g **Fat** (17 g **Sat**) | 7 g **Pro** | 69 g **Carb** | 45 g **Sugars** | 1 g **Fiber** | 292 mg **Sodium**

Pumpkin Seed Brittle Line a pan with nonstick foil. In a saucepan, heat ¾ cup sugar over medium to medium-high. Cook, tilting pan, 10 minutes or until melted and amber. Remove from heat and quickly stir in ½ cup raw pumpkins seeds (pepitas) and a pinch of salt. Spread onto prepared pan with a metal spoon. Let harden, then chop. Makes 1¾ cups.

CAKE FLOUR SWAP

If you don't have cake flour, take 1 cup all-purpose flour, remove 2 tbsp and replace it with 2 tbsp cornstarch.

December

273

290

295

GOOD TO GO
Asian Wheat Berry Salad, 271
Italian Wheat Berry Salad, 271
Wheat Berries, 271

FAMILY DINNERS
Pork Schnitzel, 273
Quickie Chicken Pot Pie, 274
Italian Wedding Soup, 277
Cauliflower Gnocchi Cacio e
    Pepe Bake, 278
Thai Curry Tilapia, 281

THE 12 WAYS OF COOKIES
Basic Dough, 282
Glazed Sugar Cookies, 282
Pecan Crescents, 283
Mocha Latte Crackles, 283
Pistachio Triangles, 283
PB Slices, 284
Orange Squares, 284
Chocolate Biscotti, 284
Coconut-Cranberry Squares, 285
Peppermint Snaps, 285
Edible Stained Glass, 286
Lemony Thumbprints, 286
Herbed Shortbread, 286

BISCUIT HACKS
Strawberry Danish, 287
Pigs in a Blanket, 287
Cheese Stick, 287

**WAKE UP TO THESE
BREAKFASTS**
Overnight Ginger Rolls, 289
Deep-Dish Mushroom
    Quiche, 290
Overnight Maple-Bacon French
    Toast, 293

LATKES
Classic Potato Latkes, 295
Sweet Potato Latkes, 295
Zucchini Fritters, 295

ASIAN WHEAT
BERRY SALAD

ITALIAN WHEAT
BERRY SALAD

GOOD TO GO

Make a week's worth of wheat berries on Sunday and add ingredients each morning to spin this salad either Italian or Asian. Swap farro, quinoa or brown rice for wheat berries if you like.

Asian Wheat Berry Salad

Serves 1 **Prep** 10 min

- ⅔ cup **Wheat Berries (right)**
- ½ cup **shredded rotisserie or leftover chicken**
- ½ cup **raw riced or finely diced cauliflower**
- 1 tbsp **diced roasted red peppers**
- 1 tbsp **diced drained sun-dried tomatoes**
- 2 cups **arugula**
- 2 tbsp **Creamy Pesto Dressing (below)**

Combine Wheat Berries with chicken, cauliflower, roasted red peppers and sun-dried tomatoes. Top with arugula. Pack with Creamy Pesto Dressing.

Creamy Pesto Dressing Whisk ⅓ cup **refrigerated pesto** with ¼ cup **fresh lemon juice** and 3 tbsp **mayonnaise**. Makes scant ¾ cup.

PER SERVING 527 **Cal** | 23 g **Fat** (2 g **Sat**) | 38 g **Pro** | 45 g **Carb** | 5 g **Sugars** | 11 g **Fiber** | 659 mg **Sodium**

Italian Wheat Berry Salad

Serves 1 **Prep** 10 min

- ⅔ cup **Wheat Berries (right)**
- ½ cup **shredded rotisserie or leftover chicken**
- ¾ cup **broccoli slaw**
- 1 tbsp **sliced scallions**
- 2 cups **arugula**
- 2½ tbsp **Ginger-Soy Dressing (below)**
- 2 tbsp **toasted sliced almonds**

Combine Wheat Berries with chicken, broccoli slaw and scallions. Top with arugula. Pack with Ginger-Soy Dressing and almonds.

Ginger-Soy Dressing Whisk ¼ cup **rice vinegar** with 3 tbsp **light soy sauce**, 2 tsp **sesame oil**, 1 tsp **sugar** and ½ tsp grated **fresh ginger**. Whisk in ¼ cup **vegetable oil** and **hot sauce** to taste. Makes ¾ cup.

PER SERVING 407 **Cal** | 12 g **Fat** (2 g **Sat**) | 35 g **Pro** | 43 g **Carb** | 7 g **Sugars** | 8 g **Fiber** | 629 mg **Sodium**

Wheat Berries

Makes 3¼ cups **Prep** 5 min
Pressure cook 30 min **Stand** 15 min

- 1¼ cups **red wheat berries**
- 1 tsp **salt**
- 3⅔ cups **water**

In an Instant Pot, combine wheat berries, salt and water. Seal and set to pressure cook on Manual 30 minutes. Let pressure release naturally 5 minutes, then vent. Unlock cooker and drain wheat berries.

To cook wheat berries on the stovetop, combine wheat berries, salt and 3¾ cups water in a large saucepan over high; bring to a boil. Cover and reduce heat to medium; simmer until tender, 35 to 45 minutes. Remove pan from heat and let sit, covered, 15 minutes. Drain excess liquid.

PORK
SCHNITZEL

FAMILY DINNERS

Because you've gotta get food on the table.

Pork Schnitzel

Serves 4 **Prep** 20 min **Cook** 18 min

8	oz egg noodles
½	cup all-purpose flour
1¼	tsp salt
½	tsp black pepper
2	large eggs
1	cup panko breadcrumbs
4	boneless pork chops (about 1 lb)
½	cup plus 1 tbsp vegetable oil
2	cups arugula
1	tbsp lemon juice
2	tbsp unsalted butter
1½	tbsp thinly sliced chives
	Lemon wedges

1 Bring a large pot of salted water to a boil; add egg noodles and cook per package directions, about 10 minutes.

2 Meanwhile, in a shallow pie plate, whisk flour, ½ tsp salt and pepper. In a second dish, beat eggs. Place panko in a third dish. Pound chops until ¼ inch thick.

3 Working in 2 batches, dredge chops in seasoned flour, then dip in egg. Dredge in panko, turning to coat well.

4 Heat ½ cup oil in a large stainless-steel skillet over medium-high. Add 2 chops and cook until browned and crispy, about 2 minutes per side. Repeat with remaining chops, adding additional oil if needed.

4 In a medium bowl, toss arugula with lemon juice, 1 tbsp oil and ¼ tsp salt. Toss cooked noodles with butter, chives and ½ tsp salt.

5 Top schnitzel with arugula and serve with noodles and lemon wedges.

PER SERVING 662 **Cal** | 28 g **Fat** (7 g **Sat**) | 34 g **Pro** | 67 g **Carb** | 4 g **Sugars** | 3 g **Fiber** | 747 mg **Sodium**

SCHNITZEL WHAT YOU WISH

The pounding and breading method in our pork recipe works for other proteins as well.

- To make a classic wiener schnitzel, follow the directions at left, replacing the chops with veal cutlets.

- Try boneless, skinless chicken breasts, making sure they're cooked through.

- Opt for boneless beef round steaks for a lemony take on traditional chicken-fried steak.

PASTRY TOPPER

• Thaw 1 sheet frozen puff pastry per package directions. Cut sheet into 6 even rectangles.

• Whisk 1 egg with 1 tbsp water; brush each piece with some egg. Sprinkle with a little thyme, if desired.

• If you want to get a bit fancy, score each piece of pastry with a paring knife to create a design.

• Bake on a parchment-lined baking sheet at 400° until puffed and browned, about 20 minutes.

Quickie Chicken Pot Pie

Serves 6   **Prep** 15 min   **Cook** 30 min
Bake 20 min

2	tbsp unsalted butter
1	small onion, diced
1	medium carrot, diced
1	large rib celery, diced
¾	tsp salt
¼	cup all-purpose flour
1	can (15.5 oz) unsalted chicken broth
1½	lb boneless, skinless chicken thighs
½	lb Yukon gold potatoes, diced
1½	tsp finely chopped thyme
	Cracked black pepper
½	cup frozen peas, thawed
	Pastry Topper (left)

1 In a large heavy pot, melt butter over medium-high. Add onion, carrot, celery and ¼ tsp salt to pot and cook until beginning to brown, about 5 minutes. Whisk in flour and cook about 90 seconds. Add broth, whisking constantly.

2 Sprinkle chicken all over with ½ tsp salt and add to pot with vegetable mixture. Stir in potatoes, thyme and cracked pepper to taste. Reduce heat to medium and simmer, covered, until potatoes are tender and chicken is cooked through, about 20 minutes, stirring occasionally to prevent sticking. Transfer chicken to a cutting board.

3 Stir peas into vegetable mixture. Chop chicken into bite-size pieces and stir into vegetable mixture. Remove from heat and adjust seasoning to taste. Serve with warm Pastry Topper.

PER SERVING 390 **Cal** | 18 g **Fat** (8 g **Sat**) | 28 g **Pro** | 35 g **Carb** | 3 g **Sugars** | 3 g **Fiber** | 683 mg **Sodium**

**QUICKIE CHICKEN
POT PIE**

ITALIAN
WEDDING
SOUP

Italian Wedding Soup

Serves 4 **Prep** 20 min **Cook** 21 min

2	**tsp vegetable oil**
1	**small onion, chopped**
1	**large carrot, diced**
1	**rib celery, sliced**
1	**tsp salt**
8	**cups unsalted chicken broth**
1	**cup orzo**
12	**oz fully cooked meatballs**
¾	**tsp salt**
¼	**tsp dried oregano**
	Cracked black pepper
5	**oz escarole or baby spinach, chopped**
	Shaved Parmesan cheese

1 Heat oil in a large heavy pot over medium-high. Add onion, carrot, celery and ¼ tsp salt; cook 5 minutes. Pour in broth; bring to a boil. Reduce heat. Cover and simmer 4 minutes.

2 Return to a boil; stir in orzo, meatballs, ¾ tsp salt, oregano and cracked pepper to taste. Cook 8 to 10 minutes, adding escarole the last 2 minutes.

3 Ladle soup into bowls. Top servings with Parmesan cheese.

PER SERVING 507 **Cal** | 17 g **Fat** (5 g **Sat**) | 33 g **Pro** | 59 g **Carb** | 6 g **Sugars** | 6 g **Fiber** | 1,294 mg **Sodium**

MAKE IT VEGETARIAN

Swap the chicken broth for vegetable broth and replace the meatballs with meatless meatballs, chopped veggie sausage or white beans.

Forgot to thaw? Our Cacio e Pepe bake works just as well with frozen gnocchi and broccoli, but you'll need to bake it 10 to 15 minutes longer before broiling.

Cauliflower Gnocchi Cacio e Pepe Bake

Serves 4 **Prep** 15 min **Microwave** 40 sec **Bake** 35 min **Broil** 3 min **Stand** 10 min

- **3 tbsp unsalted butter**
- **1 cup part-skim ricotta**
- **½ cup milk**
- **¼ cup plus 2 tbsp grated Parmesan**
- **1 tbsp all-purpose flour**
- **1 tsp cracked black pepper**
- **½ tsp salt**
- **2 bags (12 oz each) frozen cauliflower gnocchi, thawed**
- **1 box (10 oz) frozen broccoli, thawed and chopped**
- **½ cup frozen peas, thawed**
- **⅓ cup plus ½ cup shredded mozzarella**

1 Heat oven to 350°. In a large microwave-safe bowl, melt butter at 100% in two 20-second intervals. Whisk in ricotta, milk, ¼ cup Parmesan cheese, flour, cracked black pepper and salt. Stir in gnocchi, broccoli and peas.

2 Transfer half the gnocchi mixture to a greased 11 x 7-inch baking dish. Sprinkle with ⅓ cup mozzarella and 1 tbsp Parmesan cheese. Top with remaining gnocchi mixture and sprinkle with ½ cup mozzarella, 1 tbsp Parmesan cheese and cracked pepper to taste.

3 Bake, covered, until bubbly, about 35 minutes. Uncover and broil until browned, about 3 minutes. Let stand 10 minutes.

PER SERVING 503 **Cal** | 25 g **Fat** (14 g **Sat**) | 21 g **Pro** | 41 g **Carb** | 5 g **Sugars** | 11 g **Fiber** | 1,220 mg **Sodium**

CAULIFLOWER GNOCCHI CACIO E PEPE BAKE

THAI CURRY
TILAPIA

Go fish. You can replace the tilapia with 1½ pounds of any mild fish, such as catfish, trout, snapper or bass.

Thai Curry Tilapia

Serves 4 **Prep** 15 min **Bake** 30 min

1	**can (13.66 oz) coconut milk**
3	**tbsp red curry paste**
2	**tbsp chopped cilantro**
1¼	**tsp salt**
4	**tilapia fillets (about 1½ lb)**
½	**lb green beans, trimmed and halved**
2	**cups warm cooked rice**
	Torn cilantro leaves

1 Heat oven to 350°. In a small bowl, whisk coconut milk, curry paste, chopped cilantro, lime juice and ½ tsp salt. Pour into a 13 x 9-inch baking dish.

2 Pat dry tilapia with paper towels and season with ½ tsp salt. Place fish on curry sauce in the baking dish. Top fish with green beans and sprinkle with ¼ tsp salt. Lightly press beans and fish into curry sauce.

3 Bake, covered, until fish is cooked through and beans are tender, about 30 minutes.

4 Serve with warm rice and sprinkle with torn cilantro leaves.

PER SERVING 408 **Cal** | 18 g **Fat** (14 g **Sat**) | 28 g **Pro** | 30 g **Carb** | 6 g **Sugars** | 3 g **Fiber** | 1,590 mg **Sodium**

THE 12 WAYS OF COOKIES

With the easiest tweaks, one basic dough becomes
a dozen holiday-ready treats.

Basic Dough

Makes about 48 cookies
Prep 20 min **Refrigerate** 1 hr

2 **cups all-purpose flour**

¾ **tsp baking powder**

¼ **tsp salt**

1 **stick unsalted butter, at room temp**

¾ **cup sugar**

1 **large egg**

¾ **tsp vanilla extract**

1 In a large bowl, whisk flour,
baking powder and salt. With an
electric mixer, beat butter until
smooth. Beat in sugar until blended
and fluffy, scraping down sides of
bowl. Beat in egg and vanilla.

2 On low speed, beat flour
mixture into butter mixture
until combined.

3 Gather dough into a ball, flatten
into a disk and wrap in plastic;
refrigerate until easy to handle,
about 1 hour. Let dough sit at
room temperature 30 minutes if
rolling out.

Glazed Sugar Cookies

Makes 54 cookies **Prep** 30 min
Refrigerate 2 hr **Bake** 13 min
Cool 30 min

Make **Basic Dough** and refrigerate
2 hours or overnight. Heat oven
to 350°. Roll to ⅛-inch thickness.
Cut into 1-inch, 1¼-inch and
1½-inch circles using round cookie
cutters. Bake on parchment-lined
baking sheets 11 to 13 minutes.
Cool completely and spread with
glaze: Beat 2 cups **confectioners'
sugar** with ⅛ tsp **cream of
tartar** and 3 tbsp **2% milk**. Tint to
desired colors.

PER COOKIE 62 **Cal** | 2 g **Fat** (1 g **Sat**) |
1 g **Pro** | 11 g **Carb** | 7 g **Sugars** | 0 g **Fiber** |
21 mg **Sodium**

ICING TIPS FOR GLAZED COOKIES

1. Keep it fresh. Store icing in a
medium lidded bowl and spoon
into smaller bowls as needed.

2. Brush up on decorating. Use
inexpensive "kindergarten"
brushes for painting the cookies—
they can easily be washed in the
dishwasher.

3. Create a color palette. Dab
small drops of food coloring on a
piece of parchment. Dip brush into
a color, then mix into icing. Start
with pale shades, gradually adding
more for deeper colors.

When you like holiday goodness to be crunchy, nutty and sticky.

Pistachio Triangles

Makes 60 cookies **Prep** 30 min
Bake 15 min **Cool** 30 min

Heat oven to 350°. Make **Basic Dough**. Sprinkle liberally with **all-purpose flour** and roll out on wax paper to a 15 x 10-inch rectangle. Invert onto a greased 15 x 10 x 1-inch pan; press to edges. Bake 10 minutes. Meanwhile, in a medium bowl, whisk ½ cup **sugar**, 3 tbsp **all-purpose flour** and ⅛ tsp **salt** with 1 cup light **corn syrup**, 3 **eggs** and ½ tsp **vanilla extract**. Stir in 1½ cups **roasted salted pistachios**, chopped. Spread over dough; bake 15 minutes. Cool and cut into triangles.

PER COOKIE 85 **Cal** | 3 g **Fat** (1 g **Sat**) | 2 g **Pro** | 13 g **Carb** | 6 g **Sugars** | 0 g **Fiber** | 44 mg **Sodium**

Pecan Crescents

Makes 48 cookies **Prep** 30 min
Refrigerate 30 min **Bake** 15 min

Make **Basic Dough**, adding ¾ cup ground **pecans** and ½ cup **confectioners' sugar** to flour mixture and increasing **butter** to 1½ sticks. Refrigerate 2 hours. Heat oven to 350°. Break off tablespoonfuls of dough and shape into logs. Taper ends and bend into crescents; chill 30 minutes. Place on parchment-lined baking sheets and bake 15 minutes. Generously dust with confectioners' sugar while warm.

PER COOKIE 82 **Cal** | 4 g **Fat** (2 g **Sat**) | 1 g **Pro** | 10 g **Carb** | 6 g **Sugars** | 0 g **Fiber** | 23 mg **Sodium**

Mocha Latte Crackles

Makes 42 cookies **Prep** 30 min
Refrigerate 1 hr **Bake** 12 min

Combine ¼ cup **warm water** with 2 tbsp **instant coffee**. Make **Basic Dough**, adding ¼ cup **cocoa powder** to flour mixture and beating instant coffee mixture and ¼ cup **chocolate syrup** in with egg. Refrigerate 1 hour. Heat oven to 350°. Shape into 1-inch balls between your palms and roll in **confectioners' sugar** to coat. Place on parchment-lined baking sheets and bake 12 minutes.

PER COOKIE 70 **Cal** | 2 g **Fat** (1 g **Sat**) | 1 g **Pro** | 11 g **Carb** | 6 g **Sugars** | 0 g **Fiber** | 27 mg **Sodium**

Imagine the best of the dessert coffee drinks . . . in cute crackly-cookie form.

Double your chocolate with both cocoa powder and chocolate chips.

Chocolate Biscotti

Makes 30 cookies   **Prep** 30 min
Cool 30 min   **Bake** 35 min

Heat oven to 375°. Make **Basic Dough**, adding ½ cup **cocoa powder** to flour mixture, increasing **baking powder** to 1½ tsp and adding 1 more **egg**. Stir ½ cup **mini semisweet chocolate chips** into dough; divide in half. With floured hands, shape each half into an 11 x 2½-inch log on a parchment-lined baking sheet. Bake 20 to 25 minutes. Cool slightly on a rack; lower oven to 325°. Cut into ½-inch slices on a slight diagonal. Place, cut sides down, on baking sheets. Bake 10 minutes; turn over and bake 10 minutes more. Cool completely. Melt 1 cup mini semisweet chips with ½ tsp **vegetable oil** per pkg directions. Drizzle over cookies; let dry on wax paper.

PER COOKIE 128 **Cal** | 6 g **Fat** (4 g **Sat**) | 2 g **Pro** | 18 g **Carb** | 10 g **Sugars** | 1 g **Fiber** | 52 mg **Sodium**

PB Slices

Makes 64 cookies   **Prep** 30 min
Refrigerate 2 hr   **Bake** 12 min

Make **Basic Dough**, adding 3 tbsp **PB powder** to flour mixture and ¼ cup **peanut butter** to butter mixture. Divide into quarters and roll into 6-inch logs. Finely chop 1 cup **honey-roasted peanuts**. Spread nuts on a board in a 7 x 5-inch rectangle. Brush logs with **egg white**, then roll in peanuts, pressing into sides. Wrap logs in plastic and refrigerate 2 hours or overnight. Heat oven to 350°. Slice each log into 16 pieces. Bake 12 minutes.

PER COOKIE 57 **Cal** | 3 g **Fat** (1 g **Sat**) | 1 g **Pro** | 6 g **Carb** | 3 g **Sugars** | 0 g **Fiber** | 31 mg **Sodium**

Orange Squares

Makes 42 cookies   **Prep** 30 min
Refrigerate 2 hr   **Bake** 13 min

Make **Basic Dough**, adding 1 tsp grated **orange zest** to butter mixture. Refrigerate at least 2 hours or overnight. Heat oven to 350°. Roll out dough to ¼-inch thickness. Cut into 2-inch squares. Transfer to parchment-lined baking sheets and brush with a layer of **sweet orange marmalade**. Finely chop 4 slices **Trader Joe's Sweetened Dried Orange Slices** and sprinkle on cookies. Bake 13 minutes.

PER COOKIE 70 **Cal** | 2 g **Fat** (1 g **Sat**) | 1 g **Pro** | 11 g **Carb** | 7 g **Sugars** | 0 g **Fiber** | 27 mg **Sodium**

You've got your zest, your marmalade—and some pretty candied slices.

Coconut-Cranberry Squares

Makes 26 bars **Prep** 30 min
Bake 26 min

Heat oven to 325°. In a large mixing bowl, beat 3 **large egg whites** with ½ tsp **cream of tartar** and 3 tbsp **sugar** to stiff peaks. Make **Basic Dough**. Fold half the egg white mixture into dough to lighten, then fold in remainder. Chop ¾ cup **Craisins**. Fold 1 cup **sweetened flake coconut**, ¾ cup **white chocolate chips** and ½ cup chopped **Craisins** into dough. Spread into a **greased** 15 x 10 x 1-inch baking sheet. Top with remaining chopped Craisins. Cover with greased foil and bake 18 minutes. Uncover and scatter ½ cup **white chocolate chips** on top. Bake 8 minutes. Cool and cut into squares.

PER COOKIE 147 **Cal** | 6 g **Fat** (4 g **Sat**) | 2 g **Pro** | 21 g **Carb** | 14 g **Sugars** | 1 g **Fiber** | 55 mg **Sodium**

White chocolate chips, Craisins, coconut flakes. We're just gonna say: Can't stop, won't stop.

Go for a hot-cocoa-with-candy-canes vibe.

Peppermint Snaps

Makes 54 cookies **Prep** 30 min
Refrigerate 2 hr **Stand** 15 min
Bake 10 min **Cool** 30 min

Make **Basic Dough**, adding ½ cup **cocoa powder** to flour mixture and ¼ cup **milk** and ½ tsp **peppermint extract** to butter mixture with vanilla. Divide dough in half, wrap in plastic and refrigerate 2 hours or overnight. Let dough stand at room temperature 15 minutes. Heat oven to 350°. On a floured surface with a floured rolling pin, roll to ⅛-inch thickness. Cut into 2¼ x 1¼-inch rectangles. Bake 10 minutes. Cool. Melt one 11-oz bag **white chocolate chips** with 1 tsp **vegetable oil** per pkg directions. Crush 26 **starlight mints** (about ⅔ cup) with a meat mallet. Dip cookies in chocolate, then cover with crushed candy. Let dry on wax paper.

PER COOKIE 89 **Cal** | 4 g **Fat** (2 g **Sat**) | 1 g **Pro** | 13 g **Carb** | 8 g **Sugars** | 0 g **Fiber** | 27 mg **Sodium**

When Jolly
Rancher goes
all holly jolly!

Herbed Shortbread

Makes 48 cookies   **Prep** 30 min
Refrigerate 2 hr   **Bake** 13 min

Heat oven to 325°. Make **Basic Dough**, adding ⅓ cup **cornstarch** and 1½ tsp each chopped **fresh thyme** and **rosemary** to flour mixture and increasing **butter** to 1½ sticks. On a floured surface, divide dough into quarters. Press into 6-inch circles on a parchment-lined baking sheet. Prick all over with a fork and press tines around edges. Cut each circle into 12 wedges; do not pull apart. Bake 25 to 27 minutes, rotating pans halfway through. Remove from oven and recut through lines.

PER COOKIE 62 **Cal** | 3 g **Fat** (2 g **Sat**) |
1 g **Pro** | 8 g **Carb** | 3 g **Sugars** | 0 g **Fiber** |
23 mg **Sodium**

Edible Stained Glass

Makes 48 cookies   **Prep** 30 min
Bake 9 min

Stir 2 tbsp additional **all-purpose flour** into **Basic Dough**. Divide dough in half, wrap in plastic and refrigerate at least 2 hours. Heat oven to 325°. Crush 24 **Jolly Rancher candies** (6 of each color) with a meat mallet, keeping colors separate. On a floured surface, roll out half the dough to ⅛-inch thickness. Cut out 2-inch shapes and transfer to parchment-lined baking sheets. With smaller shapes, cut out centers and remove. Reroll scraps. Fill each cookie center with ½ tsp crushed candy; repeat with all dough and candy. Bake 8 to 9 minutes. Cool completely on baking sheets.

PER COOKIE 57 **Cal** | 2 g **Fat** (1 g **Sat**) |
1 g **Pro** | 9 g **Carb** | 4 g **Sugars** | 0 g **Fiber** |
23 mg **Sodium**

Mildly citrusy dough goes
choose-your-own-adventure
with flavored jams.

Lemony Thumbprints

Makes 30 trio or 84 single cookies
Prep 30 min   **Bake** 12 min

Make **Basic Dough**, adding ½ tsp **lemon zest** and ½ tsp **lemon extract** to butter mixture. Refrigerate at least 2 hours or overnight. Heat oven to 350°. Shape teaspoonfuls of dough into balls and place on parchment-lined baking sheets (grouping in threes, if desired). With handle of a wooden spoon, make an indentation in each ball and fill with ⅛ to ¼ tsp of your favorite jam(s). Bake 12 minutes.

PER COOKIE TRIO 114 **Cal** | 3 g **Fat** (2 g **Sat**) |
1 g **Pro** | 21 g **Carb** | 11 g **Sugars** | 0 g **Fiber** |
42 mg **Sodium**

BISCUIT HACKS

Bust out the waffle iron and a tube of dough for simple—and seriously addictive—snacks.

Strawberry Danish

Split 1 **refrigerated biscuit dough** round and flatten into 2 thin disks. Mix **whipped cream cheese** with a little **confectioners' sugar**. Spread mixture on disks and use them to sandwich crushed **freeze-dried strawberries**. Pinch and crimp edges to seal very well. Cook biscuits in a waffle iron, seam side down, until browned and crispy, about 5 minutes. Dust with confectioners' sugar.

PER SERVING 272 **Cal** | 13 g **Fat** (7 g **Sat**) | 4 g **Pro** | 34 g **Carb** | 12 g **Sugars** | 1 g **Fiber** | 523 mg **Sodium**

Pigs in a Blanket

Cut a **hot dog** in half lengthwise and crosswise, creating 4 pieces. Split 1 **refrigerated biscuit dough** round, and flatten into 2 thin disks. Place 2 pieces of hot dog on each disk; fold into half-moons; seal. Cook 5 minutes. Serve with **mustard** for dipping.

PER SERVING 324 **Cal** | 20 g **Fat** (8 g **Sat**) | 9 g **Pro** | 26 g **Carb** | 5 g **Sugars** | 1 g **Fiber** | 884 mg **Sodium**

Cheese Stick

Cut a stick of **mozzarella string cheese** in half lengthwise, then crosswise, creating 4 pieces. Flatten each of 2 **refrigerated biscuit dough** rounds into a disk. Place mozzarella on 1 disk. Sprinkle with a pinch each **salt** and **Italian herb blend** and top with second disk. Seal; cook 5 minutes. Serve with **marinara sauce** for dipping.

PER SERVING 457 **Cal** | 19 g **Fat** (8 g **Sat**) | 14 g **Pro** | 56 g **Carb** | 12 g **Sugars** | 3 g **Fiber** | 1,543 mg **Sodium**

WAKE UP TO THESE BREAKFASTS

Our gift to you: showstopping dishes that can all be started ahead, so you can actually relax in the a.m.

Overnight Ginger Rolls

Serves 12 **Prep** 35 min **Let rise** 1 hr, 30 min **Refrigerate** overnight **Bake** 35 min **Cool** 10 min

Dough

1	**cup whole milk**
1	**stick unsalted butter, at room temp**
1	**packet (¼ oz) active dry yeast**
¼	**cup warm water (100° to 110°)**
3	**tbsp granulated sugar**
2	**large eggs**
4½	**to 5 cups all-purpose flour**
½	**tsp salt**
	Nonstick cooking spray

Filling

1	**stick unsalted butter, at room temp**
1	**cup packed light brown sugar**
2	**tbsp chopped candied ginger**
2	**to 3 tsp ground ginger**
¼	**tsp salt**

Glaze

2	**cups confectioners' sugar**
3	**to 4 tbsp milk**

1 Make dough: Heat milk and butter in a small pan over medium until it just begins to boil. Remove from heat; cool to room temperature.

2 Meanwhile, sprinkle yeast over warm water in a large bowl. Add 1 tbsp sugar and let stand until foamy, 5 to 7 minutes. Stir in eggs and remaining sugar. Stir in cooled milk mixture.

3 Gradually add 4½ cups flour and the salt, scraping down sides of bowl, until soft dough forms. Turn dough onto a floured work surface. If too sticky, knead more flour into dough as needed. Knead about 5 minutes until smooth (dough will be soft).

4 Grease a large bowl and place dough inside. Cover with plastic wrap and let rise in a warm spot until doubled in size, about 1½ hours.

5 Coat a 13 x 9-inch glass baking dish with cooking spray. Line

bottom with parchment and coat with cooking spray.

6 Make filling: Stir together all ingredients until spreadable.

7 Punch dough down and roll out on a lightly floured surface to an 18 x 12-inch rectangle. Spread filling over dough. Starting on a long side, roll up and pinch seam to close.

8 Cut crosswise into 12 pieces and arrange in prepared dish. Cover tightly with plastic wrap and refrigerate overnight.

9 Heat oven to 350°. Uncover dish and bake buns until browned and bubbly, 30 to 35 minutes. Transfer to a wire rack and cool 10 minutes.

10 Make glaze: Stir confectioners' sugar with 3 tbsp milk, adding more if needed for desired consistency. Drizzle or spread over warm buns.

PER SERVING 385 **Cal** | 13 g **Fat** (8 g **Sat**) | 6 g **Pro** | 62 g **Carb** | 32 g **Sugars** | 1 g **Fiber** | 129 mg **Sodium**

Let the first proof happen in a cozy place, then shape the rolls and leave 'em in the fridge overnight. The second rise will happen before you rise.

Sauté the mushrooms and grate the cheese the day before. Line the springform pan with crust and store it, covered in plastic, in the fridge while sugarplums dance in your head.

Deep-Dish Mushroom Quiche

Serves 10 **Prep** 25 min **Cook** 7 min **Bake** 1 hr, 15 min **Stand** 10 min

1 box (14.1 oz) refrigerated pie crusts

11 large eggs

Nonstick cooking spray

2 tbsp unsalted butter

8 oz mixed wild mushrooms

1 small shallot, finely chopped

1 tbsp chopped fresh thyme, optional

1½ cups milk

1 tsp salt

½ tsp cracked black pepper

2 cups shredded Gruyère cheese

1 Heat oven to 400°. Place 1 pie crust on work surface. Beat 1 egg and brush over pie crust. Top with second pie crust and roll out to a smooth 14-inch circle.

2 Coat a 9-inch springform pan with cooking spray. Press crust into bottom and up sides of pan. Crimp edges of crust. Line crust with parchment paper and fill with pie weights. Bake 15 minutes. Remove pie weights and parchment from crust. Reduce oven temperature to 350°.

3 Melt butter in a large stainless skillet over medium-high. Add mushrooms and shallot and cook until browned, about 7 minutes. Stir in thyme if using. Let cool 5 minutes.

4 Whisk remaining eggs with the milk, salt and black pepper. Stir in mushroom mixture and Gruyère.

5 Pour mixture into crust and bake until puffed and just set (the center will be jiggly), 55 to 60 minutes.

6 Remove quiche from oven and let stand 10 minutes before removing side of pan.

PER SERVING 374 **Cal** | 25 g **Fat** (12 g **Sat**) | 17 g **Pro** | 23 g **Carb** | 3 g **Sugars** | 0 g **Fiber** | 690 mg **Sodium**

DEEP-DISH
MUSHROOM
QUICHE

OVERNIGHT
MAPLE-BACON
FRENCH TOAST

Whisk the quickie custard and pour it over the bread to soak while Santa does his thing.

Overnight Maple-Bacon French Toast

Serves 6 **Prep** 25 min **Refrigerate** overnight **Bake** 35 min **Cool** 5 min

Nonstick cooking spray

12 **slices cinnamon-swirl or white sandwich bread**

5 **large eggs**

1½ **cups half-and-half**

¾ **tsp vanilla extract**

½ **tsp ground cinnamon**

¼ **tsp salt**

½ **cup packed light brown sugar**

¼ **cup maple syrup**

½ **cup chopped pecans**

1 **lb thick-cut bacon, cooked**

1 Spray a 13 x 9-inch baking dish with cooking spray. Lay 6 slices of bread across bottom of pan, then top with remaining slices.

2 In a medium bowl, whisk next 5 ingredients.

3 Pour mixture over bread. Cover dish and refrigerate overnight.

4 Heat oven to 350°. Stir together sugar and syrup. Fold in pecans and bacon, allowing bacon to break up naturally into large pieces.

5 Top bread in pan evenly with bacon mixture. Bake until browned and bubbly, 30 to 35 minutes. Cool 5 minutes before serving.

PER SERVING 497 **Cal** | 23 g **Fat** (7 g **Sat**) | 18 g **Pro** | 70 g **Carb** | 35 g **Sugars** | 3 g **Fiber** | 642 mg **Sodium**

LATKES

Serve any of these crispy pancakes instead of basic hash browns at your next brunch. Top them with poached or fried eggs. Or use the latkes to replace the usual English muffin halves for a spin on eggs Benedict.

Classic Potato Latkes

Makes 12 latkes **Prep** 25 min
Cook 8 min per batch

- 1½ **lb russet potatoes, unpeeled**
- 2 **large eggs, beaten**
- ⅔ **cup potato starch**
- 1 **tsp onion powder**
- 1 **tsp salt**
  Black pepper
- 1 **cup canola oil**
  Sour cream, optional
  Applesauce, optional

1 With a box grater, grate potatoes and place in a colander; press out as much liquid as possible, then squeeze dry with paper towels. Transfer potatoes to a large bowl and add eggs, potato starch, onion powder, salt and a few grinds of pepper. Stir until well combined.

2 Heat oven to 200°. In a 3-qt sauté pan heat oil over medium-high. When oil is shimmering, add four ¼-cup mounds potato mixture and lightly flatten. Cook until browned, 3 to 4 minutes on each side. Transfer latkes to a baking sheet; place in oven to keep warm.

3 If desired, serve with sour cream and/or applesauce.

PER LATKE 116 **Cal** | 5 g **Fat** (1 g **Sat**) | 2 g **Pro** | 16 g **Carb** | 0 g **Sugars** | 1 g **Fiber** | 206 mg **Sodium**

Sweet Potato Latkes

Makes 18 latkes **Prep** 25 min
Cook 6 min per batch

- 3 **medium sweet potatoes, peeled (about 1 lb)**
- 1 **large onion**
- 2 **large eggs**
- 1 **tbsp chili powder**
- ½ **salt**
- ⅛ **tsp black pepper**
- 4 **tbsp potato starch**
- ½ **cup vegetable oil**
  Sour cream, optional

1 Fit a food processor with shredding disk. Shred sweet potatoes and place in a colander. Shred onion, then add to sweet potatoes and toss to combine. Let drain 10 minutes. Transfer to a large bowl.

2 In a small bowl, whisk eggs, chili powder, salt and pepper; stir into sweet potato mixture. Sift potato starch into sweet potato mixture and mix to combine.

3 Heat oven to 200°. In a large nonstick skillet, heat oil over medium-high. Add six ¼-cup mounds sweet potato mixture to hot oil and lightly flatten. Cook until browned, 2 to 3 minutes per side. Transfer latkes to a baking sheet; place in oven to keep warm.

4 Serve with sour cream, if desired.

PER LATKE 114 **Cal** | 8 g **Fat** (2 g **Sat**) | 2 g **Pro** | 8 g **Carb** | 2 g **Sugars** | 1 g **Fiber** | 115 mg **Sodium**

Zucchini Fritters

Makes 12 fritters **Prep** 25 min
Cook 6 min

- 1 **container (7 oz) 2% plain Greek yogurt**
- 2 **tsp lime juice**
- 1 **tsp lime zest**
- ¼ **tsp salt**
- 1½ **lb zucchini**
- ⅔ **cup sliced scallions**
- ½ **cup lightly packed cilantro, chopped, plus more for garnish**
- 1 **egg yolk**
- ⅓ **cup all-purpose flour**
- 1 **tsp salt**
- ½ **tsp black pepper**
- 4 **tbsp canola oil**

1 In a bowl, stir yogurt, lime juice and zest and salt until smooth.

2 Shred zucchini and squeeze in a clean kitchen towel until moisture is absorbed. In a bowl, combine zucchini, scallions, cilantro, egg yolk, flour, salt and pepper.

3 Heat oven to 200°. In a large sauté pan, heat 2 tbsp oil over medium-high. Add four ¼-cup mounds of zucchini mixture and lightly flatten. Cook until browned, 3 minutes per side. Transfer to a baking sheet; place in oven to keep warm. (Add 1 tbsp oil to pan for each batch.) Serve with lime yogurt and garnish with cilantro.

PER FRITTER 83 **Cal** | 6 g **Fat** (1 g **Sat**) | 3 g **Pro** | 6 g **Carb** | 2 g **Sugars** | 1 g **Fiber** | 206 mg **Sodium**

INDEX

A

ALMOND(S)
Cocoa-Coconut Almond Balls, 11
Coconut-Almond Brownies, 215
Green Beans Amandine, 256
Italian Wheat Berry Salad, 271
Nut Clusters, 83
Pistachio and Raspberry White
    Chocolate Bark, 52
Romesco, 67
Turmeric Chicken Salad, 181
APPETIZERS AND SNACKS. *SEE ALSO* DIPS
Cheese Stick, 287
Greek Nachos, 195
Pigs in a Blanket, 287
Pita Chips, 124
APPLES
Apple and Fennel Salad, 157
Chicken and Apple Slaw, 115
DIY Waffle Toppings, 231
Overnight Oatmeal, 35
Roasted Celery Root and Apple with
    Pork, 30
Salted Caramel Dip, 231
ARTICHOKES
Lemon Chicken with Artichokes, 241
Parmesan-Artichoke Dip, 61
Spinach and Tortellini Salad, 192
Warm Spinach-Artichoke Dip, 129
ARUGULA
Asian Wheat Berry Salad, 271
Grilled Halloumi Salad, 190
Italian Wheat Berry Salad, 271
Lemon-Thyme Chicken Burgers, 162
Pork Schnitzel, 273
Asian Wheat Berry Salad, 271
ASPARAGUS
Orzo Salad with Grilled Shrimp, 92
AVOCADOS
Avocado-Corn Salsa, 123
Avocado Mousse, 123
Basic Guacamole, 123
B + T Guac, 123
Chunky Avocado-Citrus Dip, 123
Roasted Potatoes and Parsnips with
    Steak, 27
Turkey Taco Salad, 187

B

Baby Back Ribs, 153
BACON
BBQ Bacon Cheddar Burgers, 112
Bell Pepper, Cheddar and Sausage
    Quiche, 88
B + T Guac, 123
Caramelized Onion Dip, 127
Cheddar, Bacon and Scallion Bread, 219
DIY Waffle Toppings, 231
Fontina, Basil and Bacon Grilled
    Cheese, 202
Overnight Maple-Bacon French
    Toast, 293
Overnight Oatmeal, 35
Texas-Style Beans, 154
Warm German Potato Salad, 150
Baked Rigatoni and Meatballs, 18
BANANAS
Berry-Beet-Banana-Basil Smoothie, 33
Cherry Cooler, 179
DIY Waffle Toppings, 231
Overnight Oatmeal, 35
BAR COOKIES
Birthday Cake Cookie Bars, 212
Coconut-Almond Brownies, 215
Coconut-Cranberry Squares, 285
No-Bake Fireworks Cheesecake Bars, 172
Pistachio Triangles, 283
Raspberry Crumb Bars, 211
Salted Caramel Bars, 211
Swirled Pumpkin Spice Cheesecake
    Bars, 263
Barley Stew, Chicken and, 45
Basic Dough, 282
Basic Gravy, 252
Basic Guacamole, 123
BASIL
Berry-Beet-Banana-Basil Smoothie, 33
B + T Guac, 123
Fettuccine with Fresh Tomato Sauce, 111
Fontina, Basil and Bacon Grilled
    Cheese, 202
Pho-Style Beef Salad, 189
Rigatoni with Meat Sauce, 242
Tomato, Zucchini and Parmesan
    Fristrata, 249
Watermelon toppings, 169
BBQ Bacon Cheddar Burgers, 112
BBQ Pork Pizza, 41

**BEANS. *SEE ALSO* CHICKPEAS; GREEN
    BEANS**
Beef and Bean Chili, 74
Chipotle Corn Chili, 209
Edamame Dip, 125
Ground Turkey Quesadilla, 99
Pasta and White Bean Soup, 205
Roasted Broccoli and White Bean Pasta, 24
Seriously Sneaky Chocolate Cake, 85
Smoky Beet and Bean Dip, 125
Southern Caviar with Hominy, 125
Texas-Style Beans, 154
White Bean Dip, 125
BEEF
Beef and Bean Chili, 74
Beef and Sweet Potato Stew, 80
Beef Meatballs with Marinara, 61
Chicago-Style Burger, 150
Chili, Rice and Spinach Burrito, 209
Chipotle Corn Chili, 209
Greek Steak and Salad, 140
Instant Pot "Roast" Beef, 65
Mini Eggo Sliders, 231
Pho-Style Beef Salad, 189
Rigatoni with Meat Sauce, 242
Roasted Potatoes and Parsnips with
    Steak, 27
Smoked Brisket, 154
Stuffed Flank Steak, 21
Stuffed Mac and Cheese, 42
Tacos con Carne, 161
BEETS
Berry-Beet-Banana-Basil Smoothie, 33
Smoky Beet and Bean Dip, 125
Bell Pepper, Cheddar and Sausage
    Quiche, 88
Berry-Beet-Banana-Basil Smoothie, 33
BEVERAGES
Berry-Beet-Banana-Basil Smoothie, 33
Cherry Cooler, 179
Coffee-Chocolate-PB Smoothie, 33
Mr. Clarke's Chemistry Punch, 232
Birthday Cake Cookie Bars, 212
BLACKBERRIES
Apple and Fennel Salad, 157
Rocking Berry Roll, 176
Blackened Zucchini and Corn Tacos, 161
BLUEBERRIES
Blueberry-Maple Butter, 193
Pork with Blueberry Balsamic Sauce, 119
Red, White and Blueberry Pops, 170
Rocking Berry Roll, 176

BLUE CHEESE
Blue Cheese Dip, 58
Buffalo Chicken Dip, 131
BREADS
Cheddar, Bacon and Scallion Bread, 219
Overnight Ginger Rolls, 289
Strawberry Danish, 287
Zucchini Muffins, 185
BROCCOLI
Bell Pepper, Cheddar and Sausage
Quiche, 88
Cauliflower Gnocchi Cacio e Pepe
Bake, 278
Chicken with Garlic and Sage Sauce, 229
Halfway Healthy Spaghetti Pesto, 143
Italian Wheat Berry Salad, 271
Roasted Broccoli and White Bean Pasta, 24
Stuffed Mac and Cheese, 42
BROCCOLI RABE
Chicken Marsala, 76
Sausage and Broccoli Rabe Hoagie, 201
Sheet Pan Sausage and Broccoli Rabe, 201
Brownies, Coconut-Almond, 215
Brussels Sprouts with Poached Egg and
Parmesan, Roasted, 24
B + T Guac, 123
Buffalo Chicken Dip, 131
BURGERS
BBQ Bacon Cheddar Burgers, 112
Chicago-Style Burger, 150
Lemon-Thyme Chicken Burgers, 162
Burrito Bowl, 41
Burrito, Chili, Rice and Spinach, 209
BUTTERS
Blueberry-Maple Butter, 193
Chimichurri Butter, 193
Greek Butter, 193
Honey-Cardamom Butter, 193
Red Curry Butter, 193
Shallot-Chive Butter, 149
Sriracha-Scallion Butter, 193

C

CABBAGE
Chicken and Apple Slaw, 115
Moo Shu Pork Noodles, 13
Peppery Coleslaw, 153
Pho-Style Beef Salad, 189
Soy-Glazed Chicken Thighs, 71
CAKES
Chocolate Ganache Cupcakes, 55
Milk Chocolate Marshmallow Cake, 106
Pumpkin Spice Layer Cake, 267
Raspberry Crepe Cake, 107
Rocking Berry Roll, 176
Seriously Sneaky Chocolate Cake, 85
Upside Down Cake, The, 232
Caramelized Onion Dip, 127

CARROTS
Chicken and Barley Stew, 45
Chicken and Veggie Skillet, 139
Ground Pork Banh Mi, 147
Instant Pot Slow-Cooked Honey-Ginger
Pork, 65
Peppery Coleslaw, 153
Pho-Style Beef Salad, 189
Roasted-Vegetable Chicken Soup, 27
Salmon Veggie Bowls, 190
CAULIFLOWER
Asian Wheat Berry Salad, 271
Berry-Beet-Banana-Basil Smoothie, 33
Cauliflower Gnocchi Cacio e Pepe
Bake, 278
Salmon Veggie Bowls, 190
Vegetable Frittata, 179
Celery Root and Apple with Pork,
Roasted, 30
Chard and Sausage Stuffing, 256
CHEDDAR
BBQ Bacon Cheddar Burgers, 112
BBQ Pork Pizza, 41
Bell Pepper, Cheddar and Sausage
Quiche, 88
Cheddar, Bacon and Scallion Bread, 219
Chili, Rice and Spinach Burrito, 209
Overnight Oatmeal, 35
Sheet Pan Egg Sandwiches, 39
Stuffed Mac and Cheese, 42
Tomato and Cheddar Slab Tart, 168
Turkey Taco Salad, 187
CHEESE. SEE ALSO BLUE CHEESE;
CHEDDAR; CREAM CHEESE; FETA;
GOAT CHEESE; MOZZARELLA;
PARMESAN; RICOTTA
Baked Rigatoni and Meatballs, 18
Bell Pepper, Cheddar and Sausage
Quiche, 88
Buffalo Chicken Dip, 131
Caramelized Onion Dip, 127
Cheese Stick, 287
Chicken Enchiladas, 46
Chorizo Queso, 131
Deep-Dish Mushroom Quiche, 290
DIY Waffle Toppings, 231
Fettuccine with Fresh Tomato
Sauce, 111
Fontina, Basil and Bacon Grilled
Cheese, 202
Greek Nachos, 195
Grilled Cheese Salad, 202
Grilled Halloumi Salad, 190
Ground Turkey Quesadilla, 99
Lemon-Thyme Chicken Burgers, 162
Mushroom and Cheese Fondue, 129
Overnight Oatmeal, 35
Parmesan-Artichoke Dip, 61
Pepperoni Pizza Dip, 131

Potato Puff Casserole, 239
Rigatoni with Meat Sauce, 242
Roasted Broccoli and White Bean
Pasta, 24
Sausage and Broccoli Rabe Hoagie, 201
Shaved Vegetable and Prosciutto
Pizza, 246
Spinach-Ricotta Lasagna, 74
CHEESECAKE
No-Bake Fireworks Cheesecake Bars, 172
Swirled Pumpkin Spice Cheesecake
Bars, 263
CHERRIES
Cherry Cooler, 179
Overnight Oatmeal, 35
Cherry Tomato Salsa, 129
CHIA SEEDS
Berry-Beet-Banana-Basil Smoothie, 33
Cherry Cooler, 179
Chicago-Style Burger, 150
CHICKEN
Asian Wheat Berry Salad, 271
Baked Rigatoni and Meatballs, 18
Buffalo Chicken Dip, 131
Chicken and Apple Slaw, 115
Chicken and Barley Stew, 45
Chicken and Veggie Skillet, 139
Chicken Enchiladas, 46
Chicken Marsala, 76
Chicken Meatballs with Buffalo Sauce, 58
Chicken Piccata, 17
Chicken Ramen, 206
Chicken with Garlic and Sage Sauce, 229
Coconut Rice with Jerk Chicken and
Mango Salsa, 91
DIY Waffle Toppings, 231
Ground Turkey Quesadilla, 99
Italian Wheat Berry Salad, 271
Lemon Chicken with Artichokes, 241
Lemon-Thyme Chicken Burgers, 162
Mediterranean Bowl, 79
Mustard-Olive Roast Chicken and
Potatoes, 65
Quickie Chicken Pot Pie, 274
Roasted-Vegetable Chicken Soup, 27
Soy-Glazed Chicken Thighs, 71
Spice-Roasted Chicken Thighs, 31
Spicy Chicken Lettuce Wraps, 206
Spinach and Tortellini Salad, 192
Tacos con Carne, 161
Turmeric Chicken Salad, 181
Tuscan Chicken Cobb, 144
CHICKPEAS
Mediterranean Bowl, 79
Roasted Red Pepper Hummus, 125
Turmeric Chicken Salad, 181
Chili, Rice and Spinach Burrito, 209
Chimichurri, 67
Chimichurri Butter, 193
Chipotle Corn Chili, 209

CHIVES
Bell Pepper, Cheddar and Sausage
    Quiche, 88
Green Goddess Dressing, 67
Instant Pot Quick Shrimp Risotto, 49
Pork Schnitzel, 273
Shallot-Chive Butter, 149
Warm Crab Dip, 131
**CHOCOLATE. *SEE ALSO* WHITE
    CHOCOLATE**
Chocolate Biscotti, 284
Chocolate Chip Cookie Ice Box Cake, 196
Chocolate Cream, 196
Chocolate Ganache Cupcakes, 55
Cocoa-Coconut Almond Balls, 11
Coconut-Almond Brownies, 215
Coffee-Chocolate-PB Smoothie, 33
Ganache, 85
Marshmallow Filling and Frosting, 106
Milk Chocolate Marshmallow Cake, 106
Mocha Latte Crackles, 283
Overnight Oatmeal, 35
PB Cup Balls, 11
Peppermint Snaps, 285
Seriously Sneaky Chocolate Cake, 85
Chorizo Queso, 131
Chunky Avocado-Citrus Dip, 123
CILANTRO
Avocado-Corn Salsa, 123
Basic Guacamole, 123
Cherry Tomato Salsa, 129
Chicken Enchiladas, 46
Chimichurri, 67
Chimichurri Butter, 193
Cilantro-Scallion Dip, 127
Coconut Rice with Jerk Chicken and
    Mango Salsa, 91
Ground Pork Banh Mi, 147
Red Curry Butter, 193
Roasted Potatoes and Parsnips with
    Steak, 27
Slow Cooker Curried Lentil Soup, 225
Southern Caviar with Hominy, 125
Thai Curry Tilapia, 281
Turmeric Chicken Salad, 181
Turmeric-Yogurt Dip, 127
Zucchini Fritters, 295
Citrus Herb Turkey, 250
Classic Potato Latkes, 295
Cocoa-Coconut Almond Balls, 11
COCONUT
Cocoa-Coconut Almond Balls, 11
Coconut-Almond Brownies, 215
Coconut-Cranberry Squares, 285
Overnight Oatmeal, 35
Pistachio and Raspberry White
    Chocolate Bark, 52
Strawberry, Grapefruit and Coconut
    Pavlova, 102

COCONUT MILK
Coconut Rice with Jerk Chicken and
    Mango Salsa, 91
Saté Dip, 57
Strawberry, Grapefruit and Coconut
    Pavlova, 102
Thai Curry Tilapia, 281
COFFEE
Chocolate Chip Cookie Ice Box Cake, 196
Coffee-Chocolate-PB Smoothie, 33
Milk Chocolate Marshmallow Cake, 106
Mocha Latte Crackles, 283
COOKIES. *SEE ALSO* BAR COOKIES
Basic Dough, 282
Chocolate Biscotti, 284
Edible Stained Glass, 286
Glazed Sugar Cookies, 282
Herbed Shortbread, 286
Lemony Thumbprints, 286
Marbled Vanilla Sugar Cookies, 51
Mocha Latte Crackles, 283
Orange Squares, 284
PB Slices, 284
Pecan Crescents, 283
Peppermint Snaps, 285
CORN
Avocado-Corn Salsa, 123
Bell Pepper, Cheddar and Sausage
    Quiche, 88
Blackened Zucchini and Corn Tacos, 161
Chipotle Corn Chili, 209
Corn and Crab Salad, 149
CORNMEAL
David's No-Fail Homemade Pizza
    Dough, 246
Rhubarb Tart, 101
CRANBERRIES
Coconut-Cranberry Squares, 285
Very Berry Balls, 11
CREAM CHEESE
Blue Cheese Dip, 58
Buffalo Chicken Dip, 131
Caramelized Onion Dip, 127
Cream Cheese Frosting, 267
No-Bake Fireworks Cheesecake Bars, 172
Open-Faced Crab Sandwich, 95
Parmesan-Artichoke Dip, 61
Strawberry Danish, 287
Swirled Pumpkin Spice Cheesecake
    Bars, 263
Warm Crab Dip, 131
Warm Spinach-Artichoke Dip, 129
Creamy Pesto Dressing, 271
Crepe Cake, Raspberry, 107
Crispy Tofu with Peanut Sauce, 226
CUCUMBERS
Greek Steak and Salad, 140
Ground Pork Banh Mi, 147
Mediterranean Bowl, 79

Salmon Veggie Bowls, 190
Tzatziki, 67
Cupcakes, Chocolate Ganache, 55
Curried Lentil Soup, 14

D

David's No-Fail Homemade Pizza
    Dough, 246
Deep-Dish Mushroom Quiche, 290
**DESSERTS. *SEE ALSO* BAR COOKIES;
    CAKES; COOKIES; PIES AND TARTS**
Chocolate Chip Cookie Ice Box
    Cake, 196
Pumpkin Flan, 259
Pumpkin Mousse Parfaits, 264
Raspberry Crepe Cake, 107
Red, White and Blueberry Pops, 170
Strawberry, Grapefruit and Coconut
    Pavlova, 102
Swirled Meringue Sorbet Sandwiches, 175
DILL
Greek Steak and Salad, 140
Green Goddess Dressing, 67
Orzo Salad with Grilled Shrimp, 92
Tzatziki, 67
Whipped Feta Dip, 127
DIPS
Avocado Mousse, 123
Basic Guacamole, 123
Blue Cheese Dip, 58
B + T Guac, 123
Buffalo Chicken Dip, 131
Caramelized Onion Dip, 127
Chorizo Queso, 131
Chunky Avocado-Citrus Dip, 123
Cilantro-Scallion Dip, 127
Edamame Dip, 125
Green Pea Dip, 129
Mushroom and Cheese Fondue, 129
Olive Tapenade, 129
Parmesan-Artichoke Dip, 61
Pepperoni Pizza Dip, 131
Roasted Red Pepper Hummus, 125
Salted Caramel Dip, 231
Saté Dip, 57
Smoky Beet and Bean Dip, 125
Sour Cream and Leek Dip, 127
Southern Caviar with Hominy, 125
Turmeric-Yogurt Dip, 127
Warm Anchovy Dip, 131
Warm Crab Dip, 131
Warm Spinach-Artichoke Dip, 129
Whipped Feta Dip, 127
White Bean Dip, 125
DIY Waffle Toppings, 231
Dry Rub, 153

E

Edamame Dip, 125
Edible Stained Glass, 286
EGGS
Bell Pepper, Cheddar and Sausage
Quiche, 88
Deep-Dish Mushroom Quiche, 290
Perfect Ramen Eggs, 206
Potato Puff Casserole, 239
Roasted Brussels Sprouts with
Poached Egg and Parmesan, 24
Sheet Pan Egg Sandwiches, 39
Tomato, Zucchini and Parmesan
Fristrata, 249
Tuscan Chicken Cobb, 144
Vegetable Frittata, 179
Veggie-Feta Egg Cups, 82
Enchiladas, Chicken, 46

F

Fennel and Apple Salad, 157
FETA
Greek Nachos, 195
Greek Steak and Salad, 140
Orzo Salad with Grilled Shrimp, 92
Salmon Pasta, 186
Veggie-Feta Egg Cups, 82
Whipped Feta Dip, 127
Fettuccine with Fresh Tomato Sauce, 111
FISH. SEE ALSO SALMON; SHELLFISH;
SHRIMP
New England Fish Dinner, 245
Salmon Pasta, 180
Salmon Veggie Bowls, 190
Thai Curry Tilapia, 281
Tuna Kebabs, 166
Warm Anchovy Dip, 131
Fondue, Mushroom and Cheese, 129
Fontina, Basil and Bacon Grilled
Cheese, 202
French Toast, Overnight Maple-Bacon, 293
FROSTINGS AND FILLINGS
Chocolate Cream, 196
Cream Cheese Frosting, 267
Ganache, 85
Marshmallow Filling and Frosting, 106

G

Ganache, 85
GARLIC
Chicken with Garlic and Sage Sauce, 229
Grilled Shrimp Caesar, 116
Sour Cream and Leek Dip, 127
GINGER
Chicken Ramen, 206
Ginger-Soy Dressing, 271

Glazed Delicata Squash, 256
Instant Pot Slow-Cooked Honey-Ginger
Pork, 65
Overnight Ginger Rolls, 289
Overnight Oatmeal, 35
Pork Meatballs with Hoisin Sauce, 57
Salmon Veggie Bowls, 190
Saté Dip, 57
Slow Cooker Curried Lentil Soup, 225
Glazed Delicata Squash, 256
Glazed Sugar Cookies, 282
Gnocchi Cacio e Pepe Bake, Cauliflower, 278
GOAT CHEESE
Salmon Pasta, 180
Vegetable Frittata, 179
GRAINS. SEE ALSO CORNMEAL; OATS;
POLENTA; RICE
Asian Wheat Berry Salad, 271
Chicken and Barley Stew, 45
Italian Wheat Berry Salad, 271
Mediterranean Bowl, 79
Turmeric Chicken Salad, 181
Wheat Berries, 271
GRAPEFRUIT
Chunky Avocado-Citrus Dip, 123
Strawberry, Grapefruit and Coconut
Pavlova, 102
GRAPES
Upside Down Cake, The, 232
GRAVY
Basic Gravy, 252
Vegan Mushroom Gravy, 252
Wine and Herb Gravy, 252
Greek Butter, 193
Greek Nachos, 195
Greek Steak and Salad, 140
GREEN BEANS
Chicken and Veggie Skillet, 139
Chicken with Garlic and Sage Sauce, 229
Green Beans Amandine, 256
New England Fish Dinner, 245
Thai Curry Tilapia, 281
Green Goddess Dressing, 67
Green Pea Dip, 129
GREENS. SEE ALSO ARUGULA;
CABBAGE; KALE; SPINACH
Chard and Sausage Stuffing, 256
Italian Wedding Soup, 277
Grilled Cheese Salad, 202
GRILLED RECIPES
Baby Back Ribs, 153
Blackened Zucchini and Corn Tacos, 161
Chicago-Style Burger, 150
Greek Steak and Salad, 140
Grilled Halloumi Salad, 190
Grilled Maine Lobster, 149
Grilled Salmon, 157
Grilled Shrimp Caesar, 116

Hobo Packs, 137
Lemon-Thyme Chicken Burgers, 162
Orzo Salad with Grilled Shrimp, 92
Pork with Peaches and Pecans, 165
Smoked Brisket, 154
Tuna Kebabs, 166
Tuscan Chicken Cobb, 144
Ground Pork Banh Mi, 147
Ground Turkey Quesadilla, 99

H

Halfway Healthy Spaghetti Pesto, 143
HAZELNUTS
Apple and Fennel Salad, 157
Overnight Oatmeal, 35
Herbed Shortbread, 286
Hobo Packs, 137
Hominy, Southern Caviar with, 125
Honey-Cardamom Butter, 193

I

Instant Pot Quick Shrimp Risotto, 49
Instant Pot "Roast" Beef, 65
Instant Pot Slow-Cooked Honey-Ginger
Pork, 65
Italian Wedding Soup, 277
Italian Wheat Berry Salad, 271

K

KALE
Chicken and Apple Slaw, 115
Curried Lentil Soup, 14
Tuscan Chicken Cobb, 144

L

Lasagna, Spinach-Ricotta, 74
LATKES
Classic Potato Latkes, 295
Sweet Potato Latkes, 295
Leek and Sour Cream Dip, 127
LEMON(S)
Lemon Chicken with Artichokes, 241
Lemon Tart, 132
Lemon-Thyme Chicken Burgers, 162
Lemony Thumbprints, 286
Spice-Roasted Chicken Thighs, 31
White Bean Dip, 125
LENTILS
Curried Lentil Soup, 14
Slow Cooker Curried Lentil Soup, 225

M

MANGOES
Coconut Rice with Jerk Chicken and
Mango Salsa, 91

Pistachio and Raspberry White
    Chocolate Bark, 52
Marbled Vanilla Sugar Cookies, 51
Marshmallow Filling and Frosting, 106
MEATBALLS
    Baked Rigatoni and Meatballs, 18
    Beef Meatballs with Marinara, 61
    Chicken Meatballs with Buffalo
        Sauce, 58
    Fettuccine with Fresh Tomato Sauce, 111
    Italian Wedding Soup, 277
    Pork Meatballs with Hoisin Sauce, 57
Mediterranean Bowl, 79
Milk Chocolate Marshmallow Cake, 106
Mini Eggo Sliders, 231
MINT
    Apple and Fennel Salad, 157
    Green Pea Dip, 129
    Pho-Style Beef Salad, 189
Mocha Latte Crackles, 283
Moo Shu Pork Noodles, 13
MOZZARELLA
    Cauliflower Gnocchi Cacio e Pepe
        Bake, 278
    Cheese Stick, 287
    Ground Turkey Quesadilla, 99
    Pepperoni Pizza Dip, 131
    Shaved Vegetable and Prosciutto
        Pizza, 246
    Tuscan Chicken Cobb, 144
    Warm Spinach-Artichoke Dip, 129
Mr. Clarke's Chemistry Punch, 232
Muffins, Zucchini, 185
MULTICOOKER RECIPES
    Instant Pot Quick Shrimp Risotto, 49
    Instant Pot "Roast" Beef, 65
    Instant Pot Slow-Cooked Honey-Ginger
        Pork, 65
    Slow Cooker Curried Lentil Soup, 225
MUSHROOMS
    Beef and Sweet Potato Stew, 80
    Chicken and Barley Stew, 45
    Chicken Marsala, 76
    Deep-Dish Mushroom Quiche, 290
    Mushroom and Cheese Fondue, 129
    Shaved Vegetable and Prosciutto
        Pizza, 246
    Spinach Salad with Warm Sausage
        Dressing, 96
    Stuffed Flank Steak, 21
    Stuffed Mac and Cheese, 42
    Vegan Mushroom Gravy, 252
    Vegetable Frittata, 179
Mustard-Based Rib Sauce, 153
Mustard-Olive Roast Chicken and
    Potatoes, 65

N

New England Fish Dinner, 245
No-Bake Fireworks Cheesecake Bars, 172
NOODLES
    Chicken Ramen, 206
    Pork Schnitzel, 273
Nut Clusters, 83

O

OATS
    Cocoa-Coconut Almond Balls, 11
    Coffee-Chocolate-PB Smoothie, 33
    Overnight Oatmeal, 35
    PB Cup Balls, 11
    Raspberry Crumb Bars, 211
    Very Berry Balls, 11
OLIVES
    Greek Nachos, 195
    Mediterranean Bowl, 79
    Mustard-Olive Roast Chicken and
        Potatoes, 65
    Olive Tapenade, 129
ONIONS
    Caramelized Onion Dip, 127
    Cheddar, Bacon and Scallion Bread, 219
    Cilantro-Scallion Dip, 127
    Pickled Red Onion, 27
    Sriracha-Scallion Butter, 193
Open-Faced Crab Sandwich, 95
ORANGE(S)
    Chunky Avocado-Citrus Dip, 123
    Citrus Herb Turkey, 250
    Orange Squares, 284
    Spice-Roasted Chicken Thighs, 31
OREGANO
    Chimichurri Butter, 193
    Hobo Packs, 137
    Pork with Blueberry Balsamic Sauce, 119
    Rigatoni with Meat Sauce, 242
    Roasted Pepper Salsa, 195
Orzo Salad with Grilled Shrimp, 92
Overnight Ginger Rolls, 289
Overnight Maple-Bacon French Toast, 293
Overnight Oatmeal, 35

P

PARMESAN
    Cauliflower Gnocchi Cacio e Pepe
        Bake, 278
    Green Pea Dip, 129
    Ground Turkey Quesadilla, 99
    Halfway Healthy Spaghetti Pesto, 143
    Instant Pot Quick Shrimp Risotto, 49
    Parmesan-Artichoke Dip, 61
    Roasted Brussels Sprouts with
        Poached Egg and Parmesan, 24
    Spinach-Ricotta Lasagna, 74

Tomato and Spinach Mini Ravioli, 205
Tomato, Zucchini and Parmesan
    Fristrata, 249
Warm Crab Dip, 131
Warm Spinach-Artichoke Dip, 129
PARSLEY
    Baked Rigatoni and Meatballs, 18
    Beef and Sweet Potato Stew, 80
    Chard and Sausage Stuffing, 256
    Chimichurri, 67
    Chimichurri Butter, 193
    Cilantro-Scallion Dip, 127
    Corn and Crab Salad, 149
    Green Goddess Dressing, 67
    Grilled Shrimp Caesar, 116
    Lemon Chicken with Artichokes, 241
    Mediterranean Bowl, 79
    New England Fish Dinner, 245
    Parmesan-Artichoke Dip, 61
    Roasted-Vegetable Chicken Soup, 27
    Shrimp Fra Diavolo, 222
    Stuffed Flank Steak, 21
    Tomato and Spinach Mini Ravioli, 205
    Warm German Potato Salad, 150
Parsnips with Steak, Roasted Potatoes
    and, 27
PASTA. *SEE ALSO* NOODLES
    Baked Rigatoni and Meatballs, 18
    Fettuccine with Fresh Tomato Sauce, 111
    Halfway Healthy Spaghetti Pesto, 143
    Italian Wedding Soup, 277
    Lemon Chicken with Artichokes, 241
    Moo Shu Pork Noodles, 13
    Orzo Salad with Grilled Shrimp, 92
    Pasta and White Bean Soup, 205
    Pho-Style Beef Salad, 189
    Rigatoni with Meat Sauce, 242
    Roasted Broccoli and White Bean
        Pasta, 24
    Roasted-Vegetable Chicken Soup, 27
    Salmon Pasta, 180
    Shrimp Fra Diavolo, 222
    Soy-Glazed Chicken Thighs, 71
    Spinach and Tortellini Salad, 192
    Spinach-Ricotta Lasagna, 74
    Stuffed Mac and Cheese, 42
    Tomato and Spinach Mini Ravioli, 205
Pastry Topper, 274
PB Cup Balls, 11
PEANUT BUTTER
    Coffee-Chocolate-PB Smoothie, 33
    Crispy Tofu with Peanut Sauce, 226
    PB Cup Balls, 11
    PB Slices, 284
    Saté Dip, 57
PEANUTS
    PB Slices, 284
    Pho-Style Beef Salad, 189

PEAS
- Cauliflower Gnocchi Cacio e Pepe Bake, 278
- Green Pea Dip, 129
- Halfway Healthy Spaghetti Pesto, 143
- Instant Pot Quick Shrimp Risotto, 49
- Moo Shu Pork Noodles, 13
- Quickie Chicken Pot Pie, 274

PECANS
- Nut Clusters, 83
- Overnight Maple-Bacon French Toast, 293
- Pecan Crescents, 283
- Pork with Peaches and Pecans, 165

Peppermint Snaps, 285

Pepperoni Pizza Dip, 131

PEPPERS, BELL
- Bell Pepper, Cheddar and Sausage Quiche, 88
- Corn and Crab Salad, 149
- Ground Turkey Quesadilla, 99
- Hobo Packs, 137
- Instant Pot Slow-Cooked Honey-Ginger Pork, 65
- Roasted Pepper Salsa, 195
- Roasted Red Pepper Hummus, 125
- Romesco, 67
- Sheet Pan Sausage and Broccoli Rabe, 201
- Shrimp and Sausage Skillet, 74
- Southern Caviar with Hominy, 125
- Tuna Kebabs, 166
- Veggie-Feta Egg Cups, 82

PEPPERS, CHILE
- Avocado-Corn Salsa, 123
- Basic Guacamole, 123
- Bell Pepper, Cheddar and Sausage Quiche, 88
- Chicago-Style Burger, 150
- Chipotle Corn Chili, 209
- Chorizo Queso, 131
- Saté Dip, 57
- Smoky Beet and Bean Dip, 125
- Southern Caviar with Hominy, 125

Peppery Coleslaw, 153

Perfect Ramen Eggs, 206

Pho-Style Beef Salad, 189

Pickled Red Onion, 27

PIE PASTRY
- Pastry Topper, 274
- Prebaked Crust, 132

PIES AND TARTS
- Lemon Tart, 132
- Pumpkin Meringue Pie, 260
- Rhubarb Tart, 101
- Tomato and Cheddar Slab Tart, 168

Pigs in a Blanket, 287

PINEAPPLE
- Overnight Oatmeal, 35
- Tuna Kebabs, 166

PISTACHIOS
- Mediterranean Bowl, 79
- Overnight Oatmeal, 35
- Pistachio and Raspberry White Chocolate Bark, 52
- Pistachio Triangles, 283
- Watermelon toppings, 169

Pita Chips, 124

PIZZA
- BBQ Pork Pizza, 41
- David's No-Fail Homemade Pizza Dough, 246
- Shaved Vegetable and Prosciutto Pizza, 246

POLENTA
- Chicken Piccata, 17
- Sheet Pan Sausage and Broccoli Rabe, 201

POMEGRANATE
- Berry-Beet-Banana-Basil Smoothie, 33
- Chunky Avocado-Citrus Dip, 123
- Mr. Clarke's Chemistry Punch, 232
- No-Bake Fireworks Cheesecake Bars, 172

PORK. *SEE ALSO* **BACON; PROSCIUTTO; SAUSAGES**
- Baby Back Ribs, 153
- BBQ Pork Pizza, 41
- Burrito Bowl, 41
- Ground Pork Banh Mi, 147
- Instant Pot Slow-Cooked Honey-Ginger Pork, 65
- Moo Shu Pork Noodles, 13
- Pork Meatballs with Hoisin Sauce, 57
- Pork Sammies, 41
- Pork Schnitzel, 273
- Pork with Blueberry Balsamic Sauce, 119
- Pork with Peaches and Pecans, 165
- Roasted Celery Root and Apple with Pork, 30
- Sheet Pan Pork, Butternut Squash and Potato, 221
- Slow Cooker Pulled Pork, 41

POTATOES. *SEE ALSO* **SWEET POTATOES**
- Bell Pepper, Cheddar and Sausage Quiche, 88
- Chicken Marsala, 76
- Classic Potato Latkes, 295
- Curried Lentil Soup, 14
- Hobo Packs, 137
- Mustard-Olive Roast Chicken and Potatoes, 65
- New England Fish Dinner, 245
- Potatoes Anna, 257
- Potato Puff Casserole, 239
- Quickie Chicken Pot Pie, 274
- Roasted Potatoes and Parsnips with Steak, 27
- Sheet Pan Pork, Butternut Squash and Potato, 221
- Warm German Potato Salad, 150

Pot Pie, Quickie Chicken, 274

Prebaked Crust, 132

PRESSURE COOKER RECIPES
- Curried Lentil Soup, 14
- Instant Pot Quick Shrimp Risotto, 49
- Instant Pot "Roast" Beef, 65

PROSCIUTTO
- Shaved Vegetable and Prosciutto Pizza, 246
- Tuscan Chicken Cobb, 144

PUMPKIN
- Pumpkin Flan, 259
- Pumpkin Meringue Pie, 260
- Pumpkin Mousse Parfaits, 264
- Pumpkin Spice Layer Cake, 267
- Swirled Pumpkin Spice Cheesecake Bars, 263

PUMPKIN SEEDS
- Avocado Mousse, 123
- Chicken and Apple Slaw, 115
- Pumpkin Seed Brittle, 267

Q

Quesadilla, Ground Turkey, 99

QUICHE
- Bell Pepper, Cheddar and Sausage Quiche, 88
- Deep-Dish Mushroom Quiche, 290

Quickie Chicken Pot Pie, 274

R

RADISHES
- Ground Pork Banh Mi, 147
- Turkey Taco Salad, 187

RASPBERRIES
- No-Bake Fireworks Cheesecake Bars, 172
- Pistachio and Raspberry White Chocolate Bark, 52
- Raspberry Crepe Cake, 107
- Raspberry Crumb Bars, 211
- Red, White and Blueberry Pops, 170
- Rocking Berry Roll, 176
- Very Berry Balls, 11

Red Curry Butter, 193

Red, White and Blueberry Pops, 170

Rhubarb Tart, 101

RICE
- Burrito Bowl, 41
- Chicken and Veggie Skillet, 139
- Chili, Rice and Spinach Burrito, 209
- Coconut Rice with Jerk Chicken and Mango Salsa, 91
- Crispy Tofu with Peanut Sauce, 226
- Instant Pot Quick Shrimp Risotto, 49
- Shrimp and Sausage Skillet, 74
- Thai Curry Tilapia, 281
- Tuna Kebabs, 166

RICOTTA
Baked Rigatoni and Meatballs, 18
Cauliflower Gnocchi Cacio e Pepe Bake, 278
Green Pea Dip, 129
Pepperoni Pizza Dip, 131
Shaved Vegetable and Prosciutto Pizza, 246
Spinach-Ricotta Lasagna, 74
Watermelon toppings, 169
Rigatoni with Meat Sauce, 242
Roasted Broccoli and White Bean Pasta, 24
Roasted Brussels Sprouts with Poached Egg and Parmesan, 24
Roasted Celery Root and Apple with Pork, 30
Roasted Pepper Salsa, 195
Roasted Potatoes and Parsnips with Steak, 27
Roasted Red Pepper Hummus, 125
Roasted-Vegetable Chicken Soup, 27
Rocking Berry Roll, 176
Romesco, 67
ROSEMARY
Herbed Shortbread, 286
Sheet Pan Pork, Butternut Squash and Potato, 221

S

SAGE
Chicken and Barley Stew, 45
Chicken with Garlic and Sage Sauce, 229
SALAD DRESSINGS
Creamy Pesto Dressing, 271
Ginger-Soy Dressing, 271
Green Goddess Dressing, 67
SALADS
Apple and fennel Salad, 157
Asian Wheat Berry Salad, 271
Chicken and Apple Slaw, 115
Corn and Crab Salad, 149
Greek Steak and Salad, 140
Grilled Cheese Salad, 202
Grilled Halloumi Salad, 190
Grilled Shrimp Caesar, 116
Italian Wheat Berry Salad, 271
Orzo Salad with Grilled Shrimp, 92
Peppery Coleslaw, 153
Pho-Style Beef Salad, 189
Spinach and Tortellini Salad, 192
Spinach Salad with Warm Sausage Dressing, 96
Turkey Taco Salad, 187
Turmeric Chicken Salad, 181
Tuscan Chicken Cobb, 144
Warm German Potato Salad, 150

SALMON
Grilled Salmon, 157
Salmon Pasta, 180
Salmon Veggie Bowls, 190
SALSA
Avocado-Corn Salsa, 123
Cherry Tomato Salsa, 129
Roasted Pepper Salsa, 195
Salted Caramel Bars, 211
Salted Caramel Dip, 231
SANDWICHES. *SEE ALSO* BURGERS
BBQ Bacon Cheddar Burgers, 112
Chicken Meatballs with Buffalo Sauce, 58
Fontina, Basil and Bacon Grilled Cheese, 202
Grilled Shrimp Caesar, 116
Ground Pork Banh Mi, 147
Mini Eggo Sliders, 231
Open-Faced Crab Sandwich, 95
Pork Meatballs with Hoisin Sauce, 57
Pork Sammies, 41
Sausage and Broccoli Rabe Hoagie, 201
Sheet Pan Egg Sandwiches, 39
Spicy Chicken Lettuce Wraps, 206
Saté Dip, 57
SAUCES. *SEE ALSO* GRAVY
Chimichurri, 67
Mustard-Based Rib Sauce, 153
Romesco, 67
Shallot-Chive Butter, 149
Tomato-Based Rib Sauce, 153
Tzatziki, 67
SAUSAGES
Bell Pepper, Cheddar and Sausage Quiche, 88
Chard and Sausage Stuffing, 256
Chorizo Queso, 131
Fettuccine with Fresh Tomato Sauce, 111
Ground Turkey Quesadilla, 99
Hobo Packs, 137
Overnight Oatmeal, 35
Pepperoni Pizza Dip, 131
Pigs in a Blanket, 287
Sausage and Broccoli Rabe Hoagie, 201
Sheet Pan Sausage and Broccoli Rabe, 201
Shrimp and Sausage Skillet, 74
Spinach Salad with Warm Sausage Dressing, 96
Seriously Sneaky Chocolate Cake, 85
SHALLOTS
Chunky Avocado-Citrus Dip, 123
Deep-Dish Mushroom Quiche, 290
Green Beans Amandine, 256
Instant Pot Quick Shrimp Risotto, 49
Potato Puff Casserole, 239
Roasted Broccoli and White Bean Pasta, 24
Shallot-Chive Butter, 149

Sheet Pan Sausage and Broccoli Rabe, 201
Sour Cream and Leek Dip, 127
Tomato and Cheddar Slab Tart, 168
Vegan Mushroom Gravy, 252
Shaved Vegetable and Prosciutto Pizza, 246
Sheet Pan Egg Sandwiches, 39
Sheet Pan Pork, Butternut Squash and Potato, 221
Sheet Pan Sausage and Broccoli Rabe, 201
SHELLFISH. *SEE ALSO* SHRIMP
Corn and Crab Salad, 149
Grilled Maine Lobster, 149
Open-Faced Crab Sandwich, 95
Shrimp Fra Diavolo, 222
Warm Crab Dip, 131
SHRIMP
Grilled Shrimp Caesar, 116
Instant Pot Quick Shrimp Risotto, 49
Orzo Salad with Grilled Shrimp, 92
Shrimp and Sausage Skillet, 74
Shrimp Fra Diavolo, 222
Tacos con Carne, 161
SLOW COOKER RECIPES
Beef Meatballs with Marinara, 61
Chicken Meatballs with Buffalo Sauce, 58
Chorizo Queso, 131
Instant Pot Slow-Cooked Honey-Ginger Pork, 65
Overnight Oatmeal, 35
Pork Meatballs with Hoisin Sauce, 57
Slow Cooker Curried Lentil Soup, 225
Slow Cooker Pulled Pork, 41
Smoked Brisket, 154
Smoky Beet and Bean Dip, 125
SMOOTHIE
Berry-Beet-Banana-Basil Smoothie, 33
Coffee-Chocolate-PB Smoothie, 33
SNACKS
Cocoa-Coconut Almond Balls, 11
Nut Clusters, 83
PB Cup Balls, 11
Very Berry Balls, 11
SOUPS. *SEE ALSO* STEWS AND CHILI
Curried Lentil Soup, 14
Italian Wedding Soup, 277
Pasta and White Bean Soup, 205
Roasted-Vegetable Chicken Soup, 27
Slow Cooker Curried Lentil Soup, 225
Sour Cream and Leek Dip, 127
Southern Caviar with Hominy, 125
Soy-Glazed Chicken Thighs, 71
Spice-Roasted Chicken Thighs, 31
Spicy Chicken Lettuce Wraps, 206
SPINACH
Chili, Rice and Spinach Burrito, 209
Ground Turkey Quesadilla, 99
Italian Wedding Soup, 277
Overnight Oatmeal, 35
Pasta and White Bean Soup, 205

Potato Puff Casserole, 239
Salmon Pasta, 180
Spice-Roasted Chicken Thighs, 31
Spinach and Tortellini Salad, 192
Spinach-Ricotta Lasagna, 74
Spinach Salad with Warm Sausage
  Dressing, 96
Tomato and Spinach Mini Ravioli, 205
Veggie-Feta Egg Cups, 82
Warm Spinach-Artichoke Dip, 129
SQUASH. *SEE ALSO* PUMPKIN; ZUCCHINI
  Glazed Delicata Squash, 256
  Sheet Pan Pork, Butternut Squash and
    Potato, 221
Sriracha-Scallion Butter, 193
STEWS AND CHILI
  Beef and Bean Chili, 74
  Beef and Sweet Potato Stew, 80
  Chicken and Barley Stew, 45
  Chipotle Corn Chili, 209
STRAWBERRIES
  Berry-Beet-Banana-Basil Smoothie, 33
  Overnight Oatmeal, 35
  Pistachio and Raspberry White
    Chocolate Bark, 52
  Rocking Berry Roll, 176
  Strawberry Danish, 287
  Strawberry, Grapefruit and Coconut
    Pavlova, 102
Stuffed Flank Steak, 21
Stuffed Mac and Cheese, 42
Stuffing, Chard and Sausage, 256
SWEET POTATOES
  Beef and Sweet Potato Stew, 80
  Ganache, 85
  Hobo Packs, 137
  Spice-Roasted Chicken Thighs, 31
  Stuffed Flank Steak, 21
  Sweet Potato Latkes, 295
Swirled Meringue Sorbet Sandwiches, 175
Swirled Pumpkin Spice Cheesecake
  Bars, 263

T
TACOS
  Blackened Zucchini and Corn Tacos, 161
  Tacos con Carne, 161
Texas-Style Beans, 154
Thai Curry Tilapia, 281
THYME
  Beef and Sweet Potato Stew, 80
  Chicken and Veggie Skillet, 139
  Deep-Dish Mushroom Quiche, 290
  Herbed Shortbread, 286
  Lemon-Thyme Chicken Burgers, 162
  Mushroom and Cheese Fondue, 129
  New England Fish Dinner, 245
  Olive Tapenade, 129

Potatoes Anna, 257
Tomato and Cheddar Slab Tart, 168
White Bean Dip, 125
Tofu with Peanut Sauce, Crispy, 226
TOMATOES
  Avocado-Corn Salsa, 123
  Beef and Bean Chili, 74
  Beef and Sweet Potato Stew, 80
  Beef Meatballs with Marinara, 61
  B + T Guac, 123
  Cherry Tomato Salsa, 129
  Chipotle Corn Chili, 209
  Fettuccine with Fresh Tomato Sauce, 111
  Greek Nachos, 195
  Greek Steak and Salad, 140
  Grilled Halloumi Salad, 190
  Mediterranean Bowl, 79
  Pepperoni Pizza Dip, 131
  Rigatoni with Meat Sauce, 242
  Salmon Pasta, 180
  Shaved Vegetable and Prosciutto
    Pizza, 246
  Shrimp Fra Diavolo, 222
  Southern Caviar with Hominy, 125
  Spinach-Ricotta Lasagna, 74
  Tomato and Cheddar Slab Tart, 168
  Tomato and Spinach Mini Ravioli, 205
  Tomato-Based Rib Sauce, 153
  Tomato, Zucchini and Parmesan
    Fristrata, 249
  Turkey Taco Salad, 187
  Tuscan Chicken Cobb, 144
  Vegetable Frittata, 179
Tuna Kebabs, 166
TURKEY
  BBQ Bacon Cheddar Burgers, 112
  Citrus Herb Turkey, 250
  Ground Turkey Quesadilla, 99
  Turkey Taco Salad, 187
Turmeric Chicken Salad, 181
Turmeric-Yogurt Dip, 127
TURNIPS
  Roasted-Vegetable Chicken Soup, 27
Tuscan Chicken Cobb, 144
Tzatziki, 67

U
Upside Down Cake, The, 232

V
Vegan Mushroom Gravy, 252
Vegetable Frittata, 179
Veggie-Feta Egg Cups, 82
Very Berry Balls, 11

W
Waffle Toppings, DIY, 231
WALNUTS
  Nut Clusters, 83
  Raspberry Crumb Bars, 211
Warm Anchovy Dip, 131
Warm Crab Dip, 131
Warm German Potato Salad, 150
Warm Spinach-Artichoke Dip, 129
Watermelon toppings, 169
Whipped Feta Dip, 127
White Bean Dip, 125
WHITE CHOCOLATE
  Coconut-Cranberry Squares, 285
  Peppermint Snaps, 285
  Pistachio and Raspberry White
    Chocolate Bark, 52
  Very Berry Balls, 11
WINE
  Beef and Sweet Potato Stew, 80
  Chicken Marsala, 76
  Chicken Piccata, 17
  Instant Pot Quick Shrimp Risotto, 49
  Mushroom and Cheese Fondue, 129
  Rigatoni with Meat Sauce, 242
  Shrimp Fra Diavolo, 222
  Wine and Herb Gravy, 252
Wraps, Spicy Chicken Lettuce, 206

Y
YOGURT
  Avocado Mousse, 123
  Cherry Cooler, 179
  Coffee-Chocolate-PB Smoothie, 33
  Greek Nachos, 195
  No-Bake Fireworks Cheesecake Bars, 172
  Red, White and Blueberry Pops, 170
  Slow Cooker Curried Lentil Soup, 225
  Turmeric-Yogurt Dip, 127
  Tzatziki, 67
  Zucchini Fritters, 295

Z
ZUCCHINI
  BBQ Bacon Cheddar Burgers, 112
  Blackened Zucchini and Corn Tacos, 161
  Halfway Healthy Spaghetti Pesto, 143
  Rigatoni with Meat Sauce, 242
  Shaved Vegetable and Prosciutto
    Pizza, 246
  Tomato, Zucchini and Parmesan
    Fristrata, 249
  Zucchini Fritters, 295
  Zucchini Muffins, 185